THE PONTIFF
IN WINTER

ALSO BY JOHN CORNWELL

Hitler's Pope

Breaking Faith

The Power to Harm

A Thief in the Night

Nature's Imagination

Consciousness and Human Identity

Earth to Earth

Hitler's Scientists

Hiding Places of God

Coleridge: Poet and Revolutionary, 1772–1804

Seven Other Demons

The Spoiled Priest

Strange Gods

THE
PONTIFF
IN WINTER

Triumph and Conflict
in the Reign of John Paul II

JOHN CORNWELL

DOUBLEDAY

NEW YORK LONDON TORONTO SYDNEY AUCKLAND

PUBLISHED BY DOUBLEDAY
a division of Random House, Inc.

DOUBLEDAY and the portrayal of an anchor with a dolphin
are registered trademarks of Random House, Inc.
Copyright © 2004 by John Cornwell

The poems appearing on pages 13 and 16–17 were quoted from *Collected Poems of Karol Wojtyla* by Karol Wojtlya, translated by Jerzy Peterkiewicz, copyright © 1979, 1982 by Libreria Editrice Vaticana, Vatican City. Used by permission of Random House, Inc.

Book design by Fearn Cutler de Vicq
Cataloging-in-Publication Data is on file with the Library of Congress.

ISBN 0-385-51484-0

PRINTED IN THE UNITED STATES OF AMERICA

November 2004
First Edition
10 9 8 7 6 5 4 3 2 1

For JGM and JS
With Love

Contents

John Paul the Great

Karol Wojtyla, Pope John Paul II, has shown himself to be a man of rare depth of soul, an evangelist of tireless energy who traveled to the ends of the earth to spread the Christian Gospel. Priest and prophet, he has acted to conserve the traditions of the Catholic Church while urging transformation in preparation for a millennial springtime of the spirit.

He raised the consciousness of his Polish countrymen, exposing the sterility of Soviet totalitarian rule. He has preached freedom as a characteristic of our humanity. But he warned of the danger in capitalist democracies of liberty that lacked moral culture. He presented to the world an original understanding of Christian humanism and saw marital sex as an icon of the Trinitarian God. He has strived for Christian unity, reaching out to Eastern Orthodoxy and the Churches and communions separated from Rome by the Reformation. All the while he has toiled, despite encroaching illness, pain, and old age, to maintain the unity and continuity of the Catholic Faith. As Shakespeare's Kent says of the passing of King Lear: "The wonder is he hath endured so long / He but usurped his life." His ardent supporters among the faithful seem justified in hailing him Karol the Great.

But there is a parallel rather than an alternative Catholic version, rarely expressed in public in deference to a taboo that forbids criticism of living and even dead popes. A widespread constituency of Catholics, men and women, clergy and bishops throughout the world, is convinced that John Paul has drawn so tightly on the reins of universal authority that he has undermined the discretion, the authority, the integrity, and the strength of the local, diocesan Church. They believe that while appearing triumphant in the world at large, he is leaving his Church in a state of weakness and conflict.

This centralizing papal dynamic over more than a quarter of a century has had profound consequences, of which the complex scenario of sexual abuse by priests is but one example. The systemic corruption of clerical sexual abuse has revealed a dimension of paralysis and vacillation on the part of local bishops and senior clergy who attempted to conceal and deny it. Undermined by years of centralizing papal rule, there was a tendency for local church leaders to look over their shoulders to Rome, where initiative and authority were deemed to reside in all matters. And yet action was not forthcoming from the papal pinnacle. Indifference and complacency were found right up to John Paul himself until world indignation left Rome no choice but to acknowledge the crisis.

His failure to recognize from the outset a complex set of crises within the priesthood, and to handle them appropriately, contrasts starkly with harsh denunciations of those who failed to achieve the high standards of sexual morality he set for Catholic laity. John Paul advocated exclusion of those Catholics who are divorced and remarried without annullment (nearly forty percent of Catholic marriages end in divorce in Western countries), or who live in unmarried partnerships or in homosexual relationships.

His hard line on all forms of contraception in any circumstances has alienated generations of the faithful, many of whom have fallen away. In Africa, while agencies were right to warn against encouraging promiscuity through free distribution of condoms to the young, he has taken an extreme stance. His insistence that condoms should not be used in any circumstances has condemned untold numbers of Catholics at risk for HIV infection to certain death. He has excluded women from any future hope of priestly ministry not only within his own pontificate but by attempting to legislate for his papal successors for all time. He has shut his ears to pleas for married clergy and rejected requests for laicization by priests who have married and started families—refusing them the sacraments.

While making a show of encouraging interfaith dialogue and urging ecumenism, he has characterized other religions (that is, non-Christian religions) as "defective," claiming that many Christian denominations, including the Anglican (Episcopalian) denominations, were not proper churches, their priests and bishops not proper priests and bishops. Despite his deep longing to come to an accord with the Russian Orthodox Church, he has established Roman Catholic dioceses in Russia in defiance of the concerns of the entire Orthodox Church.

His debility in his latter days has exposed the long-term consequences of his autocratic papal rule. He has become a living sermon of patience and fortitude, appealing to the sympathies of the entire world; but the billion-strong Church has been run increasingly by his Polish secretary and a handful of aging reactionary cardinals. We have had a papacy in which a pope utters virtual heresy, bishops and faithful are told they may not discuss women priesthood, a Curial cardinal teaches that condoms kill, prelates guilty of having shielded pedophiles are honored, and a U.S. president has exploited the papacy as an election campaign stop.

To understand John Paul, as he himself has declared often enough, is an exercise in penetrating the inner man. "They try to understand me from the outside," he once said. "But I can only be understood from the inside." Unlike his predecessor John XXIII, who spoke constantly from the heart, John Paul has revealed his personality in theatrical displays that have enraptured and beguiled his huge audiences. Exploiting modern broadcast communications to their fullest extent, his omnipresence and monopoly of the limelight have reduced within his Church all other authority, all other holiness (unless dead), all other comparisons, voices, images, talents, and virtues. The legislator, the single dispenser of blessings, beneficence, and wisdom—there has been no hidden corner of the Church where he was not present, heard, read, and where he was not absolute.

This has been a big papacy, difficult if not impossible to capture in the round. His story has been told already in many different ways. As he prepared to travel to Cuba in February 1998 to meet with Fidel Castro, *The Times* (London) judged him the most influential political figure in the world during the previous twenty years. And the paper was right, up to a point. His encouragement of the Polish people to reject Soviet communism had reverberations throughout Eastern Europe and beyond. A line of malevolent dictators—Marcos in the Philippines, Baby Doc in Haiti, Pinochet in Chile, Jaruzelski in Poland, Stroessner in Paraguay—fell from power after he had kissed the soil of their countries.

Tributes to John Paul's intellectual status have been no less ardent. He has been feted as the sole philosopher Pope in history. His biographer, George Weigel, argues that John Paul's teachings have raised him to unchallenged status in "the history of modern thought." Mr. Weigel believes that John Paul II, among many outstanding achievements, returned "the great humanistic project to its true trajectory, which aimed, he argued, straight into the Holy Trinity Itself." John Paul, by this verdict, has set the world on its true course for this new millennium.

As John Paul's papacy lengthened and the obituarists repeatedly updated their eulogies, a variety of adulatory perspectives on his life and times have emerged, enhancing the cult of his personality: John Paul the athlete, poet, playwright, pastor, theologian, prophet, politician, confessor, contemplative, preacher, ecumenist, counselor, sage, reconciler, moralist, living saint.

A number of biographies and portraits were published between 1994 and 1999 in expectation of John Paul's imminent demise. They include accounts by Michael Walsh, the late Jonathan Kwitny, the late Tad Szulz, Marco Politi and Carl Bernstein, and George Weigel. Any writer attempting a new portrait of John Paul owes a considerable debt to these authors, whether one agrees with their conclusions or not. They have brought a wealth of documentation and exclusive interview material to their portraits. But John Paul's refusal to die according to a timetable set by others (Vaticanologists have been predicting his imminent death since at least 1994) has rendered them outdated.

This new portrait of John Paul II is not a biography of comprehensive record. I do not attempt to compete with the thoroughness of earlier biographies, a comprehensiveness that tends, through sheer mass of detail, to weigh down its extraordinary subject like a diamond set in lead. I have attempted to be selective in order to emphasize connections that bring his character and contradictions to narrative life, from his childhood to the year of the new millennium. Then, picking up where the latest biography ends, I tell the story of his pontificate during the first years of this decade, a period that includes the Jubilee Year, the papal visits to Jerusalem and former Soviet republics, the 9/11 attacks in America, the War on Terror, the Iraq war, his relations with America, the continuing struggles within the Catholic Church over authority and regard for other religions, and the sexual abuse crisis in the priesthood that has rocked the Church to its foundations.

This critical post-1999 era has seen the Holy Father in the final stages of Parkinson's disease, immobile, often incapable of speech, and suffering from blank episodes of concentration and memory. Urgent questions were raised in the late 1990s about the possibility of resignation. In the first year of the millennium, John Paul set aside such suggestions by publicly avowing the mystical nature of his personal pontificate.

John Paul in his young manhood and prime defined the term "mystical" in a subtle and orthodox manner—as the spiritual meeting of two liberties: the acting human person with the person of Jesus Christ, encountered not as an object in the world but as the All. In his early years as an academic and bishop, moreover, he was preoccupied with defining the nature of the human person as "ex-centric" rather than self-centered. We become more ourselves, and more like Christ, who is the model of humanity, he said, by self-giving.

By his early sixties, however, he was inclined to entertain a more vulgar and egocentric construal of the mystical element in his life, with drastic implications for human responsibility, the meaning of history, his own divinely ordained role as Pope, and his extraordinary degree of certitude. At the same time, his inclination toward popular mysticism involved a contradiction, a denial, of those Christian humanist notions that he continued to preach into his late years.

After the attempt on his life on May 13, 1981, he began to allude to the importance of the coming millennium. He was increasingly inclined to place his trust in celestial control of history in preference to human, earthbound responsibilities. Meanwhile, over the years, he increasingly undermined the prospects for collegiality, reducing the status of his bishops ("They treat us like altar boys," said the late Cardinal Joseph Bernardin of Chicago of John Paul and the Roman Curia). Once an outstanding champion of political and religious freedom, John Paul began to place limits on liberty—limits that he alone could define: "Authentic freedom," he wrote in his key encyclical, or letter to the world, *Veritatis Splendor* (*Splendor of the Truth*), "is never freedom 'from' the truth but always freedom 'in' truth." The Catholic faith had the fullness, the monopoly, of the truth, he asserted in the Vatican address he endorsed called *Dominus Jesus* (*The Lord Jesus*, 2000).

At the same time, his pyramidal notion of the function of the papacy, the cult of his papal personality, seemed to encourage an epic self-centeredness. And the more central, holy, and absolute the pope, the less significant his bishops, his clergy, and the laity. A token of the soaring cult of his personality: In his native Poland, most churches now have on prominent show an outsize statue of John Paul. As a Polish correspondent to the international Catholic weekly *The Tablet* noted at Christmas 2003: "To my knowledge no other public figure has had so many statues erected in his lifetime, except Joseph Stalin."

He saw himself in the eye of an unrelenting, ever-expanding, global storm; his mystical vision has no doubt lent greater simplicity to the complexity and fragmentation. "In the designs of Providence there are no mere coincidences," he had declared to a mass gathering in Fatima, Portugal, in 1982. Then, in the millennium year 2000, he unfolded Fatima's prophecy in its fullness—the Third Secret, which turned out to be a prediction across the entire century about *him*, Karol Wojtyla. It was meant. It was written. As was his survival despite bullets, his Parkinson's, and his slips in the shower, along with all his grand initiatives, declarations, pronouncements, and judgments.

Papal biographer Weigel has declared John Paul "the man with arguably the most coherent and comprehensive vision of the human possibility in the world ahead." Cardinal Avery Dulles, eminent Jesuit theologian and author of *The Splendor of the Faith*, writes that John Paul's vision is "capable of encountering and respectfully challenging all opposing ideologies and spiritual movements." Such encomiums leave little room for the coherent and comprehensive vision of Jesus Christ, let alone that of the countless spiritual teachers within and outside of Christianity down the ages.

This new portrait of John Paul, written in the ominous light of the postmillennium period in which religious fundamentalism offers the greatest threat to world peace, and problems of poverty and deprivation proliferate, tells the story of a pontiff who has matched remarkable talents with corresponding frailties and foibles. His pontificate has seen opportunities crowned with success and opportunities lost. The power and timing of his initiatives in Poland were impeccable. But at a time when fundamentalist religions are in antagonistic confrontation with the West, his most tragic failure has been his refusal to acknowledge the potential for discovering within Christianity a basis for pluralist societies.

The impression, moreover, that John Paul alone is the main event in the Catholic Church has taken Catholicism in the direction of papal fundamentalism—the idea that Catholic beliefs and values are handed in a mandatory fashion top-down. He has muted the voices of the Church's many saints, theologians, bishops, and lay-men and -women who constitute the Catholic wisdom of the present and of the ages. Faced with his inevitable demise, his supporters are busy attempting the perpetuation of his papacy for generations to come.

Under John Paul the Catholic Church has become the voice of one man in a white robe pronouncing from the Roman pinnacle, rather than a conversation between past, present, and future; between many cultures, ethnicities, and spiritualities; between the Church universal and the Church local—wherever people gather for the Eucharist. The questions arise: How and why should this have come about? And what does this situation mean for the future of Catholicism?

John Paul is a human being; he is eminently, outstandingly, and impressively human. But reacting to the burdens and temptations of his ancient and impossible office, the crises of the times, and the persuasions of his devotees, he has run the papacy as if he were a Superman. But a Superman has no place in a Church of communities that require to be fully themselves in their smallest groups; that flourish and gather strength from their own local resources as well as from the Roman center. Another Superman on the throne of Saint Peter can only continue the tragic process of abdication of responsibility, maturity, and local discretion that we have witnessed in the Catholic Church this past quarter of a century.

PART ONE

HOLY THEATRE

1920–1999

"Holy Theatre" implies that there is something else in existence, below, around and above, another zone even more invisible, even farther from the forms which we are capable of reading or recording, which contain extremely powerful sources of energy.

——PETER BROOK: *There Are No Secrets:*
Thoughts on Acting and the Theatre

CHAPTER ONE

Close Encounters

There is no substitute for the living presence, the inclination of the head, the meeting of the eyes, the idiosyncratic gesture, the tone of voice. I first met Pope John Paul II privately in his halcyon days. It was a gray morning in December 1987, and I had attended Mass in his private chapel.

Accompanied by his secretary, Stanislaw Dziwisz, a Polish priest with soft gestures and undulant step, John Paul appeared in the library of the papal apartment as if he had all the time in the world. He looked utterly centered in himself.

I noticed that his cassock was a little worn and off-white, a comfortable favorite for early mornings. He gave the impression of being equally comfortable and settled in his papacy. He was wearing a gleaming gold watch that flashed, like his pectoral cross, in the strong arc lamps. He wore a pair of stiff, shiny, fashionable tan casuals; they seemed to me, at first, incongruous, unclerical. Previous popes in this modern era had floated on felt-soled scarlet slippers.

He studied me with narrowed eyes, dragging those feet in sturdy shoes along the marble floor, somewhat pigeon-toed. "Stas" Dziwisz, the "velvet power" in the papal apartment, was whispering something in his ear. Then he was next to me, deeply stooped and hugely broad-shouldered, his legs a little apart like a hill-walker

3

steadying himself. There was a discreet hint of peppermint and aftershave: I understood he liked Fisherman's Friend lozenges for his throat, and dabbed Penhaligon Eau de Cologne on his well-shaved jowls. His silver-white hair was inexpertly cut and slightly tousled. His familiar face, the most famous face in the world, looked drained, exhausted, as if he had not slept. Cinematically handsome from afar, he appeared, eminently, human up close. If he was a mystic, as many of his biographers claim, I sensed no numinous aura.

He inclined a large Slavonic left ear, inviting me to speak. His hand went out; as I grasped it and wondered whether I should kiss his ring, he managed to clutch my arm and push it away at the same time. His great square head went down until his chin was buried in his chest; then the eye opened, a steely knowing eye, scrutinizing me sideways. He was waiting for me to say something. I caught a sudden impression of the Niagara of sycophancy, persuasion, and petition that poured into that ear day by day. Then he turned full face on—a wide, fatherly, frank face. He began to speak, pointing his forefinger at me.

That first impression was of a man who was at once recollected and yet dauntingly observant; kindly, yet capable of stern authority. I sensed an unassailable integrity and openness, and yet there was something cunning, a peasant craftiness about the way he nailed you sideways with that eye when you least expected it. Above all, in that Vatican milieu of fleshy celibates, whose ambience was cushioned offices and plump prayer stools, he came across as a plain man who set no store by decorous niceties; an unaffected, integrated, informal, utterly human person.

His informality, setting him apart from a generation of prelates who stood on ceremonial and ecclesiastical dignity, was captured in another first encounter I had heard about.

The late Derek Worlock, Archbishop of Liverpool, was serving on a bishops' commission in Rome with Cardinal Wojtyla of Krakow, as John Paul then was in the early 1970s. One morning, according to Worlock, Wojtyla arrived late, soaked, having walked through driving rain across Rome, eschewing the use of the chauffeur-driven car to which he was entitled. Without the least embarrassment, as the assembled bishops and cardinals looked on, he first took off his shoes, then his sodden socks. Standing in bare feet, he squeezed out the water on the floor, placing the socks over a radiator to dry. Then he turned and said to the amazed prelates: "Well, gentlemen! Let's get on with it."

In his presence there is a sense of fathomless seriousness, a hint of inconsolable melancholy even. And yet you see in those intelligent, watchful eyes a ready sense of life's ridiculousness, held firmly in check. In the atmosphere of adulation that surrounds him, his minor jests are greeted with collapsing paroxysms of mirth, as when he said to Mayor Koch in New York: "You are the mayor. I must be careful to be a good citizen!" Rarely reported are his more outrageous pranks, aided by his thespian gifts. A Vatican monsignor who was in attendance on the Pope for some years told me the following revealing story:

> One morning, John Paul gave an audience to a phalanx of German visitors, theologians, bishops, and VIPs. They were extremely formal and uptight, typically German. After I had shown them out of the audience room, I went back in to take my leave of the Pope. He looked me fiercely in the eye, stood ramrod straight, clicked his heels, and gave a barely perceptible but quite unmistakable little Nazi salute with a slightest gesture of the hand. It was hilarious: the Polish Supreme Pontiff sending up the Krauts! I was fit to burst out loud. Instead, insanely, I forgot myself and decided to turn the joke on him. So I gave him a look of horror, my hands on my cheeks, as if to rebuke him—as if to say: "Oh you naughty, Holy Father! What would the Germans make of your little charade?" His face darkened instantly and terrifyingly. His eyes were blazing with anger. But at that moment Ratzinger, another German, swept into the room and I had to shut the doors on them, giggling nervously to myself. Later that day, John Paul and I were alone again. He

turned on me, furious, and hit me hard on the arm. It actually hurt. "I was just trying to encourage you!" he said. "Didn't you understand? I was encouraging you!" It was an odd phrase to use in English. But I understood what he meant. He meant that he was trying to amuse me or liven me up for the day. I stood there, fit to cry, because I loved him so much and I could see that I had offended him deeply. But how could I tell him that of course I had been "encouraged," that I was just engaged in a little lighthearted irony in return? I just had to let it go, leaving him to think that I was a sanctimonious, humorless idiot.

Whatever the character of the man who becomes pope, the papal role, in time, begins to take over the human being, the personality of the individual elected to the strangest, most impossible and isolating job on earth. Paul VI, Pope in the 1960s and 1970s, described the isolation thus: "I was solitary before, but now my solitariness becomes complete and awesome. Hence the dizziness, the vertigo. Like a statue on a plinth—that is how I live now."

We will never know the solitude, the psychological fragmentation, the inner sufferings that have afflicted John Paul in consequence of his papal office. But there are clues. Eamon Duffy, the Cambridge church historian, relates a story told him by a theologian friend who had been invited to dinner with John Paul II in the days when young priests were invited regularly to the papal table. This friend found himself sitting next to John Paul and decided to strike up a personal conversation rather than try to find something arresting or important to say.

He said: "Holy Father, I love poetry and I've read all your verse. Have you written much poetry since you became Pope?" To which the Pope said: "I've written no poetry since I became Pope." So the theologian said: "Well, why is that, Holy Father?" The Pope cut him dead, turning to the person on his other side.

Twenty minutes later, John Paul turned to the theologian and said curtly: "No context!" That was all.

As the dinner party broke up and the guests were departing,

Duffy's friend, on taking his leave, said somewhat rashly: "Holy Father, when I pray for you now, I'll pray for a poet without context." The Pope did not respond. He just froze.

John Paul clearly felt that he had laid bare a very private part of his life. But he had imparted a tragic truth perhaps. The papal office takes over the whole person. That is what the job demands. When he said there was no "context" for poetry, he seemed to be acknowledging that in the depths of his soul, deep down where the poetry is written, there lies a terrible, vertiginous solitude.

There are many millions who have never met the Pope in the flesh but who have encountered him in their dreams. Graham Greene, toward the end of his life the most famous Catholic writer in the world, had been a friend of Pope Paul VI, who had read all Greene's books and admired them. But Greene never received a call to meet with John Paul II. When I talked with Greene not long before he died, he told me: "I dream about John Paul II. There is a recurrent dream. I am in St. Peter's Square and there are tens of thousands of people, nuns and priests and laypeople. They are all groveling on their knees, venerating him in the most repulsive fashion. And he is in their midst dispensing communion from a huge ciborium. Only, he is not dispensing the communion bread but ornate, overrich Italian chocolates." And there was another dream: "I am sitting on my balcony in Antibes having breakfast. I open up the newspaper and there's this headline: 'John Paul Canonizes Jesus Christ.' I sit there, astounded that this pope could be so arrogant as to make a saint of our Savior." Then Greene said, as if he had got to the bottom of John Paul's character: "He had a lot in common with Ronald Reagan. They were both world leaders who were in fact just actors."

Greene's antipathy toward John Paul, encapsulated in those dreams, represents a familiar reaction among many sophisticated, liberal Catholics: John Paul arrogant and autocratic, patting the heads of the faithful, John Paul obsessed with saint-making, John Paul acting a part. One wonders, though, how Greene, with his novelist's antennae, might have judged John Paul had he actually met him in the flesh.

Not everyone was bowled over by John Paul; and John Paul, we are told, could shut a person out, totally and finally, when he felt that his interlocutor was behaving inappropriately. On my second private meeting with him, I too dared to ask him about his creative writing. His response was to feign deafness. I asked again, and he pointedly made an unrelated observation in order to change the subject.

But the inescapable reaction of those who have had dealings with him, person to person, and this was certainly my own impression, is dynamic paradox and contradiction. Anna-Teresa Tymieniecka, the philosopher who worked with him on his book *Acting Person* in the 1970s, was probably in love with him. Sexually attractive, subtle, with great force of character, she spent hundreds of hours with him, sometimes with his secretary present, but often alone. She was under no illusions about John Paul's foibles; her percipient description of his character, given in an interview with Marco Politi and Carl Bernstein, is as memorable as it is moving:

> He has developed in himself an attitude of modesty, a very solicitous way of approaching people. He makes a person feel there is nothing else on his mind, that he is ready to do everything for the other person. Owing to his innate personal charm, which is one of his great weapons, he has in addition a poetical nature, a captivating way of dealing with people. These are all evidences of his charisma—even the way in which he moves, though it is no more now that he is an old gentleman. He had a way of moving, a way of smiling, a way of looking around that was different and exceedingly personal. It had a beauty about it.

Yet, Dr. Tymieniecka went on to say: "If there is one trait of character which I can observe in him it is love of contradiction." She says: "People around him see the sweetest, most modest person." Then she adds: "He is by no means as humble as he appears. Neither is he modest. He thinks about himself very highly, very adequately . . . This is an extremely multifaceted human being, extremely colorful."

CHAPTER TWO

Stagestruck

Like a moth to a flame, the boy Karol Wojtyla was drawn irresistibly to theatre. From the age of eight, tall for his age and plump in the face, he was stagestruck: running errands for an amateur dramatic society, helping to build stage sets, aspiring to be a prompter. At home, alone in the privacy of his bedroom, he performed another kind of playacting: priestly rituals in make-believe vestments sewn by his seamstress mother, Emilia. When his brother, Edmund, fourteen years his senior, became a doctor, Karol solo-acted scenes for the patients in the hospital wards. By the time he left school, Karol had directed and acted in ten productions, invariably in the lead role.

He had a taste for patriotic drama, statuesque postures, and grandiloquent bardic monologues. Years later, Wojtyla would declare that the tradition of Polish drama puts Shakespeare in the shade. Polish theatre, he explained, preserved the existence of the nation through all the annexations and occupations inflicted by barbarous neighbors. The Catholic Faith and Polish drama blended indistinguishably: Liturgy, pilgrimage, theatre had greater reality and power than the ebb and flow of armies and dictators. And the fount and origin of Polish nationhood was the motherhood of the Virgin Mary. For Catholic Poles, history was not shaped by the vanity of human ambitions but by Mary's intercessions and miraculous initiatives.

And yet, as with all patriotism and nationalism, there are continuities with xenophobia and ethnic hatreds, as Poland's Jews could confirm. There is no doubting Karol Wojtyla's ease with the Jewish community in the town of his birth. His home in Wadowice was owned by Jews; his best friend, Jerzy Kluger, was a Jew, and Karol could bandy Yiddish with Jewish kids on the street. But it was Cardinal Hlond, Catholic primate of all Poland, who declared in 1936, when Karol Wojtyla was sixteen and Hitler's Reich was but three years in existence: "There will be the Jewish problem as long as the Jews remain."

Nor were the Poles unknown to execute preemptive military strikes. In 1920, three months after Karol Wojtyla was born, in a bid to form an empire that would take in the Ukraine, Byelorussia, and Lithuania, Poland took on the Red Army. To be sure, Poland had much to fear from Russia and its satellites. Lenin had stated: "The path to world conflagration passes over the corpse of Poland." Tearing up the Versailles settlements following the end of the Great War, Poland's military dictator, Jozef Pilsudski, seized the great city of Kiev from the Bolsheviks. In retaliation Lenin ordered the invasion of Poland, bringing four massive armies to the gates of Warsaw, outnumbering the Polish army virtually three to one. A call went out from every pulpit rallying Polish manhood to the defense of the native soil. The Poles were weary, and many of her soldiers were no more than children and went barefoot. But the blood of the nation was up. On the day after the Feast of the Assumption of the Virgin Mary, August 16, 1920, the Red Army was routed in an orgy of carnage on the banks of the Vistula River. Some 15,000 Russians were slaughtered and 65,000 taken prisoner. A further 30,000 fled across the nearest border into Prussia and were disarmed. The victory was owed in popular imagination neither to the courage of the citizen army nor to Pilsudski's tactics, which were as brilliant as they were bold, but to the direct intervention of the Virgin Mary. She would be accorded credit for stopping the sweep of atheistic communism into the West. The battle was to be known in future years as the Miracle of the Vistula. Patriotism and religious fervor, piety and violence, were at fever pitch.

Karol Wojtyla was born on May 18, 1920, in Wadowice, a scruffy provincial town some twenty miles southwest of Krakow, not far from the Czech border. His father, Karol Senior, was a noncommissioned officer, formerly in the Austro-Hungarian army, now a quartermaster in Poland's militia; his mother, Emilia, an invalid for much of her adult life and inconsolable following the loss of a baby daughter, Olga, took in sewing to make ends meet.

Karol Senior, seldom out of uniform, was a self-disciplined martinet with carefully proportioned mustachios. He mapped out his sons' days, scheduling even their leisure hours. He was pious and controlling. Karol Junior's upbringing under a strict father ("He was so hard on himself that he had no need to be hard on his son," remarked Wojtyla with fond approval) was imbued with devotion to the Virgin, her feast days, cults, shrines, privileges, and perpetual acts of succor. Poland is the country, Wojtyla would one day declare, where one may "hear the beating of the heart of the nation in the heart of the Mother." He knelt before the statue of the Virgin in the parish church every day on his way to school, where he was taught by a succession of dedicated priests.

Nearby, on the summit of a hill, was a discalced, or barefoot, Carmelite community, austere monk-friars who practiced both the contemplative and the active missionary life. He became an early devotee of the Carmelite scapular, two pieces of cloth to be worn over one's breast and back, signifying Mary's protection. Those wearing the scapular at their deaths, it was believed, were excused their due in Purgatory and would rise straight to heaven the Friday following their passing.

The greatest of Poland's shrines was the monastery at Jasna Gora, "Bright Mountain," housing the miraculous icon of "The Black Madonna" in the city of Czestochowa. The wood on which the icon is painted is reputed to be the board of the table, crafted by St. Joseph, on which the holy family ate; St. Luke, the evangelist, is credited with having painted the image. Prince Ladislaus Opolszyk brought it to Czestochowa in 1382, and Prince Jagiello built the monastery and church for the Paulite Fathers, whose task in perpetuity was to venerate and protect the sacred object. After the monastery repulsed an attack by antipapist Swedes in 1656, Our Lady of Czestochowa was proclaimed Queen of Poland. The icon became the rallying sign of Polish nationalism. On a visit to Jasna Gora, June 6, 1979, Wojtyla, as Pope, would inform his listeners that as a schoolboy he had been granted "special interviews" with Our Lady at the shrine. The icon would become the inspiration for Henryk Grecki's Opus 36, *Symphony of Songs of Complaint,* which bears comparison with Britten's *War Requiem* and Shostakovich's *Leningrad Symphony* as memorials to the victims of World War II.

Then there were the shrines of the Christ and Virgin of Kalwaria situated in steep woodland between Wadowice and Krakow—chapels and grottoes commemorating the House at Nazareth, the Mount of Olives, Mount Calvary, the Brook of Kedron, the tomb of Mary: twenty-four shrines in all. Each year the young Wojtyla and his father attended the richly somber annual Marian Festival: "The Funeral and Triumph of the Mother of God," conducted on the eve of the feast of her Assumption into Heaven. All through the night Karol, among a host of pilgrims bearing lamps, trudged up and down the steep hills following an open coffin in which lay an effigy of the dead Mother of God. Parallel with the Way of the Cross, celebrated on Good Friday each year, her destination was the burial place from whence she would be assumed on the morrow, body and soul into heaven. The ritualistic insistence on the death of Mary was no small matter along these borderlands where the Latin rite antagonistically confronted the Eastern Orthodox schismatics who insisted that Mary merely slept rather than died before she was conducted to heaven by an angelic host.

It was to the altar in the basilica at Kalwaria that Wojtyla's father and his two sons repaired in 1929 to pray for the soul of Emilia, Karol's mother. She had died alone, away from home, aged forty-five. Karol was just nine years of age. All we know for certain is that she had been under treatment for kidney and heart disease. When the father learned of her death, he had marched over to Karol's school, conveyed the information to a duty teacher, and departed, leaving the boy to receive the news of his mother's death without paternal consolation. It was remembered that Karol, dry-eyed, told the teacher: "It is God's will." Ten years later, Karol Wojtyla, poet, dramatist, and actor, would write a poem to her:

> *On your white tomb*
> *Blossom the white flowers of life.*
> *Oh how many years have already vanished*
> *Without you—how many years?*
> *On your white tomb*
> *Closed now for years*
> *Something seems to rise:*
> *Inescapable as death.*
> *On your white tomb*
> *Mother, my lifeless love . . .*

Karol grew up a pensive soul, although not introverted. One of his acting friends, Danuta Michalowska, says that when things went well during rehearsal he would cartwheel across the stage. Three years after the death of his mother, Edmund the doctor, Karol's beloved older brother who had carried him everywhere on his shoulders, died from scarlet fever contracted from a patient. Edmund's death made a deeper impression on Karol than the death of his mother, he would recall, "because of the dramatic circumstances in which it occurred and because I was more mature." His brother died in agony and anger. The senior hospital physician who stood by his bed related that Edmund had cried out repeatedly in his death throes: "Why me? Why *now*?"

Karol Wojtyla had the answer. He solemnly reminded those who attempted to commiserate that it was "the will of God." Throughout his pontificate, John Paul has kept his brother's stethoscope in a drawer in his desk.

Death, suffering, and separation were inescapable, as the poem he wrote in honor of his mother emphasized. But the Motherhood of Our Lady exemplified a suffering that brought consolation and promise of succor. Her heart, too, had been pierced with sorrows. She too had died, but she would not allow death to separate her from her children. Her motherly care beyond death was demonstrated by her frequent visitations, her real presences on this earth, as if she were on pilgrimage to the promised era of the third millennium.

Such were the Marian meditations that would take shape in Karol Wojtyla's soul on his strange and eventful path to the priesthood, and in time to the very pinnacle of the Catholic Church. He would articulate his particular insight into her earthly apparitions "through space and time, and even more through the history of souls." Ruminating on the great shrines dedicated to her apparitions in his encyclical letter to the world, *Mater Redemptoris* (*Mother of the Redeemer*, 1987), he would make special mention of Guadalupe (Our Lady of the Americas outside Mexico City), Lourdes, Fatima, and his own Polish Jasna Gora, a "specific geography of faith," as he called it, not forgetting "all those places of pilgrimage where the People of God seek to meet the Mother of God in order to find, within the radius of the maternal presence of her who believed, a strengthening of their own faith."

*

In August 1938, when Karol was eighteen, he arrived in the city of Krakow with his father. They had inherited the lower ground floor of a house in which his mother had once owned a share. "Day after day," Wojtyla would write later of his father, "I was able to observe the austere way in which he lived. After my mother's death, his life became one of constant prayer. Sometimes I would wake up during the night and find my father on his knees." Small wonder he would refer to his home life in Krakow as a "kind of domestic seminary." For the serious young drama king Karol, however, the comparison was entirely a favorable one.

He stood out among the first-year students at the university. With his long hair, open-necked collars, and extravagant hand gestures, he looked every inch the artist. He was yet to master the minimalism that would bring the house down in later years. His bearing was "full of dignity"; one informant speaks of his wearing fashionable knicker-bockers and trendy brown shoes of above-ankle cut. He continued to be stagestruck, and so when he enrolled at the Jagiellonian University he was drawn to courses in the history of the Polish language, Polish literature, and Polish drama. He took voice training and joined yet another local drama group. Halina Krolikiewicz, the Polish actress with whom he collaborated in the theatre at school and afterward, has commented: "He analyzed everything, thought everything through. But he also had a sparkle, an ironic sparkle in his eye."

*

Disaster leading to global catastrophe struck as Karol Wojtyla entered his second year at the university. On September 1, 1939, Hitler invaded Poland with overwhelming superiority in arms, exploiting the Wehrmacht's new military blitzkrieg strategy. On September 17, the Red Army, under the bitter and tyrannical deal struck with Hitler, swarmed into eastern Poland, greatly accelerating the bloody defeat of the country. But Poland's agony was just beginning, particularly for the nation's Jews, millions of whom were transported to concentration camps in Poland. By the end of the war, in addition to the uprooting of populations, starvation, and repression, some six million Poles were to suffer death or physical injury. Hans Frank, the Nazi governor general, planned to make Poland a slave state, destroying its culture and liquidating the entire intellectual and academic class, as well as its priesthood. Contemplating Karol Wojtyla's profound abhorrence of contraception and abortion, it is crucial to remember that as a young man, having lost his mother, sister, and brother, he witnessed the tidal wave of hatred that threatened to crush the life out of an entire people. Small wonder he saw in every indication of thwarted life a type and exemplification of that lust for annihilation that he came to call a "culture of death."

Wojtyla's university teachers and many students were rounded up and sent to concentration camps. The brutality of the occupation gave greater impetus and point to Wojtyla's passion for theatre. Working during the day in a quarry where minerals were mined for the Solvay chemical plant, which made explosives for the Nazis, he was entitled to a permit that allowed him to remain in Krakow. In his spare time, he helped found a secret drama society that staged readings of patriotic poetry and new writing. The group regarded their readings and clandestine improvisations as a form of resistance more effective than the violent tactics of the partisans who hid in the woods and came at night to kill Germans and collaborators. The theatrical material included a genre known as Polish Messianism, work of traditional "prophetic" bards that exemplified the suffering and resurrection of Poland as a parallel to Christ's sacrifice for the human race. Poland was the Christ, scourged and nailed to the cross.

Living amid death, cruelty, privation, and oppression—and, in time, evidence of genocide from the smoking chimney stacks beyond the barbed wire of Auschwitz, thirty miles distant from Krakow—Wojtyla's secret theatre assumed the proportions of an alternative world, an alternative reality. Nor were their dreams restricted to central Europe. The Polish Messianists dreamed of a Slavic Pope who would one day reform the papacy and spread Catholicism eastward across the globe. The young Wojtyla would have heard many times the lines of the patriotic dramatist Juliusz Slowacki (1809–49):

> *Armed discord God strikes*
> *At a bell immense,*
> *For a Slavic Pope*

He opened the throne . . .
Behold the Slavic Pope is coming
A brother of the people.

It was in 1940, the second year of the war, that Karol's religious life blossomed and combined, indivisibly, with his love of theatre. He would come to believe that in the contrast between what one is and what one aspires to be consists the thrilling drama of human existence. He came to believe, moreover, that our personal religious dramas are part of the ultimate drama, written and directed from all eternity by God, who inhabits the center stage of the cosmos.

It was as if the flames of two candles were conjoining, feeding on each other and producing an ever-fiercer brightness. A devout youth, serious by nature, solemn in bereavement, oppressed by Nazi occupation, he was irresistibly drawn to a deep, all-embracing religious commitment. Carrying stones in the quarry by day (how he must have thought of the Good Friday Way of the Cross pilgrimage at Kalwaria, when young men carried rocks while following the Christ), working in the clandestine theatre when time allowed, he found spiritual sustenance in the devotions of the parish of St. Stanislaw Kostka in Krakow. Under the Nazi onslaught, priests were being arrested, tortured, and murdered; as the numbers of the clergy declined, laymen were encouraged to step in. One such pastoral worker was a pious bachelor, Jan Tyranowski, aged forty years at the time that Wojtyla met him in the second year of the war.

To some, Tyranowski came across as mentally unstable. An autodidact, he spoke with stilted language in a high, piping voice. A curious gloss on his bachelordom notes that he had rebuffed the overtures made by various women in his youth. There was an occasional hint of gay ostentation. A picture of him taken around the time he first met Wojtyla reveals him dressed in a white nightgown, sitting bolt-upright in bed between starched lace sheets, like the risen Christ, gazing wide-eyed into the camera. Wojtyla, however, revealing a taste for spiritual chiaroscuro, saw him as one of those "unknown saints, hidden amid the others like a marvellous light at the bottom of life, at a depth where night usually reigns."

Tyranowski, who worked as a tailor alongside his father and brother, lived amid drifts of books and three sewing machines. Having taken a vow of celibacy, he devoted himself to a determined pursuit of sainthood. He had ransacked the works of Father Adolf Alfred Tanquerey, author of the redoubtable *The Spiritual Life*, widely read in seminaries throughout the world. But his crucial mentor in the realms of mysticism was St. John of the Cross, the seventeenth-century Carmelite poet-mystic. Tanquerey's work, which was mechanical and systematic, came out of the late-nineteenth-century scholastic revival led by Leo XIII—characterized by abstract reasoning, logic, questions, objections, and carefully parceled theses. Tanquerey eschewed visions, voices, levitations, and consolations in prayer, or at least put them firmly in their place. His recommendations for growth in the spirit bore a strong resemblance to the self-disciplined exercises of an athletic workout. In contrast, John of the Cross stressed suffering on the path to mystical union but employed the poetic imagery of romance, sexual passion, betrothal, marriage, the evocative images of unrequited lovers wandering lovelorn in the night: the tantalizing spiritual melodrama of the Dark Night of the Soul.

It has often been repeated in pious accounts of the life of Karol Wojtyla that he was a mystic and that he had been guided thence by Jan Tyranowski. Spiritual directors in the first half of the twentieth century were conscious of the woolliness that passed for the pursuit of the mystical, the hazards of narcissism and self-absorption in pursuit of the state known as contemplation or unitive prayer. Who is called to contemplation? Can it be acquired by our own efforts? Or is it a gift of the Holy Spirit? Is one even aware of the gift? At the heart of such questions was a curious paradox, much debated in the schools of mysticism: One might only consider oneself a recipient of divinely infused knowledge should one remain entirely unaware of having received such a gift. A reassuring sign, although by no means a guarantee, was a continuing thirst for mystical union with God despite the absence of "lights," or revelations, in prayer.

Wojtyla began reading St. John of the Cross under Tyranowski's earnest tutelage, and he embarked on a course in Spanish in order to read the poet-mystic in the original. Was Wojtyla in the process of being enticed by Tyranowski into the miasmas of mystic woolliness? By every account, it would seem that Tyranowski was an authentic guide in these hazardous regions of the spirit. Wojtyla would come to understand, under his guidance, that the high point of contemplation was the meeting of two liberties, two personal wills: the human person and the person of Jesus Christ.

But there was another crucial dimension. On arriving in Krakow, Wojtyla, in a bid for independence and maturity, had thought to scale down his devotions to the Virgin Mary so as to concentrate exclusively on the person of Jesus. That was until Tyranowski placed in his hands a copy of the works of St. Louis de Montfort, the seventeenth-century French "vagabond" missionary, founder of the Company of Mary, and author of *True Devotion to Mary* and *The Secret of Mary*. De Montfort had developed an enthusiasm for Marian devotion that many thought extravagant, couching his prayers to Mary in baroque language aimed at drawing in like-minded devotees (while correspondingly, it has to be said, deterring the many not so minded). From de Montfort, Wojtyla would one day borrow his papal motto: *Totus Tuus,* All Yours, indicating the gift of his entire self, not to the People of God, but to the Virgin in emulation of her gift of self to her children. For it was Mary, always Mary, Wojtyla came to trust, despite his brief hesitation, or perhaps because of it, who points us in the direction of the Lord. As the de Montfort prayer has it:

My powerful Queen, you are all mine through your mercy, and I am all yours.
    Take away from me all that may displease God and cultivate in me all that is pleasing to Him.

Tyranowski's influence, as it happened, had begun with an intense practical Marian devotion conducted in the parish. He had recruited Wojtyla into a prayer circle known as the "Living Rosary." The gatherings in church, or in the privacy of the devotees' homes, were composed of fifteen members, corresponding to the fifteen meditations of the rosary, which involves the repetition of Hail Marys, 150 in all, counted out on "rosary beads." By establishing a "living" rosary, the church of St. Stanislaw Kostka had created an unusual form of spiritual and social solidarity in those dark and dangerous times.

Tyranowski's influence was to increase through the war years—even more so after February 1941, when Karol Wojtyla Senior died alone, age sixty-two, of a heart attack in the basement apartment. He was found by Wojtyla and a friend when they arrived one evening with food and medicine. Wojtyla wept copiously, regretting that he was absent at his father's passing. He spent the night in prayer beside his father's corpse. More than half a century later, he remembered: "I never felt so alone . . ." Many years later, he would confide that almost all his memories of childhood and adolescence were connected with his father. "The violence of the blows that struck him opened up immense spiritual depths in him; his grief found its outlet in prayer. The mere fact of seeing him on his knees had a decisive influence on my early years."

Distraught in his sorrow, entirely alone in the world, Wojtyla walked several miles every day to Krakow's military cemetery after finishing work in the quarry in order to kneel and weep and pray in the mud by his father's grave. Wojtyla's contemporary of those days, later to become a priest, Mieczyslaw Malinski, would say many years later that he feared that Wojtyla might lose his mind. Malinski has confirmed that it was Jan Tyranowski who sustained him. And it was under the auspices of the "mystic" tailor that Wojtyla's priestly vocation now began to grow and flourish. Addressing seminarians in Krakow as a young bishop twenty years later, he said of Tyranowski: "I don't know whether it is to him that I owe my priesthood calling, but, in any event, it was born within his climate, the climate of the mystery of supernatural life."

Karol Wojtyla was at first tempted to give his all and plunge into a Carmelite vocation, a spirituality famous for its contrast: meditative prayer on the mountaintop, alternating with evangelism in the marketplace. Karol Wojtyla hesitated, then decided for the secular or diocesan priesthood: pastors who live in the world while not being *of* the world. Perhaps, he believed, the supreme ideal was to live simultaneously on the mountain and in the marketplace. Would that not be the pinnacle of the imitation of Christ?

By 1942, he had enrolled in a clandestine seminary housed within the Krakow palace of Cardinal Adam Sapieha. He continued to work at the Solvay plant, but he now carried in his satchel a manual of Thomistic metaphysics. His fellow seminarian Malinski recalls seeing Wojtyla in blue overalls and clogs without socks, puzzling over the abstract theses. "It's hard going," he would say. "I sit by the boiler and try to understand it—I feel it ought to be very important to me." We are told that sometimes Wojtyla wept with frustration as he studied the philosophical texts in the midst of chemical fumes, quarry explosions, and clashing machinery. And he would have been in no doubt of the danger that attended a clandestine training for the priesthood. Sapieha had links with the Polish underground resistance, which was taking orders from the Polish government in exile in London. The Nazis would kill some 2,500 Polish priests and five bishops by the war's end. Sapieha believed that effective retaliation involved not armed resistance but the training of priests who would restore Poland's Church from the ashes in the aftermath of war. For the rest of his life, Wojtyla would believe that the Catholic priesthood involved heroism, discipline, and ultimate self-sacrifice. As Pope, he would show no sympathy for priests who abandoned their vows of celibacy in order to marry.

Karol came through the war physically unscathed, save for a near-fatal road accident when he was knocked down by a truck and almost left for dead. A woman acquaintance on a passing tram leapt into the road and had him borne to a hospital by a passing army vehicle. Lying in a hospital bed, he was convinced that his priestly vocation had been supernaturally confirmed by his survival. And what more supernatural confirmation did he need of the special providence in his regard, when he considered the deaths of so many of his contemporaries, friends, acquaintances, and teachers?

It is uncertain to this day just what Karol Wojtyla did and did not do to help Jewish victims during the war. One thing we know for certain: A woman called Edith Tszierer, still alive at the time of this writing, declared that she owed her life to him. As a teenager she had been in the Sakrzysko-Kammiena labor camp. Released at the end of the war, she was too weak to walk. Karol Wojtyla gave her bread and tea and carried her on his back for three kilometers to a railway station. In Jerusalem on March 23, 2000, she broke down in tears as she thanked him at the Yad Vashem memorial center.

He was ordained on the Feast of All Saints, November 1, 1946, aged twenty-six—a ceremony not unmixed with sadness, since his father was not there to witness the greatest day of his life, nor Jan Tyranowski, who was seriously ill. His first three Masses were celebrated in a black chasuble, the vestments worn at Masses for the dead, in the St. Leonard's chapel in the crypt of Wawel Cathedral. It was the Feast of All Souls, the one day in the year when it was possible under the old dispensation to celebrate Mass three times. In an extended meditation on his first Masses on the golden anniversary of his priesthood, he recalled the tombs in that crypt: "All those people are 'great spirits' who led the nation through the ages. In their ranks are found not only sovereigns and their consorts, or bishops and cardinals, but also poets, great masters of the language, who were extremely influential in my education as a Christian and a patriot." He dedicated the Masses for his dead family—mother, father, and brother—but with the oils of ordination not yet dry on his hands, he was already conscious of his relationship with the great and the good of the history, culture, and public life of his nation.

The Eternal City

Two weeks after being raised to the priesthood, young Father Wojtyla was making his way by train across Europe, via Paris, to Rome. We have glimpses of the young priest in photographs, wearing spectacles (later he would use contact lenses), broad-shouldered, slightly stooped, strong-jawed, mature for his years.

He had been granted barely eighteen months to pursue studies for a doctorate in divinity, although the Roman doctorate in those days was more akin to an M.A. dissertation. It was not given to every young priest to be funded for a postgraduate Roman education, especially in destitute countries like Poland where every priest was needed. Cardinal Sapieha evidently judged Wojtyla a potential ecclesiastical highflyer, and in the traditional manner was boosting his future clerical career by acquainting him with *Romanitá*—the "Roman thing."

Cardinal Sapieha had enrolled Wojtyla at the Dominican house of theological studies known as the Angelicum, where he was supervised by Father Reginald (nicknamed "The Rigid") Garrigou-Lagrange, the well-known French Dominican scholar. Garrigou-Lagrange was a specialist in spirituality, the author of a three-volume work on St. John of the Cross, and a preeminent champion of conservative interpretations of Thomas Aquinas, whose philosophy and theology had been deemed virtually dogma since Pope Leo XIII in the last decade of the nineteenth century. Hans Küng, the dissident theologian, a young Roman seminarian in the postwar era, reports sitting alone with just one other student while "The Rigid" droned through St. Thomas's *Summa,* line by line. Küng had been frustrated by the conservatives at the Jesuit Gregorian University and had gone to the Angelicum in search of something more progressive. "By comparison," observes Küng, however, "the theses at the Gregorian seemed even modern to us." Placing Father Wojtyla under the tutelage of the great Garrigou-Lagrange seemed to indicate his bishop's decision to keep Wojtyla out of liberal harm's way.

Yet for the young priest who had never left Poland, the Roman experience was an opportunity to broaden his horizons. Lodged in more than a hundred national seminaries in Rome were students and scholars from all over the world. He trudged the Eternal City, acquainting himself with its churches, catacombs, and antiquities. He learned Italian, which he came to speak fluently albeit in a heavy Polish accent. He also brought his Latin to a high level of competence, which was to help him years later during the sessions of the Second Vatican Council in the 1960s. When he became Pope he would be hailed as The Man from a Far Country: Few suspected how completely at home he was in Rome, the center of Church governance.

Meanwhile, Garrigou-Lagrange was a strong influence, being at the eye of a fierce theological storm that would rage for years to come. In the 1930s, a group of French theologians, led by the Jesuit Henri de Lubac (1896–1991), had begun a work of theological renewal. They were striving to end a period of Catholic anti-modern and anti-Protestant bias in France while combating Nazi neopaganism and anti-Semitism. In the process they were returning, in their view, to the roots of Christian belief. De Lubac believed that Catholicism was in danger of losing a sense of the communion of humankind, its solidarity through God's incarnation in Jesus Christ. De Lubac was seeking in his prewar writings to convince Catholics that Christianity was a social religion.

In the very year Wojtyla arrived in Rome, Garrigou-Lagrange had delivered a shockingly intemperate attack against de Lubac and his colleagues. "What do they propose to put in the place of Thomas?" Garrigou-Lagrange fulminated in an article in the Angelicum's journal. "Where is the New Theology going with the new teachers who inspire it? Where is it going, if not on the paths of skepticism, fantasy and heresy." Evidently, there could be no worse insult than "new," "newness," "the new." Not surprisingly, before allowing Father Wojtyla to proceed with his doctoral thesis, Garrigou-Lagrange set the young Polish priest to work, augmenting and invigorating his knowledge of St. Thomas according to the prevailing views at the Angelicum.

Garrigou-Lagrange had a profound impact on many of the students who came in contact with him. He had a soaring, mystical view of the priesthood as conferring a transcendental, indelible character on the soul of the recipient of ordination. Such notions reveal the extent to which he had distanced himself from the "social Christianity" of de Lubac and his colleagues. Wojtyla's views of priesthood, when he came to be Pope, would reflect his mentor's view that the priest enjoys supernatural charisms that privilege him and separate him from the rest of humankind. In his book *The Priest in Union with Christ,* Garrigou-Lagrange argued that ordination is a calling to the highest vocation on earth, higher than the archangels, in union with the great High Priest, Jesus Christ, himself of whom the Holy Father was Vicar. Later generations of progressive vocational advisers would question this approach, arguing that it put an unbridgeable gulf between clergy and the laity, especially female laity. The high status of ordination would be criticized as privileging men, who might well be fragmented and inadequate, with a dangerous degree of unwarranted self-regard, thus exacerbating their immaturity.

But there were other perspectives on the priesthood at that time. Cardinal Sapieha was keen that Wojtyla and a companion Polish student from the diocese of Krakow, Stanislaw Starowieyski, should travel to acquaint themselves with the worker-priest movement in France, where priests had been forced into factories and labor camps by the Nazis during the war. A former worker-seminarian himself, Wojtyla warmed to this project. He consequently traveled through France and Belgium during his vacations, meeting worker-priests. Yet the question, still, was how to live in the world yet not be *of* the world. Father Wojtyla, we learn, believed the Paris Metro to be an excellent place in which to practice spiritual meditation (it would be remembered years later by members of Opus Dei, an organization beloved of Pope John Paul II, that their founder, Josemaría Escrivá de Balaguer, had his deepest mystical experience on a tram). In those years at Solvay, Karol Wojtyla had mastered the art of being in one place physically and elsewhere mentally. But was this what the worker-priest apostolate was about: to be present and yet detached in spirit? The French worker-priests were rather more coarse-grained and gritty than Father Wojtyla's aspiration to mysticism on the Metro implied. The worker-priests, in fact, were soon to be disbanded for the threat they seemed to pose to traditionalist notions of priesthood, being in the world but not of the world, as promoted by Garrigou-Lagrange and Pope Pius XII.

After 1950, worker-priests were ordered by Pius XII to abandon the communities in which they worked and to take up residence in priests' houses or religious communities. They were required to do only part-time jobs and drop their union memberships. Lost in the eventual abolition of the worker apostolate, according to those who espoused the movement, was a more social, humane Church reaching out to a post-Christian France. The vision of an elevated sacralized, separate, priestly caste was to win the day. In years to come, it was clear that the seeds sown by Garrigou-Lagrange and the culture of Pius XII would survive and thrive, for both better and worse, in the soul of Karol Wojtyla.

*

The research topic for Wojtyla's doctorate, when he finally embarked on it under the close scrutiny of his eminent Thomistic supervisor, was "The Doctrine of Faith in St. John of the Cross."

John of the Cross was at that time being scrutinized for elevation to the status of Doctor of the Church by Pius XII. The point of Father Wojtyla's thesis, it seems, was to demonstrate that the mystic saint saw eye to eye with the Angelic Doctor, Thomas Aquinas, on the theology of faith. As it turned out, Garrigou-Lagrange was not entirely satisfied with Wojtyla's thesis. The issue between them was a technical aspect of the prayer of contemplation, or unitive prayer; at the same time, we see Wojtyla's early absorption in the meaning of personhood, the individual self. Wojtyla was insistent that one does not come to Christ in unitive prayer as one seeking an object among other objects in the world (for how could God be a mere object), but as a free act of will—a free person meeting the person and will of Christ as the All. The personal and free nature of an individual's capacity to meet Christ is central, he insisted, to what it means to be human. Garrigou-Lagrange, however, following Thomas Aquinas, as he thought, insisted on the objective nature of human apprehension, even when one was referring to God. Wojtyla dug in his toes and declined to reconsider or rewrite. Although Father Wojtyla received high marks, he never was granted a Roman doctorate for his thesis. He would present it on his return to Poland at the Jagiellonian University, where he successfully graduated to Doctor of Divinity.

Here at the completion of his Roman studies, however, was the foundation of his ideas of "personalism" that Wojtyla would build on through the rest of his life: that the human person is essentially a unique individual with the capacity for communion with God. The drama of human existence consisted in the struggle of each individual soul to realize union with *Him*. Taking God out of the equation of humanity, as Soviet communism was striving to do in his homeland, was to deny not just belief in God but our essential humanity. The works of St. John of the Cross were to have a deep and lasting effect on Wojtyla beyond the growth of his own personal spirituality. But there was a further dimension. He believed with St. John of the Cross that suffering, doubt, and prayer can lead to an infusion of divine knowledge. As the late Cardinal John Krol of

Philadelphia would say admiringly of John Paul II, "He studied theology on his knees."

On the question of kneeling, as it happens, students at the Belgian college, where he was lodged, had noticed that Father Wojtyla spent many hours on his knees in chapel, where it was noted that his prayer posture was singular: Unlike his companions, Wojtyla made a point of kneeling on the bare floor of the chapel, eschewing the comfortable kneelers provided.

*

In 1947, when Father Wojtyla was still in his first year of residence in Rome, he took a step in the direction of another kind of mysticism, less intellectual than the rarefied ratiocinations at the Angelicum but nonetheless incendiary to the soul of the young Polish priest. With travel funds provided by Cardinal Sapieha, Wojtyla and his companion Stanislaw embarked on a tour of shrines and sacred curiosities, an important destination, San Giovanni di Rotondo in southwest Italy, marking his early inclination for the physical phenomena of popular mysticism.

The years following the Second World War had seen the expansion of the cult of a Franciscan friar called Padre Pio, who was credited with mystical charisms: healing, stigmata, prophecy, bilocation, unusual discernment, and paranormal occurrences such as demonic attacks courageously withstood in the night. Padre Pio was born Francesco Porgione near Naples in 1877. He entered a Franciscan seminary at the age of fifteen and was ordained by the age of twenty-three. Not long after ordination, he began to experience the wounds of Christ in his hands, feet, and side. His status and reputation, however, were controversial. Ecclesiastical detractors accused him of inflicting the stigmatic wounds upon himself with carbolic acid, which, they said, had been found under his bed along with eau de cologne.

Without moving from his friary at San Giovanni di Rotondo on the Gargano peninsula, Padre Pio more than any holy man in

Catholic Christendom in the twentieth century seemed to provide tangible and abundant proof, according to his enthusiastic devotees, that God intervenes in direct and observable ways in human affairs. Indeed, he was credited with performing miracles at great distances around the globe, leaving a distinctive aroma behind. He was even said to have appeared to Allied pilots during air battles, warding off Luftwaffe fighter planes.

The high point of the day was the celebration of his Mass. There were stories of pilgrims being bitten, knocked to the ground, and trampled in the rush to get close to the altar. When not struggling with demons or praying in ecstasy, Padre Pio would hear confessions for as long as twelve hours a day. He was known to tell penitents of sins they had either forgotten or were keeping from him.

During the Easter break from the Angelicum in 1947, Wojtyla and Starowieyski repaired to the monastery of Padre Pio. As Wojtyla traveled south, he may well have had in mind another mystic, his friend Jan Tyranowski, who had died an agonizing death in the previous month in a hospital in Krakow. Tyranowski suffered generalized infection, possibly the result of cancer, and had had an arm amputated in an attempt to stop the spread.

In San Giovanni, Father Wojtyla went to confession with Padre Pio.

Father Andrzej Bardecki, editor of the *Tygodnik Powszechny*, a semi-independent Catholic newspaper in postwar Poland, has said that Wojtyla "spoke about him with the greatest esteem—he believed that Padre Pio would [one day be made] a saint." However, Cardinal Archbishop Alfons Stickler, the Austrian prince of the church, has asserted that "Padre Pio told [Wojtyla] he would gain the highest post in the Church." Stickler added: "Wojtyla believed when he was created a cardinal, the prophecy was realized." But Padre Pio, as Wojtyla would discover in time, did nothing by halves. Wojtyla, in turn, would himself fulfill the other side of the prophecy by presiding at the Franciscan's beatification in May 1999 on the eve of the millennium.

CHAPTER FOUR

Professor and Pastor

On completing his studies in Rome, Father Wojtyla returned to an impoverished, subjugated Poland, where the Communist Party was attempting to replace the country's sense of its ancient cultural identity with a totalitarian state based on sterile ideology and fear. Poland had become a hellish hinterland where betrayal was endemic, the only theatre was the show trial, and hundreds of thousands languished in labor camps. Poland was a bureaucratically centralized satellite of the Soviet Union, its gray, brutalized postwar architecture exemplifying the cultural and aesthetic void in which the state now operated.

For the young Father Wojtyla, the enemy rose large and clear, the power of darkness in all its manifest lies and malevolence. The course of action for a priest was simple. No accommodation with communism was possible: It would be an unyielding battle for hearts and minds in every context and at every opportunity—not only in church but in the classrooms, the workplaces, even in sport and leisure activities.

Adam Sapieha was still the local bishop of Krakow, but there was a new primate of all Poland—Stefan Wyszynski, a former seminary teacher, consecrated in 1946, now raised to the archbishopric of Warsaw. Archbishop Wyszynski, patriot, former resistance leader, and Marian devotee, would lay the ground for an energetic nation-wide pastoral mission. He would encourage a powerful alternative to Soviet atheism; it would be grassroots and inspired by popular Marian piety.

Father Wojtyla was at first appointed assistant pastor in a rustic hamlet fifteen miles east of Krakow. He made the journey on foot. Crossing the boundary of his new parish, he threw himself face-down and kissed the soil. The gesture, witnessed by parishioners, would become a signature of his travels as Pope in future years. It was in emulation of the Curé d'Ars—Saint Jean-Marie Vianney, the French patron saint of parish priests, who kissed the soil of his parish every time he reentered it. During his travels through France, Wojtyla had visited the parish of Ars, where he learned of Jean Vianney's boast that he was a "prisoner of the confessional," spending up to eighteen hours a day listening to his flock confess their sins. The saintly Curé was a model of self-denial.

The young Father Wojtlya imitated the French Curé saint's poverty-stricken demeanor, trudging about the parish wearing scuffed boots and threadbare cassock in all weathers, spending untold hours in the confessional, prostrating himself on the floor of the church at night, sleeping on the bare boards of his bedroom. He gave away his only bed pillow to a woman who had been robbed of hers. His friend and fellow priest, Malinski, said he looked like a down-and-out. Always about his Father's business, we are told that he had a tendency to be late for appointments.

It was barely eight months before Sapieha brought him back into Krakow to serve in a busy city parish where his pastoral duties included caring for students at the Jagiellonian University and the city polytechnic. The stooped, emaciated, and bespectacled figure of the young priest could be seen passing with a determined step from the sanctuary to the confessional, to the hostels and garret lodgings of his student flock, then back to the confessional. He would keep a penitent in the box for an hour and more. He was a "demanding" confessor, it was said. Here was a context in which the drama of the life of the soul—who I am and who I ought to be—could be played out to the full: Father Wojtyla directing the one-on-one theatre of the soul in the darkness of the confessional.

Father Wojtyla was a tireless counselor of teenagers on questions of love and dating. He advocated self-control, and training in self-denial, with an intensity that was remembered a whole lifetime later by members of his audience. He did not scruple to involve himself intimately in the lives of his young parishioners. One of his penitents, Marie Tornowska, has said that Father Wojtyla encouraged her to woo a particular young man. When she demurred, informing the good father that the young man would not be interested in her, he insisted that she should *educate* the fellow to be her partner. Fortunately, she saw the funny side of it.

At weekends he turned theatrical impresario, renewing his old contacts at the Rhapsodic Theatre and producing medieval mystery plays. Then there were the singing rehearsals for the choir he was training to render the Gregorian Mass of the Angels. Moreover, there were nights when, despite a grueling eighteen-hour pastoral day, he would meet with his special philosophy group to plow, like his erstwhile mentor Garrigou-Lagrange, line by line through the *Summa Theologiae* of Thomas Aquinas.

He was earning admiration on every side, but it was noted that he was liable to obfuscation in the pulpit. We are told that he humbly accepted criticism and made determined efforts to be accessible. One undesirable trait in his pastoral work persisted: He was *never* on time. One of his parishioners noted that he was socially awkward. Yet such was his magnetism that a network of young people formed about him, hungry for ideas that provided alternatives to the sterile totalitarian-state auspices.

Like many a priest during this postwar period, he accompanied groups of young people on expeditions among the hills, the woods, and the lakes—hiking, kayaking, and skiing. Each day began with Mass in the open or in a barn. In the evening around the campfire, he would prompt earnest conversation. At least one member of his youth group noted that he was a good listener; and yet he was ever the paternalist. "He didn't stir up in our group any sort of intellectual discussion in a critical sense," recollected one of his young group, Karol Tarnowski.

He did not encourage overfamiliarity, but he never tired of asking questions about the romantic relationships of his young companions, either: how they felt, how they behaved, in what manner they were they attracted to each other. How far they should go. Surprisingly, none had the impression that he was voyeuristic.

He also entertained the young people in his charge, reciting long poems and chunks of prose, and singing patriotic songs in his sonorous voice. A more mature audience might have found him a trifle tedious. He had a habit of quoting lines he had memorized from a huge repertoire of literature, then saying: "Who's that?"

*

Despite the unremitting workload of parish and chaplaincy duties, Wojtyla had academic and literary ambitions. On his return from Rome, he had walked into the office of Krakow's Catholic newspaper *Tygodnik Powszechny (Universal Weekly)* and submitted a piece on French worker-priests. Thereafter the paper, which was an irritant to the Communists and at times to the Catholic hierarchy too, became an important outlet for his essays and poetry. And now Archbishop Baziak, his new bishop after Sapieha's death, granted Father Wojtyla study leave to research a second doctorate that would qualify him to apply for a university teaching post in philosophy.

Leaving the parish, he went to live in a garret in the old city with a few clothes, his books, and his skis. It was a hard time for a bishop to lose the full-time services of such a talented and energetic priest; but the Church in Poland had need of intellectual pastors to engage the party ideologues who were infiltrating Catholic communities and the universities. The Communist Party was even attempting to bring to prominence priests and bishops they felt were ideologically sympathetic to the regime. Men like Wojtyla could be a crucial antidote.

Wojtyla's new doctoral topic was on ethics. He sought to ground his philosophical meditations in the heart and the will: the mystery of the human person. His guide in this attempt, if not his guru, was the German philosopher Max Scheler, who had died in 1928. For all the years that he studied and taught philosophy, Wojtyla would have Scheler's works at his elbow.

Scheler was associated with the philosophical movement known as phenomenology. Phenomenologists were intent on studying the nature of knowledge, mind, will, consciousness, and personhood through ruminative individual subjective experience rather than the approach of scholasticism, which was strictly logical, linear, and abstract and highly objective. Scheler, son of a Protestant father and a Jewish mother, became a Catholic convert in his teenage years, but his personal life was fragmented and he was a womanizer. After divorcing his first wife and remarrying, he left the Church. The austere Polish cleric Wojtyla would have deplored Scheler's lifestyle; but he was nonetheless attracted to the philosopher's high subjective cast of thought, which tended to circle around a topic, taking observations from many different vantage points.

Wojtyla struggled with the Scheler texts, struggled with his own philosophical scruples, and wrestled with his conscience—for was not Thomas Aquinas, the Angelic Doctor, by decree of Pope Leo XIII, the foundational, definitive, and magisterial guide to Catholic thought? He wavered, and set himself the task of combining the insights of Aquinas with those of Scheler. Surely, the circuitous, less disciplined thoughts of Scheler would benefit from alignment with the highly logical, time-honored foundations of Thomas Aquinas.

The conflict between two such contrasting philosophical force fields gave impetus to a current of contradiction that would run through Wojtyla's thinking for the rest of his life. As for style, the Scheler-Aquinas combination made for a poorly reconciled combination of phenomenological ducking and weaving, and scholastic goose-stepping. Wojtyla's apologists down the years would claim that he thus redressed and enlivened the inflexibility and austerity of scholasticism. Yet, to others, he had adopted the worst of both worlds. As one Jesuit scholar commented on John Paul's philosophical writing, with feline acerbity: "I often have the impression of banging into scholastic steel as I wander through the phenomenological fog."

His poems, which he began to publish under pseudonyms from 1950 onward, also suffer from frequent obfuscation and the baffling syntactical innovations popular at the time among modernists and experimentalists. The tendency to obscure his meaning may well have been a measure of his need to throw his materialist antagonists off balance; and yet a literary critic might be forgiven for considering some of his efforts merely affected.

His plays are more transparent, and yet they lack the interaction between characters familiar in conventional drama. His best-known play, *The Jeweller's Shop,* written during the 1950s, is composed of monologues delivered in the presence of statuesque, unresponsive others, with occasional asides from a chorus offstage, sometimes from a nameless bystander. Characters talk relentlessly to themselves. They meet outside a jeweler's shop window where wedding rings are displayed in order to deliver platitudes about their hopes and fears for future or past marriages. It is a wooden piece lacking dramatic tension or resolution. Had a pope not written it, the piece would surely have been consigned to oblivion long before.

There is an element of unself-critical autodidacticism in Wojtyla's thinking, which persisted beyond his time in Rome, where he was supervised by Reginald "the Rigid," to be sure, but where he did not enjoy a seminar-style peer-group education. Wojtyla never benefited in his student life from a sustained period of genuine routine challenge. His seminary days were fragmented and passed in the midst of emergencies. He worked alone and emerged a full-fledged guru from the outset. He tended to mix with younger people who were in awe of him. But even among equals it was said of him that he would listen carefully, sagely, with kindness, then reach his own conclusions without reference to anything that had been said. We know that he took the draft of his book on sexual ethics, *Love and Responsibility,* to the mountains and had students of medicine and philosophy respond to the material chapter by chapter. There is no evidence, however, that he altered a line as a result of their observations.

We do know, however, that he shared views on sexology with at least one individual at this time—Dr. Wanda Poltawska, a remarkable psychiatrist who had been the victim of medical experiments in the Ravensbrück concentration camp during the war. She treated Wojtyla for flu in 1956, and they found a common interest in her determined rejection of sex outside of marriage, and contraception. She believed that contraception caused neurosis and was conducting empirical research to make her point. She also believed that there was an equivalence between contraception and abortion, in that the contraceptive mentality led to abortion if contraception failed. They shared a common acceptance that chastity was formed by *ascesis*— self-discipline and exercises in self-denial.

Their friendship would be sealed with an instance of the religious paranormal. Several years after their first meeting, Dr. Poltawska was diagnosed with terminal cancer. Father Wojtyla immediately wrote to Padre Pio at his monastery in San Giovanni di Rotondo, beseeching him for his prayers. Before she was due to have an operation for the removal of the tumor, the doctors performed an X-ray and discovered that the growth had vanished. Father Wojtyla, who by this stage was a bishop, about to depart for the Second Vatican Council, was convinced that a miracle had been performed at the holy stigmatic's intercession.

Meanwhile, these years of university teaching in Krakow and Lublin and under the Soviet yoke were immensely challenging to the young priest, so much so that he was driven to the brink of exhaustion. We see him in a shabby soutane and old green overcoat, always late for lectures, forever in transit, taking trains in the early hours between Lublin and Krakow, two hundred miles apart, juggling research with teaching and pastoral work. He was not one for small talk. His students called him "Uncle." He continued to be absent-minded. On one occasion, he and a group of students were so caught up in a class argument after the university had closed its doors for the night that they had to climb out down a drainpipe, only to have a suspicious policeman quiz them in the street.

But his summers, as ever, were spent tramping and kayaking in the mountains. He was away on a distant trip on the lakes of Mazuria when he received the news that he had been nominated an auxiliary bishop in the diocese of Krakow. At thirty-eight years of age, he would be the youngest bishop in the country.

CHAPTER FIVE

Bishop and Cardinal

There is a story that when Cardinal Wyszynski summoned him to ask whether he accepted the Pope's nomination, Father Wojtyla indulged in none of the usual modest preliminaries, such as pleading for due time to pray and reflect. Without hesitation, Wojtyla said: "Where do I sign?" Another story has it that Wojtyla commented that he was rather young to be a bishop, whereupon Wyszynski quipped, "This is a weakness of which we are quickly cured."

Later that day, he entered the chapel of the Ursuline convent in Warsaw on the bank of the Vistula. According to the nuns, he prayed for eight hours, stretched out full length on the chapel floor before the Blessed Sacrament, without taking food or drink. When a nun begged him to take sustenance, he told her that he had "a lot to discuss with the Lord" and was to be left alone. The act was in keeping with his character—the active contemplative; only a cynic could object that the edifying spectacle was performed in the gaze of suitably impressed witnesses.

It seems that Wojtyla was the choice of his own bishop, Eugeniusz Baziak, rather than Cardinal Wyszynski. Wyszynski had his doubts about Wojtyla's pastoral style, suspecting that he was a dreamer and not a doer; Baziak, who originally came from the Ukraine and had spent three years under house arrest, evidently saw a different side to the man. Wojtyla, who had by now gotten that tendency to obfuscate under control, was excelling as a preacher both in church and among professional groups and workers. Talking to medical doctors the year before his consecration as bishop, he told them: "The redemption of mankind means assisting man to achieve the greatness he is meant to possess." He was preaching freedom and the best of all possible alternative worlds within a Communist regime. He was promising rain for famished lands.

He was consecrated bishop in Wawel Cathedral, where he had said his first three Masses twelve years earlier, in 1946. A man in the congregation, a former co-worker in the Solvay chemical plant, called out during the service: "Lolek! Don't let anything get you down!" Lolek, or Charlie, chose as his motto that de Montfort phrase *Totus Tuus*—All Yours.

As the new academic year began, Wojtyla continued to teach on a reduced timetable while drastically expanding his pastoral duties. In order to cut down on the number of visits to Lublin, he would teach for as long as six hours, which left him free to travel the diocese conducting confirmations, ordinations, and retreats, and leading parish and institutional visitations. His constant theme was renewal in the life of Christ. Renewal was in the air—in Poland and far beyond.

A month after Wojtyla had been made bishop, Pope Pius XII, Eugenio Pacelli, the wartime Pope, died after a pontificate of almost twenty years. His successor was John XXIII. Aged, potbellied, and congenial, he had been elected as a stopgap, but he was about to shake the Church to its foundations. Pacelli had bequeathed a centralized citadel, with the Supreme Pontiff in sole charge—forever the ultimate and initiating authority, communing alone with God. But this monolithic, triumphalist Church was out of joint with much of the rest of the world in which it thrived. Pacelli had found it hard to dissociate social democracy from Bolshevism, pluralism from relativism. He had been criticized for appearing to favor Nazism and Fascism over communism. Lover of Hitler and Nazism he was not. But on behalf of Pius XI, he had taken benefits from the tyrant in the early 1930s while appearing aloof from Hitler's regime. In any case, as he was quick to point out, the Communists burned down churches and killed far more priests than the Nazis. He only grudgingly acknowledged in the 1950s that the Christian Churches owed their freedom and expansion to the pluralist environment of more or less democratic societies in the West. Spain under Franco and Portugal under Salazar characterized his notion of ideal societies for partnership with Holy Mother Church. After Pacelli's death, there was an irresistible groundswell for change among the faithful. Catholics yearned for a different kind of Church; they wanted an end to the legalistic, centralized Church that had been shaped and governed by the great Piuses through the twentieth century.

Angelo Roncalli, the man who was John XXIII, was the son of a peasant of Bergamo. He had spent much of his priestly life as a nuncio and knew the Eastern Churches well. He had tried to help the Jews during the war. One of his first acts as Pope was to seek forgiveness of the Jews for Christian anti-Judaism. Just three months after his election on January 25, 1959, he called a general Council with a view to pastoral renewal and the promotion of Christian unity.

There was opposition from within the Vatican. When senior officials of the Curia, the Vatican civil service, failed to stop the initiative, they attempted to put a stranglehold on its deliberations and decisions. The old guard wanted it to be a Council that condemned modern heresy. Pope John intervened to ensure that there would be no anathemas or excommunications, that representatives of other Christian Churches would be present. His insistence on the principle of *aggiornamento* (that the Church should develop and change with society and history) signaled the potential for radical reform. A question that loomed large from the outset was what stance the Council fathers should adopt in relation to Soviet communism. The Polish bishops, representing the Catholic Church behind the Iron Curtain, would be critical of the *ostpolitik* of the Council, which tended toward dialogue. Bishop Wojtyla was as intransigent against compromise, if not more so, as any of them.

Preparations for the Second Vatican Council began at once. The world's 2,400 bishops were required to return a questionnaire stating their priorities for consideration during the sessions. Wojtyla's remarks focused on his philosophical preoccupation with "personalism": how the individual human soul could discover transcendence; how it was that human beings with a destiny toward God should produce Auschwitz and the Gulag. He wanted to have a greater role for the laity; he was concerned about discipline within the priesthood and liturgical reform. It comes as no surprise that he should urge the Council planners to emphasize the pastoral opportunities for theatrical activities and sport. By comparison with the huge opportunities afoot to transform the Church, Bishop Wojtyla's contribution at that stage might have seemed muted—although hardly in retrospect, when one considers the full flowering during his papacy of his contribution to Christian humanism. He was still only thirty-nine years of age when he returned his questionnaire, but by comparison with many other episcopal returns his contribution was impressive. For example, the Archbishop of Washington, Patrick O'Boyle, wanted the Council to consider, among other things, the possibility of intelligent life on other planets. As at least one wag was to comment that it might have been more appropriate for the good archbishop to consider the possibility of intelligent life in his own diocese.

As Bishop Wojtyla left for the first session of the Council, which opened on October 11, 1962, he noted: "I set out on this road with the deepest emotion, with a great tremor in my heart." He was also moved to write a poem, brimful with emotion despite the gaucheness of the conceit:

> We shall be poor and naked
> Transparent as glass
> Which not only reflects but cuts
> And may the world thus split open
> Recompose itself beneath the lash
> Of the consciences that have chosen the backdrop of this temple.

Arriving in Rome with his fellow Polish bishops, who were accustomed to disciplined discretion essential to dealing with the Communist regime, Wojtyla was stunned by the apparent anarchy and disarray that marked the early sessions of the Council. What was this? Bishops quarreling, lobbying, criticizing, and even attacking one another verbally! Wojtyla would by no means emulate them. He especially deplored the leaks to the press, the tittle-tattle and back-biting, the distortions and the spin. This was not how the Church had survived in Poland as it grappled with its totalitarian enemy. A Church that was to survive stood like a porcupine against all comers. And where was the sense of reverence for the magisterium, the Church's dogmatic teaching? The Church's inerrancy down the ages? As Pope, many years later, he would move to prevent free discussion among the bishops at the regular synods, which were intended to give the local Church a greater say in curial governance. And he would forbid executive officers in the Curia to speak to the press without express permission. More than forty years later, at a special conference to gauge the effects of Vatican II, he insisted that the press should be excluded. The Polish bishops would not hinder the impetus to renewal, but they might lend strength to conservation.

The Council was in session every year from 1962 through 1965, between October and December. Bishop Wojtyla, fit from his strenuous summer vacations, attended every session, making copious notes, listening carefully when there was something important afoot, drafting poems when he was bored. Outside the sessions, he was intent on making the acquaintance of important players. His guide was his old friend and former seminary companion Andrzej Deskur, now a shrewd member of the Curia who headed the commission for social communications. Deskur would ask him once a week whom he wanted to meet, and Bishop Wojtyla would give him his list.

Wojtyla had become an important figure in his own right by 1964, when he leapt over a number of altars to become archbishop of his own diocese following Archbishop Baziak's death. He had not been Polish primate Wyszynski's first choice, nor even his sixth choice. The cardinal evidently did not trust Wojtyla, thinking him too ratiocinative. In the end, the primate succumbed to the wishes of the canons of the diocese, who were keen to have Wojtyla, and his name went forward to Rome. He would not countenance such local discretion when he became Pope. The Communists were delighted with the choice, suspecting that they could manipulate Wojtyla to undermine the primate. How wrong they would be proved!

His voice was now heard at the Council with attention, especially on the issue of religious liberty: Five of Wojtyla's twenty-four conciliar interventions concerned freedom of conscience. It was a tightrope. For the traditionalists, it was important to avoid indifferentism—the idea that one belief is as good as another. For a Catholic bishop in a Communist country, people held their beliefs at the risk of torture and martyrdom. Wojtyla allayed the anxieties of the conservatives while insisting on the inviolable rights of individuals to follow their consciences.

He insisted: "It is not the church's role to lecture unbelievers. We are involved in a quest along with our fellow men . . . Let us avoid moralizing or suggesting that we have a monopoly of truth." He would drastically modify this declaration nearly forty years later. In the meantime, while he did not support a condemnation of communism, he saw no reason to talk over the fence with atheists. Nor did he agree that the Church had anything to gain by dialogue with the opposition. "It is not possible to speak to those who are outside the Church, those who are fighting against it, and those who don't believe in God, using the same language that one speaks to the faithful." But what did it mean to be "outside" the Church? And whose God? And whose "same" language? He voted with his brother Poles and the Germans against the final draft of the document *Gaudium et Spes* (*Joy and Hope*), which counseled reaching out to the world, attempting to seek common ground with those who held different views from Catholics; but the antidialoguists lost the day, 2,333 in favor and 251 against. Paul VI, who had followed John XXIII on the throne of St. Peter on June 21, 1963, enthused: "No one in the world is a stranger, no one is excluded, no one is far away."

It was a different matter with the question of contraception, the most vexing issue in the Catholic Church as far as the laity was concerned, and already giving rise to a massive split between practice and teaching. The question had been placed outside the competence of the Council by papal decree. A year after the Council ended, a specially appointed commission on the issue reported to Paul VI advocating that the Church's opposition to contraception "could not be sustained by reasoned argument" and that the practice was not "intrinsically evil." Nine bishops voted in favor, three against, and there were three abstentions. Archbishop Wojtyla was on that commission, but mysteriously he was not present on the day of the vote, thus remaining aloof from any future identification with yea-sayers or nay-sayers. He did not remain aloof, however, from censure for having evaded, or at least avoided, responsibility. In the end, urged by the reactionary Rome-based Curia members, Paul went his own way and wrote his 1968 encyclical letter *Humanae Vitae* (*Of Human Life*), confirming the ban on contraception in line with his predecessors.

Wojtyla's mind, however, was already made up. He had expressed his view clearly and uncompromisingly in his book *Love and Responsibility*. With his usual aptitude for inelegant phraseology, he focused his thinking on what he called "the personalist norm": We should not avail ourselves of sexual pleasure without total self-donation. Curiously, he placed the emphasis on the "pleasure-object" in the love between man and woman entirely on the male abuse of the female. But he went further than Paul VI. His "anthropological" notion of self-donation, giving oneself without reservation to another, deriving from the theology of the Trinity, is striking, if idealistic, and yet a far more anthropological reading of sexual love than the Aristotelian-Thomistic biological means-to-ends espoused by Pius XI and Paul VI. And yet, while his prose comes across as labored and detached from lived experience, his intransigent opposition to contraception in every circumstance was a response, it seemed, to the perverse Soviet propaganda advocating free love and abortion in his native Poland.

*

Few human beings got as close to the mind and heart of Wojtyla, before he became Pope, as the phenomenologist Anna-Teresa Tymieniecka. She was a vivacious, highly intelligent married woman, Polish, and yet cosmopolitan, who would collaborate with him during the mid-1970s, spending many hundreds of hours in his presence over three years while she helped him with his major philosophical work, *Acting Person*. Early in their relationship, she studied *Love and Responsibility* in depth. She has described to Marco Politi and Carl Bernstein her reaction to that work. "He is a man in supreme command of himself, who has elaborated his beautiful, harmonious personality," she said. And therein lay the problem, in her view. "To have written [as he has] about love and sex is to know very little about it. I was truly astounded when I read *Love and Responsibility*. I thought he obviously does not know what he is talking about. How can he write about such things? The answer is he doesn't have experiences of that sort." The book, originally published in 1960, reads at times like field notes on a study of human sex practices by an anthropologist from Mars—a mishmash of ethics, anatomy, physiology, fertility charts, clinical descriptions of female orgasm, and abstract analysis of relationships and emotions gleaned from his contact with the young. It is like an essay on the phenomenology of color by a color-blind physiologist. The underlying theme—that we should not use people as if they were things—is of course unexceptionable. The notion of self-donation is theologically sound but fails to take account of lived experience in time, transient emotions, weaknesses, and unequal drives and compulsions.

Dr. Tymieniecka was not saying that the Polish archbishop was a naive man. "He's innocent sexually, but not otherwise. To be a cardinal under the Communists he had to be extremely shrewd. There is no naiveté. This is a very clever person who knows what he is doing." His theological imaginings about sex, however, were to have far-reaching consequences for the individual consciences of countless millions of Catholics, including those Catholics infected with the HIV/AIDS virus in Africa and South America. For if Father Bardecki, the editor of the Polish journal *Tygodnik Powszechny*, is to be believed, when Paul VI came to write *Humanae Vitae,* some sixty per cent of the document found its origins in the views of Archbishop Wojtyla (almost certainly an exaggeration, but with a seed of truth). Wojtyla's support in helping Paul VI confirm the ban on contraception, first proposed by Pius XI in the 1930s in his encyclical letter *Casti Connubii (Of Chaste Marriage),* was essentially a male celibates' charter, reiterating a magisterial view that could not be altered without damaging the integrity of papal magisterium.

CHAPTER SIX

Combating Communism

Back in Poland, despite Wyszynski's misgivings and the Communist regime's complacency about him, Archbishop Wojtyla began to prove himself a redoubtable adversary of the Communist leadership. The immediate occasion was the thousandth anniversary of the advent of Christianity in Poland in 1966. Combining liturgy, pilgrimage, and special Masses, the year of the Jubilee became a non-stop celebration of Catholicity and spiritual renewal. As the great two thousandth anniversary for the whole of Christendom approached thirty years later, Wojtyla might well have cast his mind back to the Polish millennium, which became a catalyst for a nonviolent moral insurgency that in time, with other trends and influences, internal and external, would lead to the breaking of the Soviet yoke.

The rallying point was the icon of the Madonna of Czestochowa, the "Queen of Poland," a copy of which toured the parishes of the country and was everywhere received with outpourings of emotion. Meanwhile, countless pilgrims made the journey to the shrine of the original at Jasna Gora. The Communist regime attempted to disrupt the mass demonstrations of fervor by scheduling sports events to distract the people. But Archbishop Wojtyla celebrated no fewer than fifty-three Masses, extolling Mary's privileges before vast crowds. Finally, the regime ordered the icon returned to its monastery. In protest, people throughout the country venerated empty frames representing the absent icon.

The administration under party chief Wladyslaw Gomulka had hoped to put a wedge between Wojtyla and Wyszynski. They had seen Wojtyla as aloof from politics and social action. In a secret police memorandum dated 1967, it was observed that Wojtyla "has not so far engaged in open anti-state political activity. It seems that politics is not his strong suit; he is over-intellectualised. He lacks organising and leadership qualities, and this is his weakness in the rivalry with Wyszynski." How wrong he would prove them in the long term! In the shorter term, reality dawned when in 1967 Wyszynski was denied a visa to attend a Synod of Bishops in Rome, whereas Wojtyla was allowed to go. Wojtyla refused to leave the country, demonstrating inseparable solidarity with his primate. He did, however, journey to Rome to receive his cardinal's hat that year. Having shown his fellow feeling toward Paul VI, the two men became ever closer. Eyes were increasingly on the new Polish archbishop, prince of the Church at the age of forty-seven.

The late 1960s now saw a renewed period of struggle in Poland as the epoch of youth culture and affluence in the West began to affect the aspirations of the younger generation behind the Iron Curtain. At the same time, workers, and especially miners and dockworkers, were feeling the pinch of lower wages and shortages in basics; prices for meat, a staple food of Polish manual workers, were especially high. Meanwhile, students were reading daily about the power of public protest in the West. There were flashpoints—in particular, the government ban on the anti-Soviet play *The Forefather's Eve,* which resulted in demonstrations on the streets. Students were beaten and universities closed. Adding to the nastiness of the reprisals, the regime blamed Jewish factions and sacked Jews from the civil service and the teaching profession. Matters deteriorated fast after Polish troops were drawn into the invasion of Czechoslovakia and the repression of the Prague Spring uprising. But again, it was an increase in food prices that precipitated mass unrest. Across the country, but especially in the Gdansk shipyards, there were strikes and demonstrations, culminating in violence and the deaths of hundreds of workers.

Archbishop Wojtyla began a careful balancing act. While avoiding provocative confrontation, which could lead to further outbreaks of violence and repression, he found ways of raising the morale of the people, engendering an indignation based on human rights and freedom. Freedom was ever on his lips: "the right to freedom . . . an atmosphere of genuine freedom; an atmosphere of inner freedom, of freedom from fearing what may befall me if I act this way or go that place."

When Edward Gierek came to power, Wojtyla turned the screws harder. At a time when Paul VI and the Vatican were contemplating dialogue with the repressive regime, Wojtyla showed that compromise with the Communists, comparable to Italy's *compromesso storico* in the late 1960s, was unacceptable in Poland. In the face of nationwide hostility, Gierek's regime appeared to soften. He would attempt to give the people what they wanted. He raised loans in the West. But the deeper the country plunged into debt, the more Wojtyla put on the pressure, petitioning the authorities with requests for expensive schemes: new schools, new seminaries, new churches. At the same time, he took on the government over every item of repression—from bans on catechism classes, to conscription of seminarians, to lack of paper for Catholic periodicals.

We see him during these days, never hurried, never agitated, but a powerhouse of contemplative and pastoral energy. From 5:30 A.M., for five and a half hours every morning, he prayed and wrote in silence, now in his private chapel, now in the Franciscan church across the way, then back in his chapel, with just a short break for breakfast. From eleven o'clock he was in his office receiving a stream of visitors; then lunch and a ten-minute catnap. Then he was off around his huge diocese with its 329 parishes. As he drove, according to his chauffeur, he worked at a specially installed desk that had a reading lamp. He never picked up a newspaper—a self-

denying ordinance he maintained into old age. Not for him the theological instruments of the great theologian Karl Barth: a Bible in
one hand, a newspaper in the other! Bardecki, the editor, would keep
the archbishop abreast of the news with a digest of leading stories
and opinions. Evenings he would sometimes spend time with
friends over a beer or a glass of wine. But there were nights when he
would summon his chauffeur and drive out to shrines in the hills of
Kalwaria. Leaving the car behind, he would tramp for miles, meditating on his feet until the small hours.

The uneasy years of the 1970s continued tense and restless until
the fatal year of 1976, when demonstrations against rising food
prices resulted in violent clashes with workers in different parts of
Poland. Now Wojtyla showed his consummate skill as a politician.
When union leaders called a general strike, which could only precip-
itate Soviet intervention, Wojtyla persuaded the workers to return to
work. At the same time, in return, he dissuaded the regime from
punishing the dissidents and strike organizers.

"Human rights cannot be given in the form of concessions,"
Wojtyla told a massed congregation of young people on the Feast of
Corpus Christi in 1977. As the Polish cardinals saw it, there was danger in the fashionable sympathies for Marxism being exhibited by
left-wing Christians in the West and their counterparts in liberation
theology in South America. Such flirtations could work to undermine the struggling Church in Eastern Europe. Wojtyla master-
minded a report for the polish bishops' conference criticizing a
"conformist attitude to Marxism" in Vatican texts. Did not this
accommodation to Marxism, he wrote, indicate an infiltration of
totalitarian ideas bringing "a new form of human captivity"?

Wojtyla became closely involved with the dissident Committee
for the Defense of the Workers (KOR). KOR was essentially an
intellectual movement, but the organization formed underground
seminars on human-rights issues for workers. Wojtyla encouraged a
synergy between the parish networks and worker organizations to
create a mass nonviolent insurgency at the grass roots. He raised

consciousness in one dimension by attacking censorship and defending freedom of speech; in another dimension, he preached the fundamental rights of human beings in civil society. He harped on the fact that after decades of oppression, disruption, and suffering, Poland had earned the right to self-determination and freedom.

There was something of Martin Luther King about him as he preached throughout his diocese, now attacking the regime for its lack of moral leadership, now invoking the memory of St. Stanislaw, Poland's martyr bishop who defied a tyrannical king and paid with his life.

CHAPTER SEVEN

Signs of Contradiction

During these troubled times in Poland in the mid-1970s, Cardinal Wojtyla continued to grow as an intellectual. Ever since the Second Vatican Council, he had been attempting to write about the nature of personhood as a philosopher. This was no simple catechetical exercise, exploiting orthodox theology and Scripture, but a remarkably ambitious attempt to make an original contribution to twentieth-century thought. He wanted to explore the human person from a more modern philosophical perspective than that allowed by St. Thomas Aquinas, and in the light of the historical context of an epoch that had witnessed the descent into Nazi barbarism and the oppression of the Soviet ideology.

"St. Thomas gives us an excellent view of the objective existence and activity of the person," he wrote, "but it would be difficult to speak in his view of the lived experiences of the person." Wojtyla had been inspired by the pastoral constitution *Gaudium et Spes* (*Joy and Hope*) in the Second Vatican Council that has deep relevance for a new understanding of personhood. *Gaudium et Spes* states that human beings are the only creatures that God wills for their own sake, and that they come to full realization only through self-giving.

At the same time, he had been influenced in his second doctorate, as we have seen, by the phenomenological method of Max

Scheler. Scheler's work had led Wojtyla to see personhood in terms of lived experience rather than objectively as an abstract universal concept. And now, in the midst of his whirlwind of pastoral activities as archbishop of Krakow, he had found time to produce a manuscript for a book initially titled *Person and Act* but eventually to be renamed *Acting Person* after considerable editing and collaboration.

The theme was characterized in a letter Wojtyla wrote in 1968 to the French Jesuit theologian Henri de Lubac:

> I devote my very rare free moments to a work that is close to my heart and devoted to the metaphysical significance and the mystery of the PERSON. It seems to me that the debate today is being played on that level. The evil of our times consists in the first place in a kind of degradation, indeed in a pulverization, of the fundamental uniqueness of each human person.

The fragmention of personhood Wojtyla had in mind found its origins, in his view, in the "evil of the times": the greed and hedonism of the capitalist West, the atheistic materialism of the Soviets, the reductive existentialists such as Jean-Paul Sartre, and the rising influence of the French literary theorists who were offering a new generation of students the deconstruction of both the self and of meaning. He would articulate the nature of his quest on a number of occasions in the coming years, especially in his stated conviction that the evil in the world often seemed greater than ourselves, as if he apprehended a cosmic, mystical sense of evil at work in the world.

The book he planned would deal somewhat historically, and from a detached philosophical perspective, with such topics as consciousness, self-determination or will, the unitary nature of the person (in other words, the embodiment of the soul rather than body-soul "dualism"), and the social nature of the person. The ambition involved in such a huge canvas, in which he was seeking not polemic but a whole reworking of the mystery of the person, was prodigious. Each of these topics on its own represents formidable areas of philosophy for any professional specialist, let alone a part-time academic running one of the largest dioceses in East Europe in a time of major political and economic crisis.

In December 1970, the earlier printed version of the work, published in Poland, was the subject of a symposium at Lublin University involving twenty participants, most of whom were professors more senior in academic status to Wojtyla. The criticisms of five of the members of the symposium were severe. One even protested that he had read the book twice but still did not understand it. So much for the lavish praise of others less qualified to judge a philosophical work as good or bad, including the comment of his auxiliary bishop, Jerzy Stroba, that the book made a difficult philosophical problem accessible to the simple faithful. As the book became required reading by the clergy of his diocese (naturally!), the barbed joke did the rounds that Archbishop Wojtyla must have known that he would one day be Pope and had written the text as a punishment for priests in Purgatory.

George Huntston Williams, a Harvard professor of philosophy of religion and author of *The Mind of John Paul II,* has studied the symposium commentaries and summarized the main criticisms: "The book was neither a rounded anthropology nor a developed ethics of action . . . it mingled without due care to discrimination the intersecting vocabularies of two philosophical languages, Thomist and phenomenological . . . the author too readily equated Aristotle and Thomas [Aquinas] on man." There were other criticisms, more or less harsh, complaining of lack of clarity and lack of consistency and precision in the use of philosophical terms. Then this devastating observation: He was more often involved in "the etymological hermeneutics of words than in the hermeneutics of the realities signified." This rare dousing of cold water from a peer group evinces Wojtyla's problem as an aspiring philosopher: that he was well-meaning, clever, undoubtedly original, bold—but essentially an autodidact and, academically, completely out of his depth.

But all was not lost. Just as the prospects for the book looked hopeless, an individual appeared on the scene who had the time, expertise, and desire to help him realize the ideas he was attempting to shape and articulate. Dr. Anna-Teresa Tymieniecka made herself known to him two years after the punishing Lublin symposium.

Tymieniecka was by all accounts sexually appealing, highly intelligent, the daughter of a landed Polish family. More to the point, she was a serious professional philosopher with privileged links into philosophical circles around Europe; she seemed to have met everybody and to have read everything. Giving the opening address at a philosophical colloquium in Montreal in 1974, she managed to cite, in the hour allowed to her, Samuel Beckett, Italo Calvino, James Joyce, Franz Kafka, Giacomo Leopardi, Kurt Vonnegut, Slawomir Mrozek, Jean-Paul Sartre, with brief references to a huge circuit of philosophers and a variety of historians, in particular Oswald Spengler, as well as a line of dramatists harking right back to Aristophanes.

Tymieniecka was born in 1925 in Poland on a prosperous estate in Masovia; the estate was later broken up by Communists. Her curriculum vitae reads like a tour of scholastic Europe and North America. At Krakow's Jagiellonian University at the end of the war she was a student of Roman Ingarden, who had been a student of Edmund Husserl, founder of the phenomenological movement. She then studied philosophy of mathematics at the Sorbonne, followed by residence under the Dominicans at the Catholic University of Fribourg in Switzerland, where she completed her doctorate. She taught and continued to research at Berkeley, Oregon State, Yale, Penn State, and Bryn Mawr.

The topic of her first doctorate gives us a hint of her preoccupations: the ontology of the phenomenological structuralist Roman Ingarden and the German ethicist Nicolai Hartmann. She proceeded to a scholarly investigation of the phenomenology of "creative inwardness" in the poet Paul Valéry. Such were the researches and meditations of Dr. Tymieniecka when she became president of the World Institute for Advanced Phenomenological Research, picking up on the way the editorship of the journal *Analecta Husserliana*.

This phenomenological prodigy, with her miniskirts, blond ponytail, cosmopolitan links, and aristocratic background, was captivated by Wojtyla and his project—*Acting Person*. So she gate-crashed into Cardinal Wojtyla's life, informing him that he had written a book of vital importance, which she wished to bring to the notice of the world. In short, she wanted to dedicate her life to him and his book until the project came to fruition with publication in English—after suitable amendments, of course.

How could he resist!

Luckily, she enjoyed the indulgence of a complaisant American husband who seemed content to allow her to roam the world for months on end pursuing a variety of projects in the world of phenomenology. She was as at home in Paris as she was in Krakow, Naples, Bologna, Montreal, Washington, D.C., and New York. During the mid-1970s, she was to spend inordinate amounts of time with Wojtyla in Poland, Italy, and in the United States, where she entertained him at her rural retreat in the woods of Vermont. Cardinal Wojtyla, amid the crises of Poland and increasing calls to attend synods and commissions in Rome, took to the charmed life of American privilege, picknicking on the lawn and bathing in a nearby lake—all in the interest of his magnum philosophical opus. Her collaboration on the book (it remained extremely difficult to read even in final form) is of great importance, as is the light it sheds on Wojtyla's character. At the heart of the recast work are leading and exalted notions: of personhood as created in the image of God; will and self-donation as the realization of our full humanity; notions of human dignity, freedom, and love, derived from a Christ-based anthropology and humanism. Over the next thirty years, the core ideas would return again and again through his writings with ever-greater force, especially in relation to sexual morals. It is not too much to say that Dr. Tymieniecka helped to bring into greater focus, and even made available to Wojtyla, some of his most powerful ideas as Pope, although, as we shall see, this is emphatically not a notion the Vatican has been pleased to acknowledge.

*

The relationship between Tymieniecka and Wojtyla began in 1974 at a conference in Naples and lasted for three years. It involved intense intellectual and editorial collaboration as she translated *Acting Person* into English and recast the entire book. Tymieniecka has said: "This was on my part a labor of love, to make him known and to bring him proper recognition as a philosopher . . . My condition was that we do it together. He wanted me to do it alone and I refused. I said 'only if we do it together.'"

According to Tymieniecka, she would go to Poland three times a year and to Rome three times a year. The Polish visits would last as long as five weeks each and the Rome visits two to three weeks each. Invariably, Wojtyla's secretary, Stanislaw Dziwisz, would be in attendance. Often, they would sit together in his car as he traveled the diocese or between cities. There were days when the three went walking in the hills and woods. The relationship was evidently more than the book itself. She has conceded: "We had a dialogue all the time between two philosophers—it went far beyond the book; that was the whole charm of this work. Had we not done this, I probably would not have developed such a devotion to the book. He was an incomparable philosophical partner."

What gave their philosophical exchanges a sense of exhilaration was the political and social relevance that had inspired his earlier philosophical model, Max Scheler. Wojtyla was in conflict with a totalitarian tyranny in which individual self-determination had been suppressed and denied. Together with Tymieniecka, he was exploring the scope of self-determination as well as its limits. For a society that stresses self-determination without social cooperation is equally doomed. Was America and the capitalist West a culture of malevolent individualism? It was Tymieniecka who brought Wojtyla to the United States in 1976, organizing visits to Washington, D.C., and to Harvard. She was hard-pressed, she tells us, to persuade him that America was not a country of greed, selfishness, and hedonism. She was not sure that she had convinced him. But aside from attending the special dinners in his honor, they worked for up to sixteen hours a day on the *Acting Person* project.

When the book was published in 1977, he acknowledged his huge debt to Dr. Tymieniecka and passed over to her the rights to the English translation. After he became Pope the following year, a commission was established to scrutinize and handle his literary work up to the point of his election. With John Paul's agreement, the commission attempted to stop publication of the Tymieniecka-Wojtyla edition. She, in turn, took legal advice about suing the Pope for copyright infringement. Part of her weaponry was a prodigious correspondence with him, which now sits under lock and key in an archive at Harvard University. She eventually went ahead and published the book as a joint work, whereupon the Vatican hit back, charging that she had usurped Cardinal Wojtyla's thoughts, reducing his Thomistic thinking in favor of a too strongly phenomenological interpretation. For a time they became estranged.

Dr. Huntstanton Williams has said: "Their work together was extremely important. And afterward the Vatican and the Pope behaved rather badly in trying to suppress knowledge of their collaboration." Referring to the encyclical *Veritatis Splendor (Splendor of the Truth)*, which he believes to be John Paul's "masterpiece," Williams declared: "He couldn't have done what he's done without that relationship. It cannot be wiped out of the biographical, intellectual account."

*

In 1976, Cardinal Wojtyla was asked by Pope Paul VI to lead the five-day Lenten retreat in the Mathilde Chapel in the Vatican. Those attending included the top officials of the Holy See: Cardinal Jean Villot, Secretary of State; Giovanni Benelli, Sostituto Secretary of State; Cardinal John Wright, American prefect of the Congregation of the Clergy; and Franjo Seper, Yugoslav head of the Congregation for the Doctrine of the Faith. Pope Paul VI, suffering from prostate cancer and heart disease, sat out of sight in an antechamber, close to the altar. It was later disclosed that he was wearing a penitential hair shirt and spike discipline to increase his suffering. The choice of Wojtyla to preach the Lenten Retreat homilies was unusual. Normally, it fell to a distinguished theologian. It seemed that the Curia, knowing full well that Paul might not have long to live, were taking a close look at this young cardinal who had been widely spoken of as papabile. Wojtyla's homilies from the retreat in time would be published as a book, titled *Sign of Contradiction*.

The gathering may well have been astonished by what they heard; some, indeed, might well have been aghast. That the majority were impressed, however, is evinced by the fact that the College of Cardinals would elect him Pope eighteen months later.

There were twenty-two talks in all, ranging across a number of interrelated themes, often couched in allusive language, apocalyptic in tone, often dark, and profoundly Marian. The underlying structure of the series of talks was based on the fifteen mysteries of the rosary and the Stations of the Cross. He conjured up dark images of the earth as "ever more a burial ground," and of God being not so much dead but unheard as a result of the cacophonies of the age and the hysterical deafness of humankind. He presented Christ, the God-Man, as the redeemer of the whole human race rather than the Messiah of an elect, thus declaring the Church as coextensive with the whole world, including all those of other religions and those of no religion. He gave comfort to Paul VI, embroiled in the controversy over contraception in *Humanae Vitae*, pulled this way and that by a Church in conflict, offering him a profoundly flattering comparison. Quoting a passage from Jeremiah—"I am become a laughing stock," "and there came in my heart as a burning fire, shut up in my bones, and I was wearied, not being able to bear it"—the cardinal observed that the prophet is often rejected by his own. He then made explicit reference to those who defended contraception, describing them as "humanistic circles linked with certain Christian traditions" and "campaigners in favor of abortion." He finally consoled the Pope with the observation that "we are in the front line in a lively battle of the dignity of man."

He finished by making a starkly melodramatic and theologically shocking peroration on the theme of Christianity's coming third millennium, just a quarter century away in the year 2000. The new millennium, he said, heralded "a new Advent for the Church and for humanity," and it would be marked by two great signs. There would be the Christ himself, "the Sign of Contradiction," and there would be the Virgin Mary, clothed in the sun "a great sign in the heavens," the Second Eve who would crush the head of the Serpent.

Strictly speaking, there can be no "new Advent" in Christian revelation without reference to a Second Fall of Man, for which there is no scriptural basis in Christian theology. The Fall of Adam and Eve, as it is understood in Catholic orthodoxy, was the result of illicit cravings in three areas of human activity: in knowledge, in stewardship of the earth, and in sexuality. Wojtyla seemed to indicate that the Second Advent of the Church would be frustrated by this new Fall, which he proceeded to identify in specific terms.

There was the illicit craving of knowledge evident in the new "structuralism," the French thought of philosophers like Jacques Derrida, "which goes much further than agnosticism or even positivism . . . This asserts that God died out of human thought as human thought underwent a process of self-criticism." Next he cites both capitalism and communism as dehumanizing, especially in the Third World. Significantly, he has no alternative to these economic and political systems (assuming that he was not suggesting a return to corporatism). But he uses the opportunity to take a swing at liberation theology, which was not going to save the Third World, he insisted, whether it came from the West or from the Soviet Second World.

Finally, he came to the cravings of the flesh. The full realization of our humanity, and hence the Advent of the Church, was being thwarted by this "aphrodisiac generation." In the liberal regimes of the First World, men have grown sick from too much prosperity and too much freedom. "Human life," he went on, "presents a saddening picture of all kinds of abuses and frustrating situations . . . dignity must not be made to consist in unbridled exercise of one's own freedom . . . the freedom sought after by the campaigners in favor of abortion is a freedom in the service of pleasure unrestrained by norms of any kind."

This was very strong stuff indeed. Could this be the stuff of which a pope to follow Paul was made of? The problem was that he was a Pole and not an Italian. What extreme circumstances would need to prevail for a Pole to leap over the phalanx of Italians who had the power to choose the next pope?

CHAPTER EIGHT

"Be Not Afraid!"

Paul VI, Pope since 1963, died on August 6, 1978. Three weeks later, after only one day's voting, the conclave elected Albino Luciani on the fourth ballot. It was the shortest conclave of the century and almost the shortest in history. He had been the Patriarch of Venice; he had a winning smile; he was sixty-six years old and had spent much of his life in pastoral work. He was neither an intellectual nor an administrator. He said of himself: "If I hadn't been a bishop, I would have wanted to be a journalist." His favorite secular reading matter was *Reader's Digest.* He took the name John Paul in memory of his two predecessors. He dispensed with the ceremonial chair on which popes are carried and spoke to the faithful with homespun simplicity. In one of his early talks at the general audience, he said: "There's more of Mama than of Papa in Almighty God!" The faithful were charmed, but the Congregation for the Doctrine of the Faith was appalled.

How did the cardinals come to their choice? One of them, Cardinal Basil Hume, said, "Once it had happened, it seemed totally and entirely right. The feeling that he was just what we wanted was so general . . . We felt as if our hands were being guided as we wrote his name on the paper!" The metropolitan cardinals of the world had evidently opted for a pope who would allow greater strength to the local

Church: Luciani was not a man to throw his weight around. A less pious view of his election was that he had been used to block the more powerful candidacies of ambitious and experienced Curial cardinals who seemed intent on reestablishing a centralized Church. But there were ominous signs even in the first few days of rejoicing. His secretary, Father John Magee, said that after the new Pope had dropped a sheaf of papers over the parapet of the apostolic palace, he found the Pontiff weeping. John Paul, it seems, was terrified of Cardinal Secretary of State Villot, who was due that afternoon to collect the documents. The secretary sent the Pope to bed to calm down. While His Holiness lay in a fetal position saying his rosary, Magee called the Vatican fire brigade to fetch papers scattered on the roofs below.

Overwhelmed by the burdens of his office, the new Pope took to gestures of unusual humility. One morning he insisted on acting as altar boy to Magee when the secretary said his private Mass. Magee thought him "a beautiful man." Archbishop Derek Worlock of Liverpool struck a chord with many members of the Curia when he said: "They've made Peter Sellers pope."

Luciani was evidently a pastoral choice who was not going to attempt to *run* the entire Church, but, in the words of one Curial official, "this team was not going to make it!" The question arose: How would he deal with the strong Curial figures around him? As Archbishop Marcinkus, head of the Vatican Bank, remarked to me in 1987: "It wasn't just that he did not know where the different departments of the Holy See were: He did not know even what they did."

But then providence, or chance, stepped in. Albino Luciani, after a pontificate of just three weeks, probably died of a pulmonary embolism on the night of September 28, 1978. The cause of death will never be known with absolute certainty, as no autopsy was performed. The rumor spread that Vatican prelates had conspired with the Mafia to put poison in his coffee. Such are the consequences of inept management of press and public affairs.

In the autumn of 1978, the cardinals gathered again to choose a new pope, no doubt pondering the possibility that Albino Luciani was crushed by sheer stress after only three weeks in the job. They would have to find a man with youth, health, and indomitable strength on his side, a pope who was not a powerful Curial figure and one perhaps who had shown immense strength as a leader of the local Church, a man who would recognize the importance of giving the local Church its head.

At the same time, they wanted a pope of the Second Vatican Council, one wholly identified with neither the progressives nor the conservatives. While none could dispute the far-reaching benefits of the Council, none could deny the resulting discord and unhappiness, marked by recrimination and counterrecrimination. From one point of view, the pride and folly of one group had brought the Church to the edge of calamity; from another, the Church stood frustrated on the threshold of an as-yet-unrealized era of grace and flourishing. The Church was dividing acrimoniously between those who felt that things had gone too far and those who felt that things had not gone nearly far enough. It was becoming obvious even to some prominent progressives that the Church risked descending into chaos liturgically, doctrinally, and institutionally. In the last years of Paul VI, extreme cases grabbed the headlines: priests celebrating Mass on coffee tables, feminist "nuns" cavorting in the aisle, priests indulging in New Age beliefs and rituals, as well as traditionalists defying Rome to restore the tridentine liturgies and traditions.

The late Peter Hebblethwaite, former editor of the Jesuit periodical *The Month,* seized on what had become a new and alarming image: "a runaway Church, lurching out of control." There was a sense of widespread fear. Most interesting was the case of Henri de Lubac, responsible in many respects for the direction of the conciliar renewal program. He summed up the problems: "The opening-up to the world to be evangelized turning into a mediocre and sometimes scandalous worldliness . . . the arrogance of theologians wishing to impose their own thinking on the Church . . . small pressure groups getting control of the information media and doing their best to intimidate the bishops . . . an insidious campaign against the papacy . . . a rejection of dogmatics, a politicization of the Gospel."

Henri de Lubac, friend of Wojtyla, was not the only prominent progressive to have taken fright. Hans Urs von Balthasar and Avery Dulles were deeply anxious. And so was the eminent philosopher Jacques Maritain, who saw the conciliar reforms degenerating into "imminent apostasy." Could the cardinals choose a pope who would act to heal the growing splits, tensions, and, above all, sense of fear, while fulfilling what the Council fathers had intended?

On the ninth ballot of the new conclave, the votes revealed an impressive 103 out of 109 for Cardinal Karol Wojtyla. On the previous evening, when it was obvious that the votes were going his way, Wojtyla was seen collapsed and weeping in the arms of Cardinal Wyszynski. After he had been elected, he was said to be totally relaxed, as if knowing that it was all meant. He sipped champagne and insisted that all the cardinals should dine with him that evening. Wyszynski, inspired by the exhilaration of the occasion, waxed prophetic; he told the new Pontiff that he was the Pope to lead the world into the third millennium. When Wyszynski fell to his knees before Wojtyla in homage, the younger Pole fell to his knees with him, presenting an affecting tableau of mutual humility.

He was the first non-Italian Pope since 1522, and at fifty-eight the youngest since Pius IX was elected at age fifty-four in 1846. When on October 16, 1978, Carol Wojtyla as John Paul II appeared on the balcony above St. Peter's Square, he was virtually unknown to the world. The Italians in the Curia below the level of cardinal were astounded. My long-term contact in the Vatican, an official I have dubbed Monsignor Sotto Voce, told me: "I'll never forget the day he was elected. I was with a crowd of Italian monsignori looking down on the square from the loggia. When his name was announced, I had the presence of mind to take a sidelong look around me to see how they'd taken it. Their faces were frozen in sheer horror—a foreigner! Then the old *bella figura* complex took over, and they grinned and clapped!"

As if to inspire a sense of confidence in all those who feared for the direction in which the Second Vatican Council was taking the Church, John Paul II's first words to the faithful in St. Peter's Square and to the world at large were: "Be not afraid!" In his first declaration as Pope, he used the word "collegiality" no fewer than five times. But he also said: "We consider our primary duty to be that of promoting, with prudent but encouraging action, the most exact fulfillment of the norms of the Council . . . what was implicit should be made explicit in the sight of the experiment that followed, and in the light of new emerging circumstances." The qualification might well have sent warning signals to those who had ears to hear.

Progressives believed, at first, that this was a Pope to continue the spirit of the Council and press forward with its unfinished reforms. The conservatives, on the other hand, trusted that a prelate reared in the traditionalist, embattled Catholicism of Poland would restore many lost disciplines and values while banishing any lingering hopes entertained by Catholics of a socialist hue. Few suspected the extent to which he would disappoint the progressive side of the growing Church divide; few suspected how this man who had with Wyszynski led the Church of Poland independently of the diplomatic aspirations and authority of Rome, would assume absolutist, centrist papal authority.

John Paul was a man who believed in self-discipline and institutional discipline. He had been a priest of the era of Pius XII, reared on exemplars like Vincent de Paul, the Curé d'Ars, and the hero of Georges Bernanos's *Diary of a Country Priest.* Looking upon the "runaway Church" from the papal pinnacle, he would not be inclined to allow matters to sort themselves out. He was going to shoulder the responsibility in its entirety; he was going to take the Church by the scruff of the neck and restore order.

That this was quite a different kind of Pope, in human terms, was immediately obvious to the previous Popes' secretary, the Irishman John Magee. In an interview in 1988, he told me that he came upon him on that first day in the papal apartment:

He was sitting at my desk. His zucchetto [skullcap] was just thrown to one side, his cassock was all unbuttoned down his chest, no collar, and he was sitting sideways onto the desk, writing, not as Pope Paul VI did, upright and elegant, but slouched, his hand on his head, like a man more used to physical action than to scholarship. I knocked, and as he turned it was the physical posture of a man of the world—it was un-Popish. This was a very human, down-to-earth man. He jumped up and came over. He wouldn't let me kiss his ring. He caught hold of me, put his arms around me. "Welcome home," he said. "Now you stay with me." He didn't ask me whether I wanted to or not. He just said, "Now you stay with me!"

His household was to be Polish. Bishop Andrzej Deskur, head of the Commission for Social Communications in the Vatican, who had suffered a stroke during the conclave and would remain an invalid for the rest of his life, became a close confidant, dining with John Paul frequently. His secretary from Krakow, Stanislaw Dziwisz, now moved into the papal apartment alongside Father John Magee to learn the secretarial ropes; a team of Polish nuns was appointed to do the domestic work within the apartments. According to Nigel West, the British intelligence expert, John Paul replaced "the so-called Irish mafia, which had run so much of the Vatican for so long," with forty Polish priests and nuns who reported to Dziwisz.

Dziwisz, who came from a village near the famous mountain resort of Zakopane, was an expert skier. Born in 1939, he was ordained in 1963. After working on a parish, he became John Paul's second secretary, or chaplain, in 1966. Highly intelligent, with an aptitude for theology, he was from the very beginning the perfect servant: faceless, gentle but firm, utterly devoted to the well-being and interests of Karol Wojtyla. Others have noted that they are like "father and son."

The new Pope quickly settled into a routine that was unvarying until he became severely debilitated with Parkinson's and arthritis by the end of the century. Rising at 5:30 A.M., he prayed in his chapel until Mass at 7:30. The congregation was composed of the nuns of his household and visitors, about twenty of them, carefully chosen by Dziwisz from many hundreds of applications. Curial members would complain bitterly in time that Dziwisz tended to choose right-wingers, especially members of Opus Dei, the Neo-Catechumenates, and the Legionaries of Christ. I suspect this criticism to be apocryphal, as I was twice chosen by Dziwisz to attend these private masses over a space of four years and on both occasions was allowed to speak with John Paul privately afterward. Nobody has ever accused me of being a right-winger, nor of association with any of the groups.

After Mass and thanksgiving, he greeted the visitors in his library, and several of them would be invited into breakfast: rolls, cheese, sausage meat, coffee, juice. By 8:30 he was at his desk, where he worked without disturbance until 11 A.M., following the pattern of his routine as Cardinal Archbishop. Every Wednesday at midmorning he greeted the public audience, about 8,000 pilgrims, each of whom would require a ticket issued by a Vatican office. VIPs, the sick, and the dying were granted a special place close to the stage. Other private audiences were held in the late morning, most days except Tuesday, for diplomats, government officials, and Church leaders, all by arrangement with the prefect of the Papal Household or the Secretary of State.

He took lunch at one, often with specialists to talk on a specific theme or issue, and usually in a particular language so that all present could participate. These were working lunches, simple Italian food with a little white wine; the numbers were normally restricted to no more than ten. They ate in a modest dining room served by his butlers. He was a congenial host, relaxed and never standing on ceremony. Although he led the discussion, he was a good listener.

Lunch was followed by a twenty-minute siesta, then back to his office to study papers for an hour or two before rising to his roof terrace high above the apostolic palace, where he walked for half an hour while saying the rosary. At 6:30 P.M., he received top-ranking Vatican officials, each of them on different days of the week: the Secretary of State on Mondays and Thursdays, the undersecretary responsible for relations with foreign countries on Wednesdays, Joseph Ratzinger on Fridays. John Paul was not as keen on paperwork as Paul VI, who would work sometimes until after 2 A.M. before retiring, so the heads of departments learned to be accordingly selective about the flow of documents.

Supper, a comparatively light meal, was taken at 7:30, usually with guests. Before nine he would go to his office to spend time reading until retiring after 11:00 P.M. He was said to have nine or ten books on the go at any one time; the preponderance of this reading was theology and philosophy. In addition to his daily duties and various services conducted in accordance with the liturgical year, John Paul made frequent visits to his private chapel through the day for silent prayer or to say his breviary and the rosary. He would keep the doors of his office open so that he was conscious of the presence of the Blessed Sacrament through the day. He confessed once a week to a Polish priest and regularly performed the Stations of the Cross. One of his secretaries, now retired, Monsignor Vincent Tran Ngoe Thu, has commented that although John Paul had two telephones he would never use them to summon his aides. "He always came to me in person, even if only to ask for paper or pencils. He has never raised his voice, and he has always asked sincerely how we are. He is a very fatherly pope."

He made space routinely through the day to write, invariably in Polish. He could use a personal computer when they came into use in the late 1980s in the Vatican, but he mostly preferred writing in longhand until an accident with his shoulder and encroaching Parkinson's made it difficult. He then tended to dictate to Dziwisz. Not all his documents and homilies were written by him, but until age and debilitation slowed him down, he would read and add his own thoughts to documents that had been written on his behalf. On Sundays, when in Rome, he greeted pilgrims at noon from his window overlooking St. Peter's Square, said the Angelus, and delivered a short homily.

An early decision made by John Paul was to have a swimming pool built up at the summer palace of Castel Gandolfo. Anticipating objections, he said that it would be more expensive to have another conclave. He suffered from a spinal condition for which backstroke swimming is recommended. His swimming complex includes a sauna, a solarium, and a gymnasium. John Paul was going to keep himself physically as well as spiritually fit.

Since Wojtyla had no favorites outside his close Polish household, unless one counts his remarkable association with Mother Teresa (they would sing boisterous hymns together), there were scant opportunities in the early days for envy and scheming. He had few pleasures save for an occasional improving movie, such as Louis Malle's *Au Revoir les Enfants*. He employed a Polish baker whom he shared with Andrzej Deskur.

*

His first foreign trip, made within four months of becoming Pope, was to the shrine of Our Lady of Guadalupe in Mexico, where he also participated at a long-scheduled meeting of the Latin American Bishops Conference (CELAM). He flew into Mexico City on January 26, 1979, and stepping onto the tarmac performed the theatrical gesture for which he would become famous throughout the world: He kissed the soil of Mexico in imitation of the Curé d'Ars, indicating that he had come to take possession of his parish.

It was no coincidence that John Paul chose Latin America for his inaugural foreign trip. Here was one half of the world's Catholic population and deep-seated problems: poverty, competition from Protestant evangelicals, conflict between Catholic religious orders and their bishops. There were oppressive, reactionary regimes on the one hand, and what John Paul saw as clerical political activists inspired by Marxism-Leninism—liberation theology—on the other.

It became immediately evident that he was not in Puebla to

observe or even to merely "participate," so much as to preside. The Pope who had experienced at first hand the oppression of Soviet communism was set to confront. Chief among his anxieties was liberation theology and its central notion that evil is the consequence of reactionary social and political structures; that human flourishing is secured by political struggle and social change. For the Pope from Poland, the truth was otherwise: Sin arose from the deep stain in our nature, inherited from our first parents, and redemption comes through Jesus Christ, His Church, and His sacraments.

Having straightened out the Latin American bishops on the dangers of mixing Marxism and the Christian message (although there was much more to be said and done before he was through with liberation theology), he proceeded to Cuilapan, where he preached to a crowd of half a million on the theme of freedom, injustice, and oppression of the powerless. Speaking with vehemence bordering on anger, he located compassion and defense of the poor under the protective mantle of papal concern. The people responded ecstatically.

*

John Paul's longed-for visit to Poland had been dreaded by the Polish Communists and the Kremlin alike. After his election, Soviet KGB chief Yuri Andropov called the local Warsaw KGB officer and asked angrily how it was possible that the Polish regime had allowed the election to happen. The officer is said to have replied that such inquiries should be directed to the Vatican. Following a KGB investigation, a report eventually found its way to Andropov's desk ludicrously claiming that the election had been a German-American plot led by Cardinal John Krol of Philadelphia and Zbigniew Brzezinski, U.S. president Jimmy Carter's national security adviser.

What was certain, John Paul had, overnight, reversed the Vatican's *ostpolitik*. Under Paul VI there had been a gentle and accommodating approach to communism exercised through his secretary of the Council for Public Affairs, Archbishop Agostino Casaroli. Casaroli favored communications with Communist governments in the expectation that one day the antireligious bias of Communist regimes would waken. "When and if that day comes," said Casaroli, "the Holy See will at least have channels of communications open and ready for use." The weakness of his argument was that should that day arrive, the personnel within the regime represented by those channels would have been swept away.

John Paul's approach to the Communist governments, however, was an intelligent and wily intransigence. He would ask no favors; he would insist on freedom of religion, the full catalogue of human rights; there would be no accommodation. But here was a source of paradox and contradiction for the future of his papacy. Just as it had arguably been a mistake for Paul VI and Casaroli to seek accommodation with totalitarians, it was evident that he was continuing to act as Poland's local Church leader. John Paul was, in 1979, at a unique historic and personal juncture. In Poland he appeared as both local pastor and universal pastor. He was a living symbol of both the particular and the universal Church. In time he came to believe that he could and should be both local and universal pastor in every circumstance throughout the Church.

In his first encyclical letter to the world, *Redemptor Hominis* (*The Redeemer of Man*), published on March 4, 1979, John Paul made a thundering appeal for universal human rights. And he made it clear that he specifically had in mind the people of Poland, who had fallen victim to the Soviet system. "These rights," he wrote, "are rightly reckoned to include the right to religious freedom together with the right to freedom of conscience."

In the same encyclical, however, there were ominous signs of what was in store for dissidents who exercised their right to freedom of conscience within the Catholic Church. He warned Catholic theologians that they should engage in "close collaboration with the magisterium," the body of doctrine approved by the papacy. There was indeed a dilemma. Should he turn a blind eye to an outer-fringe New Ageist "theologian" like Matthew Fox, a member of the Dominican order who had teamed up with the white witch Starhawk in California to create his own version of Catholicism? Should he allow Archbishop Marcel Lefebvre, the traditionalist prelate, who believed that Vatican II was a heretical council, to run a breakaway section of the Church unopposed? His determination to exert discipline unfortunately imposed heavy restrictions and penalties on creative theologians who were nonconformist and different rather than erroneous or heretical.

Before the end of the first year of his papacy, the theologian Edward Schillebeeckx was summoned to the Vatican no fewer than three times to be cross-examined. Schillebeeckx, a Flemish priest of the Dominican order, had written a three-volume account of the person of Jesus Christ in which he pondered the neglected understanding of Jesus as man, rather than the risen Christ as Son of God, and drew an equivalence between Jesus and Old Testament prophets as well as prophet figures in the great world religions. Schillebeeckx, moreover, saw the Church as the manifestation of Jesus Christ in communities that meet for worship, rather than in the Vatican and diocesan offices: This was not a message that a universal pastor would wish to be spread abroad.

Another early casualty was Hans Küng, the Swiss priest-theologian. Appealing to the documents of Vatican II, Küng emphasized the idea of a constantly moving, constantly changing Church. The Church was the pilgrim People of God, subordinate to the kingdom of God, to which it is the herald and servant. Küng boldly raised questions about the hierarchical Church and papal infallibility. In 1979, Küng's teaching license was revoked by the Vatican, but this did not halt the growth of his influence.

In the meantime, the Soviet foreign minister, Andrei Gromyko, had come into the Vatican on January 24, 1979, to talk with the new Pope and to get his measure. Gromyko, who was no stranger in the Vatican, pressed the new Pope on his commitment to peace. John Paul, however, wanted him to address the issue of religious belief and obstacles to freedom of religion behind the Iron Curtain. Gromyko, according to John Paul's recollection of the meeting, began to boast that the churches in his native Byelorussia were packed. John Paul decided not to pursue the matter further.

In April of 1979, Cardinal Secretary of State Jean Villot died, and John Paul replaced him with Agostino Casaroli, the architect of the Vatican's *ostpolitik*—characterized under Paul VI by its desire to seek dialogue with the Soviet leadership. The appointment was a brilliant move, for it meant an end to the policy and brought Casaroli, with his immense intelligence and experience of the Curia and diplomacy, much closer to John Paul. At the same time the Soviets, used to figures being un-personed when their policies failed, were still dealing with Casaroli, who knew them well.

There were difficulties aplenty for the new Secretary of State as the arrangements went forward for the first papal trip to Poland—but even more difficulties, it appeared, for the Polish party boss, Edward Gierek. Some years later, Gierek would report a telephone conversation he had with Soviet leader Leonid Brezhnev. When Gierek said that he would give John Paul a respectful but modest reception, Brezhnev declared: "Take my advice, don't give him any reception. It will only cause trouble." When Gierek said that there was no way that the Polish government would not invite the Pope, Brezhnev suggested: "He can declare publicly that he can't come due to illness." Finally, Brezhnev said: "Do as you wish. But be careful you don't regret it later."

CHAPTER NINE

The Universal Pastor

On the eve of Whit Sunday—Saturday June 2, 1979—John Paul, Pope for less than nine months, faced a congregation of more than a million in the very navel of his homeland—Victory Square, Warsaw. "Come, Holy Spirit," he intoned, "fill the hearts of the faithful and renew the face of the earth." He added, to the ecstatic roar of the multitude, "of *this* earth," indicating with a sweep of his right hand the entire country and people of Poland. If there was a defining moment in his pontificate, it was that historic declaration made in the heart of his oppressed country. Then the crowds started chanting: "We want God! We want God!" Church bells pealed throughout the nation. The writer Neal Ascherson, who was present on that day, says that a boy turned to him and said: "I feel that I never heard anybody speak before." Afterward people were weeping, walking up and down the streets as if mesmerized, stunned by what they had seen and heard.

He made forty public, highly theatrical appearances in nine days. Three of those days were spent at Czestochowa, where he held a ceremony consecrating Poland to Our Lady, "Queen of Poland." He never once mentioned the Soviet Union, but when he greeted Gierek, he declared: "It is the Church's mission to make our people more confident, responsible, creative, and useful. For this activity the Church does not desire privileges, but only and exclusively what is essential for the accomplishment of its mission."

The historian Timothy Garton Ash has referred to the trip as the "most fantastic pilgrimage in the history of contemporary Europe." John Paul traveled through his own personal Polish past and the past of the nation: He visited Gniezno, birthplace of Polish Catholicism; the shrine of the Black Madonna at Czestochowa; his beloved Krakow and the shrines of Kalwaria. Then he visited Auschwitz. He stressed that he was the Slav Pope with a mission not only to Poles but to Czechs, Slovaks, Slovenes, Serbs, Croats, Bulgarians, Ukrainians, and Russians. In reference to the various pilgrims from these countries who were turned away at the Polish border, he said: "It would be sad to believe that each Pole and Slav from any part of the world is unable to hear the words of the Pope, this Slav."

From the perspective of a Europe still divided during the Cold War, he told his countrymen something astonishing. He told them that being a Slav Pope he had a special mission: to heal the centuries-old divisions between Christianity of the East and the West. This goal, he said, was the responsibility of their generation of Poles. "The future of Poland," he declared, "will depend on how many people are prepared to be nonconformist."

*

John Paul's cinematic good looks, his presence, the sense he gave of power and yet of deep and committed spirituality, made him instantly popular. His early journeys abroad soon established him as a celebrity Pope the world over, and he was mobbed like a pop star wherever he went. *Time* magazine carried a cover calling him John Paul Superstar. The faithful were so swept away by his personality that few were concerned that, while the cameras were constantly trained on him as the main event, his bishops were accordingly reduced in stature and authority. The camera lenses only had eyes for him.

In October 1979, he spoke before the General Assembly of the United Nations in New York against the background of new fears of nuclear proliferation between the West and the Soviet bloc. He insisted that politics, whether national or international, was about human beings. It "comes from man, is exercised by man, and is for man," he said. Peace was always threatened, he argued, when the worth of people was threatened. Threats to peace, he said, came from political systems that created forms of "social life in which the practical exercise of freedom condemns man to become a second-class or third-class citizen." That night he celebrated Mass before 75,000 people, and the next morning he addressed a youth rally in Madison Square Garden. As he was driven around the arena, they started up a chant that would become a kind of mantra for the young: "John Paul II, we love you!" So it went on: In Philadelphia, he greeted a million of the faithful at Logan Circle; then on to Des Moines and Chicago.

In the Windy City, his benign appearance before the ecstatic crowds concealed a much sterner presence behind closed doors. Addressing the bishops of the United States, he urged them to denounce contraception, abortion, homosexuality, and divorce. Holiness, he said, must be "the first priority in our lives and in our ministry." Bishops had to be willing to speak the truth, he said, even in the face of cultural opposition. They must revitalize the practice of confession and reverence for the liturgy.

He was John Paul the liberator, but his message of liberation in every local setting had a careful bias. In Latin America, he had warned of the wrong kind of liberation theology; in Poland, he had called for liberation from totalitarianism; now in the United States, he was preaching against gay liberation and the forms of women's liberation that resulted, in his view, in abortion. There were constituencies in America, he well knew, that were not inclined to believe that their tendencies and life choices were inherently sinful. They wanted liberation from absolutist moral authority. He was here to disabuse them.

At a service with 700 nuns present in Washington, D.C., the world of Catholic religious got a taste of what it meant to have dialogue with John Paul. Sister Mary Theresa Kane, president of the Leadership Conference of Women Religious, wearing a suit rather than a religious habit, gave the welcoming speech. She wanted to get across to him what Catholic women were feeling. She begged him:

> to listen with compassion and to hear the call of women, who comprise half of mankind. As women, we have heard the powerful messages of our Church addressing the need of dignity and reverence of all persons. As women, we have pondered upon those words. Our contemplation leads us to state that the Church in its call for reverence and dignity must respond by providing the possibility of women as persons being included in all ministries in our Church.

When John Paul responded, he ignored everything she had said and delivered a sermon extolling the religious life as a marriage with Jesus Christ. He also gave the sisters present a ticking off for not wearing "a simple and suitable garb."

*

As he got into his stride within the Holy See in Rome, and as he traveled ever wider abroad, he appeared ever more popular with the crowds, ever more authoritarian in the presence of his bishops. The Dutch bishops had shown tendencies to act independently with a view to local problems. Their "Dutch Catechism," with its modern perspectives, had been deemed inadequate by the Curia; and they had strong views on seminary formation, which, in time, would be proved both wise and far-sighted but were deplored by Rome. John Paul established a "Particular Synod" for Holland over which he presided: It became an exercise in papal authoritarianism over every aspect of Dutch initiative, from selection of bishops to ecumenism. Everything had to be translated back into Italian so that John Paul could follow each and every word. At one point, John Paul had leaned over and whispered to the interpreter, who was not Dutch:

"Sometimes your translation is clearer than what the man actually said . . ." It was clear that the long-desired "collegiality" of his bishops was degenerating into papal crisis management.

He performed similar exercises early in his pontificate when he summoned the bishops of the Ukraine, Italy, and Hungary in order to straighten them out. He believed that the Hungarian bishops, for example, were behaving weakly, that they should behave as he had done when he was a Cardinal Archbishop in Poland. He told them without a hint of irony: "The Pope will visit Hungary when the cardinal has learned to bang his fist on the table." Then he was off again on his travels.

In May 1980, he journeyed to Africa, first to Zaire, where he fired a warning shot at those who thought he was already overstepping his papal role: "Some people," he said in Kinsasha, "think that the Pope should not travel so much. He should stay in Rome, as before. I often hear such advice, or read it in newspapers. But the local people here say, 'Thank God you came here, for you can only learn about us by coming. How could you be our pastor without knowing us? Without knowing who we are, how we live, what is the historical moment we are going through?' This confirms me in the belief that it is time for the Bishops of Rome . . . to become successors not only of Peter but also of St. Paul, who, as we know, could never sit still and was constantly on the move."

The Pope who saw himself as successor to Peter and Paul went on to Brazzaville, capital of Congo, then back to northeast Zaire, then on to East Africa and Kenya, where he said a few words in Swahili in Nairobi. Next he was proceeding to Accra, the capital of Ghana. On he went, to Upper Volta and Ivory Coast, before flying back to Rome. If there was a moment that captured the spirit of his African trip, it was at Uhuru Park, Nairobi, when he donned an ostrich-feather headdress and held a leopard-skin shield in one hand and a spear in the other. He said to the vast crowd: "Christ is not only God but also a man. As a human being, he is also an African." Despite this photo-op gesture of enculturation, he repeatedly rebuked the African bishops behind closed doors for merging of pagan practices with Catholicism.

Back in Europe, he turned his attention first to France, which in his view had sunk into indifference and secularism. He started his four-day visit to the "eldest daughter of the Church," as France was known, with an address before the delegates of UNESCO, the United Nations Educational, Scientific and Cultural Organization, on June 2. UNESCO, at the time a nest of Marxist-Leninists under its patently Communist director general, Ahmadou-Mahtar M'Bow, had been engaged in confrontation with the West, specifically in the area of freedom of speech and publishing. In the previous year, UNESCO had published a study on "Communication Problems" under the chairmanship of the Irish lawyer and aging Communist Sean McBride. McBride had proposed a controlled, Soviet-style media for the Third World and denounced the free-enterprise media as culturally imperialist. The United States, convinced that UNESCO was using its outreach to undermine democracy and capitalism, withdrew its financial support from the organization.

Here was an opportunity for a great anti-Communist liberator to nail his colors to the mast. But if there was an early sign that John Paul could veer hopelessly off course and completely misjudge an opportunity, it was his speech to the UNESCO gathering. In a turgid, meandering meditation, he launched into his own special brand of autodidactic philosophizing in execrable French, while demonstrating that he was as capable of jargon as any French Marxist literary theorist. As the delegates listened with mounting amazement, he began to refer to the human person as an "ontic subject of culture." This "ontic subject of culture," he went on, warming to his subject, "contains in itself the possibility of going back, in the opposite direction, to ontic-causal dependencies." Communication problems, the focus of UNESCO interest for several years, were painfully evident that day.

There were no such obfuscations when he gave the French bishops a tongue-lashing for hiding away in their bunkers and failing to confront secularism. What, he asked, did they think they were doing? Were they not bearers "of the Gospel and of holiness, which is a special heritage of the Church of France? Does not Christianity belong immanently to the genius of your nation?" He was no less blunt to the 350,000 who came to see him off at Le Bourget Airport: "Are you faithful to the promises of your baptism?" he harangued.

Next, on June 30, he was off to Brazil for a twelve-day visit. There were the usual rallies: Half a million youngsters greeted him in Belo Horizonte, calling him "John of God! Our King!," which became the chant throughout the vast country as he traveled from the plains to the deserts to the jungles, through villages, towns, and great cities. Everywhere he was benign, compassionate, congenial, as he walked through *favellas* and was carried along rivers. But behind closed doors with his bishops, he was the authoritarian. There was much to displease him in Brazil: mass defections to Protestant evangelism, political activism of priests, and the mix of Catholicism and local magic. In Recife, he lectured the bishops for four hours. The Church, he told them, is not of this world; they must pay heed to papal social doctrine and do all in their power to foster unity. They must love the poor but shun class struggle. He would not countenance priest revolutionaries. He left his bishops stunned.

John Paul's attitude toward liberation theology after the Puebla meeting in January 1979 had taken firmer shape. He was not about to concede to what he saw as Marxism-Leninism within the Church, nor would he grant that the papacy lacked anything but the deepest and most authentic concern for the world's poor. The key liberation-theology text was *A Theology of Liberation* by Gustavo Gutierrez, a Peruvian theologian. Following Marx, up to a point, Gutierrez insisted that the class struggle is a fact and that it is impossible to remain neutral. "As a sign of the liberation to man and history, the Church itself in its concrete existence ought to be a place of liberation," he wrote. "The break with an unjust social order and the search for new ecclesial structures . . . have their basis in this perspective."

Liberation theology clearly bore no comparison with Stalinist, Soviet-style communism. The closest historical and cultural parallel was arguably the political activism of the Church in Wojtyla's Poland. The vital difference, however, was that liberation theology advocated practical emancipation to the extent of joining armed struggles. The reality of the world, Gutierrez taught, was to be discovered in practical commitment (praxis) to the struggles of the oppressed.

In Nicaragua, for example, liberation theology had become an ideological basis of the Sandinista revolution. Four Catholic priests became members of the Sandinista cabinet, including the priest and poet Ernesto Cardenal, minister of culture. (When John Paul finally met him on his trip to Nicaragua in 1983, Cardenal, dressed in lay clothes, went down on his knee, but John Paul withdrew his hand and shook an angry finger at him. "You must straighten out your position with the Church," he said.)

Yet John Paul's opposition to priests or bishops being involved in politics was paradoxical in view of his own involvements through the 1970s in Poland. He was particularly opposed, for example, to the activities of Evaristo Arns of São Paolo, who was in conflict with the Brazilian government, accusing it of oppression of the poor. He was also against Archbishop Oscar Romero's opposition to the government in El Salvador. Romero had been gunned down by soldiers on March 24, 1980, while saying Mass in the chapel of the hospital where he lived. The day before, he had appealed to the army and police to heed their consciences and to cease torturing and killing their fellow Salvadoreans.

The striking aspect of Romero's courageous outspokenness was his earlier acquiescence. He had been a timid, conservative prelate content to yield to the regime. At the age of sixty, however, he underwent a form of conversion after the murder by death squad of his friend the Jesuit Rutilio Grande. From this point he began to listen to the *campesinos* who flocked to his office every day to tell him of their suffering and anxieties. He now began to speak out against the injustices and corruption in El Salvador, in particular against the wealthy families who rigged elections and organized military coups.

His sermons broadcast each week from his cathedral denounced human rights abuses. In this he was out of step with the rest of conservative hierarchy, and also out of step with John Paul, who judged him a "political priest."

The Jesuit Michael Campbell-Johnston, who worked in an urban parish in El Salvador, has written of Oscar Romero: "He was very much a saint for our times. He was not afraid to confront some of the major problems facing today's world: the widening gap between wealthy and poor and the violence caused fundamentally by social injustice." Romero's death had resonances with the death of John Paul's beloved St. Stanislaw, the archbishop murdered by his king. But John Paul doggedly refused to make him a martyr-saint.

In time, however, John Paul would adjust his critique of liberation theology. He would assure the bishops of Brazil that aspects of this way of thinking were "not only opportune but useful and necessary." Meanwhile, John Paul was to express a suspicion of capitalism that very year in his encyclical *Dives in Misericordia* (*On the Mercy of God*). He wrote of the "fundamental defect, or rather series of defects, indeed a defective machinery . . . at the root of contemporary economics and material civilisation," defects that imprison the human family in "radically unjust situations," leading to famine in a world of plenty.

His next visit was to another Church sorely in need of stern warnings, as he saw it: West Germany. One of the largest Churches in the developed world, West Germany had traditionally been highly educated, wealthy, and independent. He chose to lecture the bishops on sexual ethics, which, he insisted, were humanistic rather than authoritarian. They must counsel men and women against living together, or "trial marriages," as he called them, "for one cannot love only on trial, accept a person only on trial and for limited time." He told the bishops to encourage Catholic "progressives" to dispel their false dichotomy between authority and human freedom, and make the traditionalists understand that Vatican I and Vatican II were one and the same Church. He had no comment to make on the progressives' call in Germany for greater collegiality, a strengthening of the local Church, and greater local freedom in the choice of bishops.

Back in Rome, however, a crucial test of Vatican II and collegiality had been brewing with the first great synod of his reign. Paul VI had intended that the world's bishops should participate on a consultative basis in the running of the Church from the Roman center. The synods had not prospered under Paul, and now many bishops hoped that John Paul would at last bring the synods in line with the spirit of Vatican II. They were to be bitterly disappointed.

The first synod of John Paul's reign, in 1980, was on the family and sexuality. Some key synod bishops attempted to raise the issue of contraception and the anomalous situation of Catholics who had remarried after divorce and without an annulment. John Paul sat through the meetings. After a synod lasting a month, John Paul put his signature to the "Apostolic Exhortation" entitled *Familiaris Consortio* (*The Community of the Family*), reaffirming the ban on contraception in Paul VI's *Humanae Vitae*. According to the researches of Thomas J. Reese in his book *Inside the Vatican,* only fifteen percent of the exhortation was taken from the views of the bishops. Reflecting on the synod later, John Paul declared that the document reflected "the consensus of the 1980 World Synod of Bishops on the Family." If a consensus was reflected, it was such as John Paul alone determined.

Under John Paul, the power of the synod would be increasingly eroded over the years until it became nothing more than a talking shop with no authority to influence the Church. He attended all the sessions, a looming presence. At one synod, he was seen to be reading his breviary while individual bishops made their submissions, as if to make it obvious that he had no intention of listening to anything that was being said. Collegiality under John Paul was destined to be shared authority as decided by the Holy Father. From the high hopes for collegiality in the 1960s, the governance of the Church had returned to the state of affairs under Pius XII, the wartime Pope, who said famously: "I don't want collaborators, only people to execute my orders."

*

Meanwhile, in Poland, the Solidarity trade union movement was emerging as a result of a shipyard strike at Gdansk led by Lech Walesa in the summer of 1980. The unrest followed government imposition of price increases of up to a hundred percent on different meat products, prompting demonstrations for commensurate cost-of-living increases and the right to strike. In August, the dock-workers struck in Gdansk, rallying around the figure of a cross; a Mass for workers killed in the 1970 clashes created the distinctive synergy between the Church and the union.

Cardinal Wyszynski remained anxious throughout these developments, fearing a brutal Warsaw Pact invasion to break the will of the workers. He preached a sermon on August 26, feast of Our Lady of Czestochowa, pleading for the union to accept a government compromise. The following day John Paul, with the Communist world listening, encouraged the workers to hold out until their rights were met. He was quickly backed by the Polish bishops' conference. The workers finally got the sanction of the government for a legal union. And so Solidarity came gradually and painfully into being, fit-fully, and with many struggles still ahead. From that point until martial law was imposed a year and a half later, the Solidarity movement would expand until its membership reached ten million.

In the meantime, the Polish leader Edward Gierek was replaced by Stanislas Kania, a former internal security boss who aimed to return Poland to Communist "norms" and to destroy Solidarity by strangling the movement in legal red tape. But the more Kania attempted to oppress the union, the more Solidarity showed its determination to resist.

Poland's Soviet neighbors, East Germany and Czechoslovakia, made threatening moves as if to intervene, and Kania flew to Moscow. Leonid Brezhnev, however, decided to play for time. Kania's attempts to destroy the legal standing of the union were overruled by the Polish Politburo. But Moscow continued to watch the situation, while planning armed intervention should Solidarity threaten the Communist state. A plan for a swift campaign had been drawn up for December 1980 involving German, Czech, and Russian troops. Zbigniew Brzezinski, the U.S. national security adviser, was able to advise John Paul of the troop movements because of satellite intelligence. Fearing an embargo of Poland's trade, Brezhnev paused. Kania convinced him, moreover, that the Polish Politburo could solve its own problems.

Then John Paul took an initiative. He wrote directly to Leonid Brezhnev in French, in his own hand. It is a strangely worded letter, stilted and circumlocutory. In essence, he drew a parallel between a planned invasion of Poland and the Nazi invasion that sparked the Second World War. He also pointed out that an invasion would break the Helsinki Final Act of 1975, which had ratified the post-Yalta arrangements confirming the status quo of Soviet domination of East Europe.

"I ask you to do everything you can," John Paul wrote, "that all that constitutes the causes of this preoccupation, according to widespread opinion, be removed. This is indispensable for détente in Europe and in the world."

By the early months of 1981, Poland was the principal focus of John Paul's anxieties and hopes. In January, Lech Walesa arrived at the Vatican with a group of Solidarity leaders. John Paul gave them a message he wanted amplified to the entire world, and especially to the Soviet Union: that the Solidarity movement was not a negative organization battling against the status quo, but a positive force for the common good.

The following month, strikes broke out in Poland over the right of farmworkers to join the union. In the unrest, Defense Minister General Wojciech Jaruzelski became prime minister. He called for a strike-free period. Solidarity responded with a general strike. Now Jaruzelski was called to Moscow. The Politburo told the general that he must resolve the situation with martial law. By March, Poland was witnessing the most extensive protest against any Communist government in the Soviet system's brief history. Workers occupied their factories, and the Warsaw Pact began military maneuvers around Poland's borders. Tass, the Soviet news agency, spread the rumor that Solidarity was planning armed insurrection, a circumstance that would have justified armed intervention.

Kania and Jaruzelski met with KGB boss Yuri Andropov and Soviet Defense Minister Dimitri Ustinov in a railway car near Brest. The Polish leaders convinced the Russians that only Poland could resolve its own problems. Soviet intervention was averted, martial law was not imposed, and Solidarity encouraged its members back to work.

In time there would be stories whispered in the corridors of the Vatican that at the height of the crisis an inebriated Leonid Brezhnev had suggested to Andropov that the Soviet world would be all the better for the death of John Paul II. Was it Andropov, then, who set about contracting the Bulgarian government to eliminate John Paul, making sure to employ a reliable hit man, one with no connections in Europe, who would become a sleeper waiting for the right opportunity?

CHAPTER TEN

Assassination and Fatima

In the early autumn of 1980, a Turkish hit man, mentally disturbed but nonetheless effective (he had killed a Jewish newspaper editor), arrived in the Bulgarian capital of Sofia, having escaped prison in Istanbul. His name was Mehmet Ali Agca. He took up residence at the expensive Vistosha Hotel, where he stayed for almost two months, and acquired a Bulgarian passport bearing his photograph issued in the name of Frank Ozgun. He traveled around Europe for several weeks, eventually arriving in Rome in December 1980. Tracing his movements, counterespionage experts have declared that Agca was extremely shrewd, disciplined, and well-financed. His contacts were sophisticated, and he employed a high degree of calculation in his secret meetings and his ability to cross borders undetected.

On the afternoon of May 13, 1981, Ali Agca positioned himself close to one of the fountains in St. Peter's Square where John Paul was about to lead a service. At 5:19 P.M., as John Paul was being driven through the crowds of pilgrims in his Popemobile, Ali Agca fired two shots from a semiautomatic pistol at a range of nine feet. One bullet tore through John Paul's abdomen. As he fell back into the arms of Stanislaw Dziwisz, a second bullet grazed his elbow and hit two American pilgrims.

When he was arrested, Ali Agca had a piece of paper in his pocket listing five local Rome telephone numbers: two for the chancellery of the Bulgarian embassy, one for the Bulgarian consulate, another for the Balkanair airline office. The last was an unlisted number for a Bulgarian diplomat, Todor Aivazov. At first Agca claimed that he had acted alone. Later, he implicated a Bulgarian group acting on behalf of the Soviet Union. He told the Italian authorities that he was to have escaped the country in a Bulgarian embassy truck with diplomatic immunity. The details checked out.

In his book titled *The Third Secret,* Nigel West, sometimes known as the unofficial historian of MI6, sets out to solve the mystery. West fails to provide definite proof that the KGB ordered the assassination, but he declares that he had another aim in mind in writing the book. He wanted to "recount the extraordinary story of one man's dedication to the task of freeing the people of the Soviet bloc from Communist totalitarianism, the zeal with which the CIA under the leadership of Bill Casey assisted him, and the KGB's determination to stop them." Ali Agca himself has still not told his full story. When he was transferred from an Italian to a Turkish prison in 2000, he said that he would tell all "once I have been released."

Not the least of the mysteries is how he failed to kill John Paul. One explanation has it that a nun saw Agca raising the pistol and pulled his jacket, disturbing his aim. Another has it that at the moment of the first shot John Paul leaned down to hug a girl who was wearing a badge of Our Lady of Fatima. The date, May 13, was the Feast of Our Lady of Fatima. John Paul would have his own explanation for the failed assassination attempt.

An ambulance got the Pope to the Policlinico Gemelli, four miles distant, within eight minutes. By the time John Paul arrived, he had lost consciousness and six pints of blood. The bullet had missed vital organs and arteries by millimeters. A temporary colostomy procedure was started at six o'clock and went on until half past eleven.

For four days and nights, John Paul lay in intensive care. On Sunday, he managed to issue a message relayed via radio and loudspeakers to the people who had come to St. Peter's Square for the noon Angelus. He said: "Praised be Jesus Christ." Then he prayed for the injured bystanders and forgave "the brother who attacked me, whom I have sincerely forgiven." Finally, he prayed: "To you, Mary, I say again: *Totus tuus ego sum*—I am entirely yours."

John Paul was to spend about four months in and out of hospital. There were sudden mystery infections, advances and retreats in his convalescence, suspicions that the bullets—there being that Bulgarian connection—might have been poisoned (the Bulgarians had infamously murdered a native dissident of their country in London by prodding him with a poison-tipped umbrella). The injured pilgrims also suffered mystery infections.

By the autumn, he was back at work and seemingly his old self, but on a reduced schedule compared with the breakneck juggernaut of the first three years of his pontificate. The shooting had left its physical mark; strong as he was, it had brought him to the brink of death. But the experience, and his survival, was to leave a deep and lasting religious, even "mystical," impression, the consequences of which would take some years to become fully apparent.

Lying in hospital, he had pondered the coincidence that the attempt had occurred on the Feast of Our Lady of Fatima, May 13, the exact anniversary of the day—indeed, according to John Paul, the "very hour"—that Mary appeared to the children of Fatima in Portugal. On returning to the Vatican, he requested that the materials relating to the Fatima story be brought to him, including the text of the Third Secret of Fatima, which had remained a closely guarded secret since being written by the Fatima seer Sister Lucia dos Santos in 1944. What he read, in the light of the attempt on his life, shocked him to the core. The Third Secret had fascinated and terrified generations of Catholics during the Cold War, since it was believed to contain the date of the Third World War. But it was not at all about a war. It was about a pope. As he read the Third Secret, he realized that the pope referred to was none other than himself, Karol Wojtyla.

The text of the Third Secret was not to be divulged publicly until May 13 in the millennium year of 2000, nineteen years after Ali Agca's attempt on John Paul's life. The "secret" described a vision in which "a bishop dressed in white was killed by a group of soldiers who fired bullets and arrows at him." John Paul, still in convalescence, was now convinced that the Virgin Mary prophesied in 1917 that he, Karol Wojtyla, would be the victim of an assassination attempt. It mattered little that certain odds and ends did not tie up: He had not, after all, been killed. And what about the arrows? But prophecy, as well he knew, was never literal, and there were other considerations of great moment connected with the Fatima cult, not least its association with the fate of atheistic communism.

At this point, it is appropriate to recount briefly the Fatima legend, since it was to have a profound effect on John Paul's "mystical" vision of history as it played itself out to the end of the 1980s and ushered in the third millennium.

The Fatima story began in May 1915 against the background of a Communist revolution in Portugal involving the persecution of Catholics and closure of churches. The visionaries were three peasant children who claimed over a period of time that they had experienced visions of an Angel and the Virgin Mary, who imparted messages for the world.

There were three sets of visions. The first set occurred in a field near the village of Fatima in 1915 when Lucia dos Santos, aged ten, accompanied by two friends, saw a transparent white cloud that she thought to be the shape of a man. The second set involved three separate apparitions, witnessed by Lucia in 1916 while she was tending sheep. This time she was with two younger cousins (not the earlier companions)—Francisco, nine, and his sister, Jacinta, seven.

The three children saw what they thought to be an angel who called himself "the Angel of Peace," and later "The Guardian Angel of Portugal." In the last of the 1916 set, the angel was holding a chalice above which was suspended a host dripping with blood. The angel prostrated himself and prayed. He took the chalice, which was still suspended in midair, then gave the host to Lucia and the chalice to Jacinto and Francisco so that they could drink from it. It seems possible that Jacinta was the central seer in the second set, and that the vision was prompted by the fact that unlike Lucia she had not yet made her First Communion. The children did not mention the 1916 apparitions until the third set, which occurred in 1917, was being discussed with the local clergy. The second set of visions was eventually written up by Lucia dos Santos, who had by then become a nun. Her account was in the form of memories over a period of years, written between 1935 and 1941, after her cousins had died.

The 1917 visions, the third set, turned out to be the crucial ones. On May 13, 1917, the same three children—Lucia, Jacinta, and Francisco—were minding their sheep at a place called Cova da Iria when they saw hovering over a bush a woman dressed in white, "more brilliant than the sun." Lucia later described her as "a pretty little woman." She appeared to be no more than doll size. The little lady told them, according to the children's reports, to come to the same spot on the thirteenth day of each month until October of that year. She told them that they would have to suffer for the conversion of sinners, and she asked them to say the rosary. In later apparitions, five more in all, the vision identified herself as the Immaculate Heart and Our Lady of the Rosary. As the apparitions continued through that summer, large crowds began to gather at each event. As many as 50,000 were present at the last vision on October 13, when people saw the sun spinning and changing color, the "miracle of the sun." The Virgin Mary, according to Lucia, asked for a chapel to be built in her honor. Again she asked for the recitation of the rosary and stated the need for moral conversion.

After an investigation lasting seven years, the local bishop proclaimed the apparitions to be authentic.

In 1941, Lucia again took up her pen to write, belatedly, about two visions that had occurred, according to her, on July 13, 1917, in which the Virgin spoke of the end of the Great War and of a coming greater conflict. She talked about Russia spreading its atheistic errors and the need for the Holy Father to dedicate Russia to the Immaculate Heart of Mary in order to bring about the conversion of that country.

In 1944, news came of a "Third Secret." Lucia now wrote about a final and crucial message or secret. This was under no circumstances to be opened, even by the Pope, until 1960. The "secret" was in the keeping of her local bishop until 1957, when it was passed to the safekeeping of the Vatican. When John XXIII finally read the message in 1960, he had it returned to the archive without publishing it.

In the aftermath of the assassination attempt, on October 12, 1981, John Paul was quoted in the *Osservatore Romano* as saying, "Again I have become indebted to the Blessed Virgin. . . . Could I forget that the event in Saint Peter's Square took place on the day and at the hour when the first appearance of the Mother of Christ to the poor little peasants has been remembered for over sixty years at Fatima in Portgual? That day . . . I felt that extraordinary motherly protection, which turned out to be stronger than the deadly bullet." A year to the day after the attack, he traveled to Fatima and placed the spent bullet in Mary's crown at the shrine. He spoke of how one hand had guided the trigger while another, "a motherly hand," had guided the bullet so as to miss vital organs.

But there was a deeper significance that would manifest itself only at the end of the decade. As papal biographer George Weigel has put it, in response to questions posed in an interview: "John Paul II's personal answer to the question of how his papacy, and indeed his life, should be understood came in Portugal, on that visit a year after the attempt on May 12 and 13, 1982. Arriving in Fatima, the Pope succinctly summarized his view of life, history, and his own mission in one pregnant phrase: 'in the designs of Providence there are no mere coincidences.'" Weigel goes on to comment, doubtless with the endorsement of John Paul: "The world, including the world of politics, was caught up in the drama of God's saving purposes in history . . . The Church's primary task was to tell the world the story of its redemption, whose effects were working themselves out, hour by hour, in billions of lives in which there were no 'mere coincidences.'" In other words, everything is written, everything is meant: Our fates are sealed, save for our ability to pray to Mary in the hope that she will intercede with her Son.

CHAPTER ELEVEN

Back on the Road

As John Paul returned to more or less full health, he made a crucial decision in November 1981 by appointing Joseph Ratzinger to head the Congregation for the Doctrine of the Faith (CDF). Thus began a close partnership that would continue into the late years of his papacy. Small, compact, handsome with silken silver hair (and as an eminent British theologian has noted, "cruel mouth and bedroom eyes"), Ratzinger was a Bavarian born in 1927 and ordained in 1951. He was an academic theologian who served as professor in several universities in Germany before becoming a theological adviser to the German bishops at Vatican II. In those days, he was a noted progressive and enthusiast for reform.

With little pastoral experience, he was appointed to the archbishopric of Munich in 1977, the year before John Paul was elected and named a cardinal. It was at the conclave following the death of Paul VI in 1978 that he got to know Cardinal Wojtyla. They agreed that the most important task that lay ahead for the governance of the Catholic Church was the protection of the "Truth."

Cardinal Ratzinger, who reported directly to the Pope, seeing him most Fridays, would run his department, the CDF, with rigorous conservatism. Being a liberal was one thing in a seminar room; being responsible for the survival and the unity of the Catholic faith from the Vatican center was quite another. The CDF was originally the Office of the Universal Inquisition, whose purpose was to safe-guard the Faith by clarifications and by disciplining false doctrine and false teachers. To this day, the CDF investigates texts by Catholics writing in the name of the Church, and calls their authors to account if there is evidence of error, mostly by warning the local bishop or the religious superior.

As a progressive, just ten years before he took over the CDF he had insisted that theologians under investigation should have coun-sel; that they should be allowed to view the files kept on them; that secrecy should not be imposed on the investigation. He reneged on those progressive ideas when he joined the Vatican. And while he had earlier entertained a compassionate view toward remarried Catholics whose first marriage had not been annulled, as head of the CDF he excluded them from the sacraments. Civilly remarried persons, he declared, "find themselves in a situation that objectively contravenes God's law. Consequently, they cannot receive holy communion." Over the years, Ratzinger would be accused of discourtesy, lack of charity, and of being a bully in his pursuit of orthodoxy.

One of the early indications that things were tightening up in the pontificate was John Paul's decision to bring the 22,000-strong Soci-ety of Jesus—the Jesuits—into line. Since Vatican II, the Jesuits had largely abandoned their teaching role in secondary education and expanded their work in the Third World. The British province, for example, withdrew Jesuits from the country's city schools and fee-paying independent colleges and dispatched them to the jungle mis-sions of Guyana. As the Jesuits saw it, they were rediscovering their roots in the promotion of justice and peace, a direction that had been confirmed at the synod of bishops under Paul VI in 1971.

But there was an impression in the Vatican that the Jesuits had become a law unto themselves. John Paul stepped in when the Jesuit general, Pedro Arrupe, fell ill and appointed his own conservative choice for successor, Paolo Dezza. With the Society's legendary obe-dience, the Jesuits jumped to attention and renewed their loyalty to the papacy.

As his health improved, John Paul found himself once again in a whirlwind of activity. John Paul was fulfilling his self-imposed role as the missionary Pope to the world: the universal pastor. After the success of his trips to Mexico, Poland, Ireland, and the United States in 1979, there had been Hungary, Africa, France, Brazil, and West Germany in 1980. In February of 1981, he had set off on his first Asian pilgrimage—Pakistan, the Philippines, Guam, Japan—stopping at Alaska as he flew back to Europe. Having recovered from the wounds of the assassination attempt by the spring of 1982, he embarked on a visit to Britain in May, followed immediately by a trip to Argentina. Since the two countries were at war over the Argentine invasion of the Falklands, John Paul had reason to exercise skillful diplomacy.

There was an upset as a consequence of Cardinal Basil Hume accepting a dinner invitation on behalf of the Pope with the Queen. Archbishop Marcinkus has informed me that he told Hume bluntly that he had better "uninvite the Pope." The British cardinal had failed to understand that if John Paul had dined with the Queen he would be obliged to dine subsequently with General Galtieri when he arrived in Buenos Aires. The two prelates parted on bad terms.

There had been high hopes in England for reconciliation between the Anglicans and English Catholics, and John Paul conducted a joint service at Canterbury Cathedral with Archbishop Robert Runcie. John Paul said that Canterbury reminded him of Krakow. The British visit was a success, leaving Anglicans and Catholics in a glow of imminent unity; less happy were the organizers who were left with some 50,000 white and yellow umbrellas that they had failed to sell, the British weather being unusually clement during the visit. Monsignor Tom Gavin, the priest who managed the Pope's visit to the Midlands and who had purchased the umbrellas, nevertheless has a happy memory of the Pope. "In Coventry," said the monsignor, "it was a sweltering day, and the clergy and prelates were all drinking gins and sherry, which the Pope declined. Then I offered him a pint of cold Polish beer and he drank it down in one draft."

John Paul's enthusiasm for evangelization in person, and his prodigious stamina, was still in its early stages, however. During his papacy, he would make more than a hundred papal trips. His intention was to take the mission of Christ the Redeemer to the ends of the earth. And he saw his journeys as parallel with the journey of the Church toward the third millennium, which beckoned as a period of spectacular Christian renewal. "As the second millennium after Christ's coming draws to an end," he wrote, "an overall view of the human race shows that this mission is still only beginning and that we must commit ourselves wholeheartedly to its service."

*

In the years following the assassination attempt, the character of John Paul's papacy was becoming ever more apparent. Although he continued to present himself as a Pope of the Second Vatican Council, and indeed revealed himself as such in many things— liturgy, focus on Scripture, outreach to the world, compassion for the poor and the disenfranchised—he was quashing some of the most crucial conciliar agendas. John Paul had by the early 1980s revealed himself as an authoritarian rather than a collegial Pope; he was inclined to draw in the reins of power to the Vatican and to his papal office rather than release authority and local discretion to the dioceses and the local Churches. This tendency was no mere quirk of his personality or even his personal history.

The tensions between the local Church and papal authority in Rome have to be understood against the background history of the papacy through the modern era. In response to the political and social changes that gathered pace in the aftermath of the French and American Revolutions, the papacy was obliged to survive in a climate of rationalism, liberalism, science, industrialization, and the evolving nation-state.

The modernizing states of Europe were inclined to separate Church from State, throne from altar, secular from clerical. At the same time, the State was insisting on control and legislation over the Church in such matters as education, marriage, divorce, and charitable finance, bringing the Catholic Church, alongside other Christian denominations and other faiths, within an ambit of secular equivalence with people of no faith. Through the hazardous circumstances of this era, the Church found itself split internally over an issue fraught with consequences for the modern papacy.

The struggle was between those who urged an absolutist papal primacy from the Roman center and those who argued for a greater decentralization of authority to the local bishops. The triumph of the modern centrists, or "ultramontanists" (a phrase coined in France indicating papal power from "beyond the mountains," or the Alps), was sealed at the First Vatican Council of 1870 against the background of the Pope's loss of his dominions. The Pope was declared infallible in matters of faith and morals as well as undisputed *primate*—supreme spiritual and administrative head of the Church. Ultramontism, power from the center, implemented with a powerful new code of canon law, issued in 1917, and a vastly expanded Curia and diplomatic corps, created and sustained a disciplined and unified Church through the course of the next century. The model of the Church came to resemble a perfect sovereign society that existed in an imaginative universal space rather than a web of interrelated local, congregational spaces. This model of control persisted through the paroxysms of two world wars, through confrontations with, and murderous persecutions by, Nazism and Soviet communism. But this had been a legalistic, monolithic Church, with a siege mentality. The vital impulse of parish and diocesan communities, the aspirations of women and the laity, had been neglected; the local discretion and authority of bishops had been eroded, indicating enfeeblement and lack of responsibility. The fatal weakening of a local Church at its peripheries can be seen by contrasting and comparing several episodes in history.

The Catholic Church in Germany survived the Kulturkampf at the close of the nineteenth century by strong independence and local discretion. Pius IX, for all his record of absolutism, had absolved German Catholics from allegiance to the State, at the same time liberating them to act freely and independently of Rome. The German Catholic community, however, acquiesced and crumpled within weeks of the Nazis coming to power, when a centralizing

Pope, Pius XI, determined to defend the local Church through diplomatic summitry with Hitler. Speaking to the students of Collegio Mondragone on May 14, 1929, Pius XI had said: "When there is a question of saving souls or preventing greater harm to souls, we feel the courage to deal with the devil in person."

Pius XII, who had been Pius XI's instrument of diplomacy with Hitler in 1933, took a very different view of accommodation "with the devil" in the postwar period: He was prepared even to excommunicate Communists. But when John XXIII came to the throne of St. Peter, he reversed this policy, as did the Second Vatican Council and Paul VI. One of the deepest ironies of this situation, moreover, was the refusal of two Cardinal Archbishops in Poland—Stefan Wyszynski and Karol Wojtyla—to heed the pressures from the Vatican to reach accords and compromises with communism. In their view, the Council document that advocated dialogue with difference—*Dignitas Humanae*—could never have required the Church to compromise on the issue of religious liberty. Hence Paul VI's accommodating *ostpolitik*, his dialogue with Moscow, could not be defended, in the view of Wojtyla, on the grounds that it accorded with Vatican II.

Shaped by antagonistic and uncompromising confrontation with Soviet ideology, John Paul seemed incapable of distinguishing between the opposition of his erstwhile Communist enemies and the opposition of Catholic dissidents. When he became Pope, he appeared unable to countenance debate or dissent, or the least opposition, from within the Church. When he became Pope, he told the faithful: "Be not afraid!" And yet he of all people appeared to fear the consequences of collegiality, subsidiarity, pluralism, and dissent within the Church.

He evidently made a crucial decision, which does much to explain the contradictions and paradoxes of his reign. He *declared* continually that Vatican II was the program of his pontificate. Yet, while sending reassuring signals designed to pacify the conciliar progressives, he used the considerable power of his office, his travels, and the outreach of the papal media and the Curia to reverse the

Council's notion of the people of God in pilgrimage, engaging in dialogue, engaging with the world.

The progressives would become increasingly conscious of the gap between John Paul's words and his actions. For whatever the faithful thought Vatican II represented, it was not about increasing the power and influence of the Pope and Curia over the running of the local dioceses. Nor was it the wish of the Council fathers that the Pope should make virtually daily statements on myriad topics while reducing his bishops to silence. Nor was it the wish of the Council that the Pope should ignore the deliberations of the bishops' synods. Nor was it expected that the Pope should nominate every bishop in the entire world.

The practice whereby the Pope nominated every single bishop in the Church throughout the world is surprisingly recent in origin, dating back a little over eighty years to the 1917 Code of Canon Law. Throughout much of the Church's history, popes inherited the right to nominate bishops only within the Papal States and areas in the East where dioceses owed direct allegiance to the pope. The late Garrett Sweeney, in *Bishops and Writers* (1977), his study on the question, has a powerful image to illustrate the mechanism. "If 'The Church' is conceptualised as a single machine," he wrote, "with divine assistance concentrated at the top, and nothing more is required of bishops than that they should operate the machine efficiently, it is entirely appropriate that they should be appointed from Rome." Naturally, Father Sweeney did not believe that the Church is a single machine with divine assistance "at the top."

The nomination of bishops by the pope alone has had important implications for the exercise of infallible or definitive teaching by all the Catholic bishops when they teach in union with one another and the pope. Clarified six decades later, in a revised version of the Code of Canon Law (1983), infallibility currently assumes collegial pluralism. And yet as critics of the status quo point out, collegiality is a difficult ideal to attain when the pope selects every bishop according to his own views and prejudices.

John Paul's determination to discipline the Church by appointing "safe" bishops first became apparent in Holland, where the faithful vehemently resented his choices in the early 1980s. His appointment of an ultraconservative Benedictine abbot, Hans Groër, in 1986 to succeed the progressive Cardinal Archbishop of Vienna, Franz Josef König, was also hotly criticized. John Paul responded by pointing out to the Austrians: "You must not allow any doubts to arise about the right of the Pope freely to appoint bishops."

But the most controversial instance of an appointment in the 1980s was to occur in Chur in Switzerland. In 1988, the Pope would nominate Wolfgang Haas, an unpopular right-wing prelate, disliked by people and clergy alike. The Pope had vetoed the choice of the local cathedral canons and forged ahead with the appointment of Haas despite a vigorous press campaign. Demonstrating Catholics formed a human carpet before the Cathedral so that those taking part in the new bishop's ordination were obliged to step over them. At the Catholic University of Fribourg in Switzerland, students formed a cortege behind a coffin marked with the legend "Second Vatican Council."

But John Paul had many more things on his mind than pacifying disgruntled local Catholics in Holland, Austria, and Switzerland. As the 1980s progressed, the disgruntlement of his critics was increasingly eclipsed by his involvement in mighty events in Poland, Eastern Europe, and the world at large.

CHAPTER TWELVE

Poland and the Fall of Communism

For John Paul, the decade of the 1980s was the decade of Poland. Before the end of 1981, the year of the assassination attempt, the situation in Poland had exploded following a new round of food price increases, which prompted the union Solidarity to call a strike. Under pressure from Moscow, General Wojciech Jaruzelski imposed martial law and arrested the Solidarity leadership. The situation was grim: tanks in the streets, the cutting of telephone and telex lines, censorship . . . The Soviet Union did not intervene, but Jaruzelski found himself losing by degrees his attempts to enforce a Polish Communist "solution" on a country that was struggling to become itself, which was no more than the unofficial motto of Solidarity: "So that Poland shall be Poland."

John Paul gave Lech Walesa his full backing. There are indications that John Paul gave Lech Walesa's movement $50 million; the sum was probably donated through the services of the Vatican Bank, run during that period by Archbishop Paul Casimir Marcinkus, nicknamed the "Pope's Gorilla" for his tough protection of popes on foreign trips. There was a rumor that the money was passed to Solidarity via Roberto Calvi, the Mafia banker who was found on June

17, 1982, hanging under Blackfriars Bridge in London, most likely the victim of a Mafia revenge murder made to look like a suicide. When I asked Archbishop Marcinkus in 1987 to confirm the gift of money to Solidarity, he employed a fine example of equivocation: "Calvi never mentioned Solidarity to me at all. If he gave something to Solidarity, okay, but I didn't know anything about it."

In the meantime, Jimmy Carter, with whom John Paul had made a good start, had lost the presidential election in the United States, and John Paul received his successor Ronald Reagan for the first time in the Vatican. There was some small embarrassment, according to Monsignor Sotto Voce, when Mr. Reagan nodded off during a private session (it has been said that Reagan, who often took cat-naps during the day, tended to fall asleep when most excited).

Both men saw the Soviet Union in stark moral terms: For Ronald Reagan, Soviet communism was the "Evil Empire." Appropriating melodramatic language to characterize the struggle between East and West, Reagan was indulging in mere religiose rhetoric. The America that he was leading into an era of Reaganomics, low taxes, and high unemployment was hardly the Powers of Light divinely ordained to destroy the Powers of Darkness. But the two men had a strong coincidence of interest—fundamentally to challenge the Yalta agreement whereby the three great powers had carved up East and West postwar Europe. The synergy between them, including their love of acting, was remarkable. The American president made a decision to keep John Paul provided with the best U.S. intelligence information; that information might well have been crucial in fore-warning Lech Walesa as to just how far he could go without Moscow sending Warsaw Pact tanks across the border.

Was there a conspiracy between them to bring down European communism? Marco Politi and Carl Bernstein pursue this argument in their biography of John Paul, *His Holiness: John Paul II and the Hidden History of Our Time* (1996). They suggest that there was a trade-off involving, for example, John Paul's silence on the placement of NATO intermediate-range nuclear missiles in Europe in exchange for Reagan's support for Poland, even of deals to be done to bring down the government of Nicaragua. The proposition is challenged by George Weigel in his *Witness to Hope*.

The crucial perspective is how John Paul saw matters. John Paul gazed upon the world and history in terms of Faith: His sense of Poland's history, and his own destiny, was deeply imbued with the Marian traditions of protection and intervention. As he saw it, in retrospect at least, the groundwork for the collapse of Soviet domination in his homeland had been laid, pastorally, in hearts and minds, on his first trip in June 1979. After 1981, moreover, and the attempt on his life, it was not possible to propose a vision of history that excluded his understanding of the prophecies of Fatima. There were no coincidences in history.

*

John Paul longed to return to Poland almost as soon as he left it in June 1981. He was thwarted in 1982 from celebrating the six hundredth anniversary of Our Lady of Jasna Gora because of martial law, or what Jaruzelski termed "a state of war." But he returned at last in June 1983 for a week's visit.

His movements were heavily controlled by the regime. This time he looked sorrowful in his expressions and demeanor. The leaders of Solidarity, including Lech Walesa, were in jail; and John Paul was not seeing eye to eye with the Primate of Poland, Cardinal Jozef Glemp, who was far from convinced that communism was doomed and was consequently in a mood for accommodation. Neither was the Pontiff in complete accord with his secretary of state, Cardinal Casaroli. Cardinal Jean-Marie Lustiger of Paris has remarked that during dinner in Krakow in 1983 Casaroli said with exasperation: "What does he want? Does he want bloodshed? Does he want war?"

Outside Jasna Gora monastery, where John Paul addressed half a million young people, many of whom had walked through the night to be there, the old magic returned. The chanting from the crowds made it impossible for him to speak at first. Timothy Garton Ash, who was there, captured the spirit. "He preaches a love that is 'greater than all the experiences and disappointments that life can prepare for us.'" The magic he performed was to turn the brooding, potentially violent insurgency into a peaceful but no less determined transformation of consciousness. Everywhere he traveled, the cry went up: "Stay with us . . . stay with us."

Garton-Ash has grasped the charismatic appeal of his preaching on this second trip: "He speaks to the Poles through a tapestry of symbols and allusions—historical, literary, philosophical, Mariological—each of which requires at least a paragraph of explanation. It is impossible because so much depends on a theatrical delivery that John Gielgud once called 'perfect.' It is impossible because poetry is what gets lost in translation."

There was a meeting between John Paul and General Jaruzelski at the Belvedere Palace in Warsaw. The regime proposed that the Church might achieve its independence through sanctioned Catholic unions and even a Catholic "opposition" party. John Paul saw it for what it was—a divide-and-rule tactic. He refused. Political parties and labor unions, he insisted, must exercise their own independence and integrity.

Up to this point, Jaruzelski had denied John Paul access to Lech Walesa. John Paul told the general to let Walesa out of jail and to begin dialogue with him, but Jaruzelski refused. So John Paul continued to press to meet Walesa himself. At last, just before his return to Rome, a "private" assignation was arranged in a cabin in the Tatras Mountains. Walesa, accompanied by his captors, was brought in by helicopter. The meeting became an open secret, giving immense dignity and legitimacy to the labor leader.

*

It was to be another three years before John Paul returned once more to Poland, and during that time a great deal had changed in his homeland. Solidarity and the Church now had an outstanding martyr, the charismatic priest Jerzy Popileuszko. Father Jerzy was a stunning preacher whose sermons were amplified to congregations of up to 50,000 assembling outside his church in Warsaw. His theme was always the same—truth, justice, liberty for Poland. Jaruzelski's secret police, acting on orders, abducted the priest on the night of October 19, 1984. They beat him until he was dead. They put him in a plastic garbage bag weighed down with stones and dumped his body in a reservoir, where he was found ten days later. He was thirty-seven years of age. It is still not known, despite many investigations, exactly who ordered the priest's murder.

Several hundred thousand people attended his funeral. Hope could not be beaten and buried; Father Jerzy's tomb in the graveyard of his church, St. Stanislaw Kostka, became a martyr's shrine and a meeting point for Solidarity. A private TV company was set up to transmit programs without license across Poland; its first transmission was the life story of Father Jerzy. As Adam Michnik has commented, communism in Poland could no longer present itself as the human face of socialism. It was "communism with a few teeth knocked out."

Through the mid-1980s, Jaruzelski maintained an uneasy status quo while foreign debts mounted and the United States applied sanctions. The quality of life in Poland plummeted with the slow-motion collapse of the economy, prompting shortages of every kind. Police brutality was by now curbed, and all the Solidarity leaders were released from jail by 1986, but Walesa continued to refuse to cooperate with the government in the absence of political pluralism. Solidarity had formed a coalition with Poland's bishops and its vast and intricate web of parishes: Grassroots parish communities kept the people informed and sustained their morale and hope. This was the state of affairs when John Paul landed in his native country once more in June 1987.

*

On his third papal visit to Poland he was greeted in the royal palace by Jaruzelski, whom John Paul had last encountered in January. John

Paul lectured the leader on democracy and the inalienable rights of individuals. Society, he said, did not exist for the state; it was the other way around. People had the right to participate in the decisions made by the state. Poland was passing through a dark and difficult period, he said, but the crisis would not be lifted unless these principles were acknowledged. Quoting a passage from the document *Gaudium et Spes* (*Joy and Hope*) of Vatican II, John Paul said: "One must pay tribute to those nations whose systems permit the largest possible number of citizens to take part in public life in a climate of genuine freedom."

On June 12, he addressed a congregation of more than a million faithful near Gdansk, scene of the shipyard strike that had launched the Solidarity movement back in 1980. He declared that "as work contributed to the common good, workers had the right to make decisions regarding the problems of the whole of society." He ended by telling them the meaning of the common good and solidarity: "Solidarity means one another, and if there is a burden, then this burden is carried together, in community. Thus: Never one against another. Never one group against another, and never a burden carried by one alone, without the help of others."

He left Jaruzelski presiding over a collapsing regime and grasping at straws. "You will take with you," said the general, "in your heart, [Poland's] image, but you will not take with you the homeland's real problems." He finished by recommending that the Pope say something of the misery, injustice, and contempt for human rights in other countries of the world. His words, however, rang hollow. Jaruzelski's Poland was doomed.

That autumn, following the failure of Jaruzelski's national referendum for government economic reforms, there were waves of strikes. In the spring of 1988, demonstrations were met with brutal force, but it was all too late and all in vain. The Soviet Union had a new leader, Mikhail Gorbachev, who had no intention of propping up the decaying regimes of Eastern Europe. Under the pressures of exorbitant military rivalry with the United States, Gorbachev was overhauling the economic and political system of the Soviet empire. Poland would be left to its fate, and Jaruzelski could no longer threaten dissidents with a Soviet-imposed martial law. The general had no alternative but to reach an accommodation with the opposition. Such was the antagonism between the extremists on both sides of the political divide that it took many months before Solidarity once again became legal. Elections took place on June 4, 1989, setting in motion the loss of Soviet control of the satellites in Eastern Europe. All but one of the hundred seats in the Polish senate and all the free seats in the Sejm, or parliament, were won by the Solidarity-backed Citizens' Committee. Official diplomatic relations were restored between the Holy See and Poland.

The world was about to witness one of the most extraordinary paroxysms in modern history: the implosion of the Soviet system. John Paul has always said that he "merely gave the tree a good shake." Few would dispute that the inexorable and bloodless collapse had been initiated by the Polish Pope.

Would this be the fulfillment of John Paul's hopes and prayers? Had the planet entered an era that could be described as the best of all possible worlds? John Paul would soon make it clear that capitalism and democracy were in need of correctives, but there had been other major developments through the 1980s within the Catholic Church, not least an extraordinary proliferation of saints.

CHAPTER THIRTEEN

John Paul, Saints, and Scientists

In centuries to come, the papacy of John Paul II will be remembered for the enormous numbers of saints and blesseds that he sanctioned. The canonizing, or making, of a saint by the Catholic Church means that a person has been declared to be reliably in heaven by the pope, and thus worthy of a universal cult or devotion. A *beatus,* or "blessed," is also declared to be in heaven but worthy of a local rather than a universal cult. Blesseds usually graduate in time to full sainthood. In both cases their relics, usually parts of their bodies or objects that have come in touch with those bodies, are deemed to have special power—of healing, for example. The faithful are encouraged to pray to these individuals, asking for intercessions—help in life, consolation, even miracles of healing. Some saints are associated with particular efficacy: St. Anthony for finding lost objects, St. Gerard Majella for pregnant women, St. Jude for "hopeless cases." Both saints and blesseds are deemed to be exemplars of a holy life: They show us how we can achieve holiness and enter heaven.

Catholic saints and blesseds also have political and institutional significance, endowing that individual with official papal approval.

John Paul approved the beatification of many individuals killed during the Spanish Civil War, while declining to honor Archbishop Oscar Romero, deemed by John Paul to have left-leaning sympathies. Ecclesial politics also play a part. While beatifying John XXIII, the popular Pope of the Council, John Paul, for balance, beatified Pius IX, associated with the dogmas of papal infallibility and primacy of the First Vatican Council in 1870.

The huge increase in the making of saints and blesseds under John Paul II was evidently part of a strategy of evangelization—to demonstrate to the world the heroic sanctity that could be achieved by the faithful in every quarter of the globe. It was a token, too, of John Paul's conviction that the "communion of the saints" is a dimension of the Church on earth. He spoke of the saints and blesseds of his papacy as "saints for the third millennium."

By the mid-1990s, John Paul had presided over the making of almost a thousand saints and blesseds, more than the number of those canonized and beatified by all the popes put together since Pope Urban VIII started the formal process in the 1620s. The mid-1980s had seen the speeding up of the system as a result of John Paul's reform of the saint-making mechanism. Traditionally, it took many decades—if not centuries—for the making of a saint or blessed. John Paul reduced the process to a few years. In January 1983, he published the Apostolic Constitution known as *Divinus Perfectionis Magister* (*The Divine Master of Perfection*). The most significant change was the abolition of the Devil's Advocate, a lawyer charged with probing the claims of the "servant of God," as a candidate for sainthood is known. The drawn-out adversarial methods of Devil's Advocates, who questioned and scrutinized every major and minor claim of holiness, had evidently slowed down the process. Instead, the merits of a servant of God would be established by the writing of a biography, or hagiography, known as a *positio*. The new system, however, meant that it was more difficult for objections and criticisms of "the servant of God" to be brought to bear.

The most controversial beatification in John Paul's papacy has been that of Josemaría Escrivá de Balaguer (1902–1975), the founder of Opus Dei. Escrivá, a charismatic Spanish priest, was as controversial as the religious movement he established in 1941. Opus Dei, a pious association of laypeople and clergy, has a reputation for secrecy, austerity, and financial shrewdness. Questions have been raised, but not settled, about his relationship with the fascist Spanish dictator General Francisco Franco. At least nine members of Opus Dei served in Franco's cabinet. The movement's spirituality was shaped by Escrivá's famous text *The Way*, originally published in 1935 and containing 999 maxims. He encouraged members, both celibate and married, to introduce Catholic values in their everyday lives, especially in the workplace. John Paul expressed his approval of the work of Opus Dei as early as 1974 when still a cardinal, paraphrasing and praising Escrivá's crucial message: "each one sanctifying his or her work, sanctifying themselves at work, and sanctifying others through their work."

Cardinal Wojtyla had prayed at the tomb of Escrivá in Rome the night before the conclave that elected John Paul I. In 1982, he granted the movement the status of a "personal prelature," which essentially meant that the priests within the organization could operate independently of a diocese and directly under the auspices of the head of the movement and the Pope. For some critics of Opus Dei, this was a further indication of John Paul's desire to weaken the dioceses and local bishops.

The biography supporting Escrivá's beatification bid, running to a prodigious 6,000 pages, was researched and written in strictest secrecy by members of Opus Dei, a fact that raised the suspicions of many, including the former *Newsweek* religious correspondent Kenneth Woodward, author of *Making Saints*. "There was considerable evidence," Woodward has written, "that Escrivá's life had not been thoroughly researched and fairly presented, that the tribunal judges had prevented contrary witnesses from being heard, and that officials of the Congregation [for saint-making] had bowed to pressure from Opus Dei to speed the process through." According to the new rules, the process should include testimony from witnesses who oppose the cause. The names of some eleven critics were put forward to the beatification tribunal for Escrivá, but only one of these was invited to give witness, and his testimony was given skimpy prominence. Kenneth Woodward managed to interview six other witnesses who had lived and worked with Escrivá. "The examples they gave of [Escrivá's] vanity, venality, temper tantrums, harshness toward the subordinates, and criticism of popes and other churchmen," writes Woodward, "were hardly the characteristics one expects to find in a Christian saint." The beatification biography, however, made Escrivá look like a superhuman walking saint. But such suspicions and criticisms were of no avail, since John Paul went ahead and sanctioned Escrivá's beatification in record time. "Opus Dei," continues Woodward, "insisted that any criticism of [the beatification process] was criticism of the pope himself."

Josemaría Escrivá de Balaguer was beatified on May 17, 1992, before a crowd of some 200,000 devotees (ten years later, he would be canonized a saint). The speed with which he had been "raised to the altars," as the saying goes, indicated for many the influence of Opus Dei over the Congregation for Saints (the Vatican department responsible for saint-making) and John Paul himself. And yet, the Escrivá story more likely indicates John Paul's approval of Opus Dei rather than the movement's manipulation of *him*. Opus Dei has flourished in the afterglow of the honor paid to its founder, expanding its following and becoming more relaxed in its dealings with the media. The movement resembles a modern-day version of the Jesuits at the Reformation, working in education and other charitable activities throughout the world. In 1998, John Paul granted the Opus Dei institute of studies in Rome the status of a Pontifical University.

＊

Another of John Paul's reforms in the saint-making process has been to reduce the number of miracles required as a testimony or sign from heaven that the candidate is indeed a saint or blessed. During John Paul's papacy, however, the Vatican has been finding it increasingly difficult to enlist Catholic doctors and scientists to cooperate in the scrutiny of such miracles, since many experts believe that involvement in the process could damage their careers. At the same time, many holy people with public cults, like John Henry Newman, do not get beatified or canonized, despite the inflation in saint-making, because the miracle criterion is too tough.

The task of the scientific scrutineers of miracles in support of a canonization or beatification is to declare the phenomenon (usually of healing) to be "inexplicable" in terms of the laws of nature. The work of the miracle scientists has often been made all the more difficult when John Paul decided that a particular candidate or group of candidates must be put on the fast track in order to provide an excuse for making a saint or blessed on a foreign trip or anniversary.

Theories of explicability depend on current theories in science, which are never held by scientists to be immutable since they are valid only until falsified or proven otherwise. The Jesuits have been pressing the Vatican to alter its policy to admit "moral" and "spiritual" miracles—for example, the healing of a broken marriage, or the cure of an alcoholic. John Paul would not hear of it.

A more inclusive pope would likely throw out the current process of saint-making, dismantling the scientific medical panels and embracing the Jesuit suggestion of miracles that appeal to the religious imagination. This more modern notion of miracles would be paradoxically closer, as some Jesuits have been arguing for years, to the significance of miracles in the Gospels, where they exemplify narratives of Christian redemption rather than pseudoscience masquerading as religious power. A more inclusive view of the meaning of miracles and sainthood might accept that it is more difficult to change human hearts than to make tumors disappear.

*

John Paul, despite his enthusiasm for miracles that defy the known laws of the Universe, has presented himself throughout his reign as a patron and supporter of science, as well as a critic and monitor of its false claims and unethical practices. His pontificate has coincided with rapid advances in genetics, embryonic stem-cell research, reprotechnology, neuroscience, and artificial intelligence. His reign has seen profound challenges to notions of creation and human identity in the fields of cosmology, evolution, and sociobiology—all of which have engaged his interest. John Paul has enthusiastically encouraged research and conferences on all these issues, and nobody could accuse him of failing to heed the call for intellectual outreach after his 1998 encyclical *Fides et Ratio (Faith and Reason)*.

John Paul started his pontificate by paying tribute in 1979 to Galileo as a Christian, as if to heal a breach with science that had existed since the mid–seventeenth century. He has presented himself, moreover, as a major patron of academic and scholarly endeavors in the natural and social sciences. The Pontifical Academy of Sciences holds plenary sessions every two years attended by twenty-four world-class scientists. On these illustrious occasions, John Paul has announced the winner of the Pius XI medal for a young scientist. He has appointed to the academy some seventy scientists for life, mostly professors from European and American universities, including Martin Rees, the late Max Perutz, and Charles Townes. The Vatican observatory, with its Jesuit astronomers and astrophysicists, has a world-class reputation. In addition, John Paul has sponsored occasional international conferences on science and social science, and there have been notable attempts to focus on issues of immediate interest, such as neuroscience, cosmology, and bioethics.

At a neuroscience conference that I attended in the Vatican in 1990, John Paul was present at the keynote lecture given by Professor Gerald Edelman. Edelman, a Nobel Prize winner who had developed a striking new theory of mind-body development, should have been of some fascination to John Paul in light of the scientist's interest in the embodied soul. There was an amusing and telling incident prior to the lecture. John Paul, flanked by Professor Edelman and Dr. Oliver Sacks, the famous author-neurologist, paused in the lobby to gaze at a blown-up picture of a single neurone, or brain cell. After meditating for what seemed an age, John Paul said ponderously to Oliver Sacks: "So! This . . . is . . . the *brain*." Sacks did not correct him. Sacks said later that he did not think it appropriate for a mere neurologist to challenge the Holy Father on such an important topic.

However, the fact is that these initiatives in the ambit of science have had little or no impact on the clerical establishment of the Vatican and give the semblance rather than the reality of a dialogue among peers. At the neuroscience conference, the final address, given by a monsignor with no qualifications in the field, reiterated a belief in body-soul dualism, contradicting the drift of the entire meeting, with the exception of just one presentation—that of the late Sir John Eccles, widely regarded as an eccentric within the discipline.

Beyond this kind of window dressing, however, John Paul was tightening the screws on Catholic universities in the United States following the publication in 1990 of a document titled *Ex Corde Ecclesiae (From the Heart of the Church)*. He was seeking to control academics in Catholic universities and colleges in the United States who taught religion in the name of Catholicism: Religion by his definition included ethics and philosophy. The move raised delicate questions about academic freedom, separation of Church and State, academic funding, and the nature of Catholic identity. The document advocated tighter control on "orthodox" teaching and the curbing of pluralist freedoms within these areas. Catholic institutions were being asked either to opt in or opt out. Opt in, and the university could surrender control to the local bishop and ultimately Rome. Opt out, and the institution could no longer call itself Catholic. The price of opting in was high. Could any university or college consider itself free while it took its orders from an absolute sovereign in Rome? This was no trivial consideration, since Catholic universities had been attracting both Catholics and non-Catholics for several generations and were in some cases competing with Ivy League institutions. There were constitutional issues, too. Could the U.S. government, or the State, award funds to an institution that took its orders from a foreign Supreme Pontiff?

The issue came to a head in 1989 after the Vatican rebuked the long-standing "dissident" Father Charles Curran, a distinguished moral theologian at Catholic University in Washington, D.C. Curran had claimed that he was dissenting not from dogma but from aspects of the Pope's teaching that were not infallible. His license to teach theology was withdrawn by Cardinal Ratzinger, and he was consequently dismissed by his university. At a press conference, Curran declared that he had been targeted in the Pope's battle against liberal academics. He lost his civil appeal against the university for dismissal in February 1989. The events disturbed many academics in Catholic institutions, widening the gulf between the American hierarchy and Catholic academe. In November of the millennium year, the Catholic bishops of the United States would draft an affidavit to be signed by all theologians teaching in Catholic colleges and universities stating their doctrinal allegiance to the magisterium.

For John Paul, the freedoms that were intrinsic to the culture of the United States involved liberties that were in need of correction and control. As the Soviet empire faltered and collapsed, the aspects of American freedom that were, in his view, license for sin and error became an increasing focus of his attention.

CHAPTER FOURTEEN

John Paul's Conflict with Democracy

As John Paul's papacy entered the decade of the 1990s and the world witnessed the breakup of the Soviet Union and the retreat of Soviet communism, it was not to be expected that he would embrace Western capitalism uncritically. On his fourth visit to Poland, in 1991, he observed and deplored the effects of American-style capitalism and Western culture. The Polish people were inclined to see their triumph over communism as a victory not for the Church but for the union Solidarity. Solidarity had become the rallying point of national unity rather than the Virgin Mary, the Catholic Church, or John Paul II. John Paul's disappointment was profound, for how would such an inward-looking, secular view of national identity serve as the catalyst for the spiritual transformation of Poland's neighbors?

As the 1990s progressed, the influence of the Church and Jean Paul declined in Poland. Democracy was employed in John Paul's liberated Poland to legalize abortion. The fault lines of Church and State, sacred and profane, lay and clerical, familiar in the process of forming nation-states in the late nineteenth century, was repeated in post-Communist Poland. It had become fashionable to be anticlerical. How could such a betrayal of John Paul's preaching and principles have come about? Was it that the Polish people were reluctant to replace Marxist dogmatism with papal dogma?

More likely, the transformation was due to the irresistible realities of capitalist economics: The demise of communism and the advent of free enterprise had inevitable outcomes. Privatization brought foreign ownership, asset stripping, closures, and unemployment. As state property was sold off, corruption became endemic. Poland was now an open country: Its citizens, if they had the funds, could travel the world. And the Western world was now coming to Poland: mass-market paperbacks, the latest Hollywood movies, commercial television and mass-audience trivia, brash advertising, pornography, pop music, cheap imported cars purchased on unlimited credit, American-style supermarkets, McDonald's.

But all might not be lost. John Paul's message to the Polish faithful now began to concentrate on the coming third millennium of Christianity. He had seen the influence over the Polish soul of a great anniversary. He himself had set the country on fire during the millennium year of Poland's Christianization in 1966. He could do it again. The task was clear: He must reevangelize his homeland. Poland must convert in order to become a beacon of hope for the rest of Europe in the coming third millennium. Poland must rediscover its Marian piety, it must reject the false allure of materialism and excess, which were no more than new forms of slavery. It was twelve years since he had preached throughout his native land of his destiny to bring into harmony the two lungs of Christendom, East and West, employing the language of Polish Messianism. "The future of Poland," he had cried, "will depend on how many people are mature enough to be nonconformists." The future he had envisioned was of Poland as the New Jerusalem—a far cry from the reality of the Poland that was taking shape. Yet what was nonconformism if not the condition of a pluralist society, which meant the right to choose freely between whether to believe and practice one faith, or another, or none at all? Just like America.

*

The source of John Paul's dislike of the capitalist West went back many years: It had a personal component associated with his lifelong inclination toward austerity and self-denial. The priest who modeled himself on the Curé d'Ars and the young pastor in Georges Bernanos's *Diary of a Country Priest* was not inclined to take an indulgent view of Western lifestyles.

Hendrik Houthakker, the husband of John Paul's collaborator on *Acting Person*, Dr. Anna-Teresa Tymieniecka, has spoken of John Paul's gut-reaction prejudices toward the United States on his visit there as Cardinal Wojtyla in 1976. Houthakker has said: "He tended to regard Western countries and especially the United States as immoral, amoral perhaps. He had no real appreciation of the virtues of democracy. [Anna-Teresa] on at least two occasions was instrumental in telling him that he was going to sound like Savonarola in the United States."

Houthakker and Dr. Tymieniecka had genuine fears, it seems, that Cardinal Wojtyla would be ungracious to their guests in America. They evidently restrained him temporarily, but in the long run his deep antipathy toward American-style pluralism, which he associated with moral relativism, would flourish unabated, and it would have a profound effect on his social teaching.

Through the first twelve years of his papacy, John Paul wrote three important encyclicals on questions of labor, politics, and economics. The first, issued in 1981, was titled *Laborem Exercens* (*On Human Work*). It was a poetic excursion on the meaning of work by a man who had every right to opinions on the subject, considering how he had spent years carrying rocks in buckets on a yoke in a Polish quarry. Avoiding the socialist issues of ownership of means of production, he wrote glowingly of the ennobling nature of work. He was at pains to deny the biblical idea that work was a divine punishment for the original sin committed by Adam and Eve. Work was creative, he insisted, and therefore signified collaboration in the creativity of God. Nor do we simply make things through work: Work is a process of self-realization, of personal development.

By December 1987, John Paul had completed his second social encyclical, *Sollicitudo Rei Socialis* (*On Social Concern*), in which he drew a moral equivalence between capitalism and communism as "imperfect." Capitalism was in need of "radical correction." He criticized "blind submission to pure consumerism," and he pointed to the dangers of First World "selfish isolation." Had John Paul written the encyclical in the light of more recent capitalist scandals, such as Enron in the United States and Parmalat in Europe, he might have enlarged further on corporate corruption.

But what had he to put in place of the unrestrained market? Was there a third way, as yet unarticulated? One third way might be social democracy, but he would go on record to say that such a system, if it were truly socialist, would be "utopian." In any case, he pointed out, it was not the task of papal social teaching to propose ideologies or economic systems to the world.

That second encyclical drew constructive criticism from Catholic thinkers in the United States, especially from Michael Novak, who put the fruit of his critique into a book: *Catholic Social Thought and Liberal Institutions*. John Paul paid heed and consequently attempted to clarify his position on capitalism in a third social encyclical, which he published in 1991, titled *Centesimus Annus* (*The Hundredth Year*).

In the style of the popes of the late nineteenth and early twentieth centuries, John Paul proclaimed the encyclical's continuity with previous papal teaching, as if to give the impression that he was engaged with his predecessors in the weaving of a seamless doctrinal tapestry. Reflected in the title of the letter was the hundred years that had passed since the publication of Leo XIII's *Rerum Novarum* (*Of New Things*) on work, capital, and society. He also had in mind the encyclical *Quadragessimo Anno* (*Fortieth Year*—that is, forty years on from the publication of *Rerum*), written by Pius XI, the Pope of the 1920s and 1930s—the era of the rise of Mussolini.

But the passage of a hundred years had another historical significance, appealing to John Paul's propensity for discovering synchronicities that he by no means saw as mere coincidences. After all, was it not possible to interpret the hundred-year period from 1891 to 1991 as a series of abortive attempts to find an alternative to naked capitalism: Marxism-Leninism, Nazism-Fascism, and, by 1989, social democracy or welfare capitalism, all ending in failure?

In John Paul's view, the previous hundred years had measured the failure of the world to heed papal social doctrine. For the Popes—Leo XIII, Pius XI, and now John Paul II—had taught that only Catholic social doctrine could mitigate the destructive and self-destructive potential of capitalism and, indeed, democracy. Despite its centennial grandeur, however, John Paul's new document merely caused a brief stir, as new encyclicals sometimes do, and was soon forgotten.

The indifference to John Paul's writings on social doctrine at this post-Soviet, post-modern juncture in world history is remarkable, for there is much in it that is good and true. George Weigel, the papal biographer, has commented that the Pope's social doctrine is "Catholicism's best kept secret . . . rarely preached and poorly cate-chised." What could be the reasons for this neglect? he asks. Weigel, as with other right-wing American Catholics, has come to the con-clusion that John Paul's social doctrine is so in advance of its time as to be obscured by its sheer prophetic power. It is, he suggests, for another, a younger and chastened, age that will follow ours. He would have us believe that John Paul's social wisdom is a legacy for the coming decades, perhaps the coming centuries. Another expla-nation for the neglect is the problem of the legacy of his predeces-sors and the stumbling block of John Paul's own expository style.

Leo XIII, the author of *Rerum Novarum,* was successor to Pius IX, who called the First Vatican Council, 1869–1870, to debate the infallibility and primacy of the Pope. Leo was a conservative who had collaborated in the writing of the *Syllabus of Errors,* which denounced liberalism, progress, and the modern. Leo was sixty-eight when he was elected and considered a mere stopgap, but in the event, he turned out to be a Pope of energy and initiative. He was keen, despite the conservative influence of the previous papacy, to engage the modern world, and particularly the world of the worker. In the 1880s, Catholic labor groups were descending on Rome in ever-greater numbers. Appeals for guidance on issues such as unions, strikes, capitalism, and socialism prompted Leo to write his great encyclical in response to the forces released by the industrial revolution. It was the papacy's response, moreover, half a century on, to the *Communist Manifesto* and Marx's *Das Kapital*. While deploring the oppression of the poor, and usury in the hands of a "small number of very rich men," while advocating just wages and the right to organize unions (preferably Catholic ones), even in certain circumstances to strike, the encyclical is lukewarm bordering on antipathetic toward democracy. Class and inequality, according to Leo, were the unalterable features of the human condition. Socialism in all its forms he condemned as illusory and synonymous with class hatred and atheism. Leo believed that the answer to socialism was not democracy but a Christian intellectual renaissance based on faith and reason. That renaissance, he declared, was to be rooted in the thought of Thomas Aquinas.

The restoration of Thomism contributed to a striking new perspective on the organic nature of an ideal society: subsidiarity, which describes a situation in which decisions about communities and societies are made from the bottom up—in other words, in proximity to those who are affected by such decisions. In the 1930s, forty years on from Leo's encyclical, Pius XI articulated this principle in his social encyclical *Quadragessimo Anno*. But much had changed in the world by the time Pius XI, Achille Ratti, was elected Pope at age sixty-four in 1922.

Scholar, archivist, and formerly a diplomat in Poland, he was short and stocky—and a keen mountain-climber, something in common with John Paul II. Pius XI was adamant that no accommodation could be made with communism or socialism. But he was also suspicious of the free-enterprise West and, like Leo, glum about democracy, which he saw as the rule of the masses. With totalitarians of the right, it was another matter. Pius XI had shown through the 1920s a clear option for corporatism—*selection* of an elite congress, or parliament, rather than *elected* representatives chosen by popular franchise. Pius thus got into bed with Italian Fascism, although he lived to regret it. He collaborated with Mussolini in out-lawing the powerful democratic Catholic Popular Party (the Partito Populare) and colluded in sending its heroic leader, Don Luigi Sturzo, into exile. Catholics were instructed by the Pope to withdraw from politics as Catholics, leaving a political vacuum in which the Fascists thrived. Priests throughout Italy were encouraged by the Vatican to support the Fascists, and the Pope spoke of Mussolini as "a man sent by Providence."

In the place of political Catholicism in Italy, Pius XI established the movement known as Catholic Action, an anemic form of cleri-cally dominated religious cheerleading, described ploddingly by Pius XI as "the organized participation of the laity in the hierarchical apostolate of the Church, transcending party politics." In 1929, Pius XI sanctioned the signing of the Lateran Treaty, which agreed that Catholic Action would be recognized only so long as it developed "its activity outside every political party and in direct dependence upon the Church hierarchy for the dissemination and implementa-tion of Catholic principles." In time, however, members of Catholic Action would be beaten up by Fascist bullyboys.

No wonder, then, that despite being like the curate's rotten egg, good in parts, the Catholic social doctrine of Pius XI should be regarded to this day as irrelevant if not wholly discredited. Sub-sidiarity in the absence of democracy is mere rhetoric. Subsidiarity under a Fascist corporatism was a recipe for violence.

The notion, then, that *Centesimus Annus* was part of an unfolding papal symphony, which had revealed in the span of a hundred years the wisdom of papal teaching, was unfortunate to say the least. All the same, the themes of John Paul's great 1991 social encyclical are at first sight unexceptionable and even laudable. At its heart is the idea that freedom without virtue is a new form of slavery. "An *alliance between democracy and ethical relativism,*" he writes, "would remove any sure moral reference point from political and social life, and on a deeper level make the acknowledgment of truth impossi-ble." In other words, freedom self-destructs without morality. John

Paul was insistent that democracy and the free market were incapable of creating the circumstances for a flourishing society without the values offered by the Church.

Yet was it realistic for the world to accept such an analysis, given the spirit of top-down magisterial doctrine in which it was expressed? Defenders of the encyclical emphasize that the Pope merely "proposes" rather than "imposes." The problem is that the spirit of the text of the encyclical and its continuities with previous social encyclicals are at war with authentic pluralism, let alone the advocacy of subsidiarity, which he was urging along with advocacy of solidarity and the "common good." John Paul's exposition of social doctrine was handicapped by an absence of respect for the strength and virtues of pluralist culture. He saw pluralism, like capitalism, as an enemy to be engaged and conquered.

A religious leader who wished to make a historic contribution to a post-Soviet climate of pluralism, John Paul was hampered by the the fundamentalist, magisterial, top-down didacticism with which he was running the Church. Within the community of his Church he was not inclined to listen to his bishops, let alone the rich contributions of theologians outside the narrow scope of the magisterium. He had blocked the contributions of women and countless other lay dimensions that make up the complex space within the Catholic Church and its relations with other denominations and faiths. The problem with John Paul's social doctrine, and an obvious reason for its neglect, was its inescapable patriarchalism.

All of which amounted to the loss of a vital opportunity. For the unrestrained market clearly demanded a moral dimension, whether from Christian resources or from other, local traditional beliefs and value systems. In China and Asia, for example, the burgeoning market surely needed to look to Buddhism and Confucianism; the Indian subcontinent to Hinduism, Sikhism, and Islam. John Paul's failure to introduce a Christian contribution in terms that would be heard and applied in Western pluralist democracies was a calamity. And the problem lay with John Paul's growing prejudice against pluralism.

CHAPTER FIFTEEN

Pluralism and the Pope

D o we create the good society by imposing values and beliefs top-down, as do fundamentalists? Or do we opt for plural-ism: allowing individuals and groups of individuals to choose their own sets of beliefs and values? As the 1990s progressed, John Paul appeared less happy with pluralism than with fundamentalism. Throughout the decade and into the new millennium, John Paul II was deeply disturbed by the relationship between pluralism and moral truth. As he told Joseph Ratzinger at their first meeting fol-lowing the death of Paul VI, his principal concern was "Truth." But how could one endorse freedom of conscience and religion for all when such freedom signaled endorsement of error? This, for John Paul, was a crucial dilemma that would shape his papacy in its late stages. John Paul had vigorously defended freedom of belief and religious practice in Poland, but final acceptance of the pluralist society as the best of all possible worlds was another matter.

A strong papal antipluralist tradition goes back to the French Revolution and its destructive elevation of reason over faith. Pope Gregory XVI in 1832 wrote a condemnation of religious liberty entitled *Mirari Vos*: "From this evil-smelling spring of indifferen-tism," he declared, "flows the erroneous and absurd opinion—or rather insanity—that freedom of conscience must be asserted and vindicated for everyone." Another way of putting it might be that the Pope was damned if he would ever admit that error "has rights."

A striking example of just how Catholic views can develop, or be restored, over the centuries can be seen in the Second Vatican Council's remarkable *volte-face* on the question of pluralism—although, in truth, it was not so much a U-turn as the restoration of a profound Christian principle. The Council's Declaration on Religious Liberty, approved with great difficulty in the final session, urged that, while false doctrines have no rights, persons have rights, including the inalienable right of liberty of conscience. In other words, the Council argued that pluralism owes its origins to a powerful philosophical and theological Christian underpinning: We owe each other respect because we are all without exception children of God.

An important adviser in the drafting of that Council document was the American Jesuit theologian John Courtney Murray. Murray had seen clearly in the late 1940s that the issue of religious liberty offered important opportunities in the postwar era for the Catholic Church as a champion of pluralist societies, free and yet principled. But a token of the distance the Church had to travel in order to endorse this view was that Murray was silenced on this very issue by Cardinal Alfredo Ottaviani, prefect of the Holy Office under Pius XII in the mid-1950s, as being in serious error.

As we have seen, John Paul II, as Archbishop Wojtyla, was also involved in the drafting of the document on religious liberty during the Vatican Council. For a bishop in a Communist country, the importance of insisting on freedom of conscience and practice of religion was all too obvious. As Pope, his interest in freedom of conscience did not diminish after the defeat of communism in his native country.

But as globalization burgeoned in the 1990s, as Europe prepared to expand its union of nations, the question as to how Catholic thinking might accord with, enrich, and sustain the principles of pluralism in North America and the European Union were increasingly urgent for him. *Centesimus Annus,* John Paul's most important social encyclical, proposed, as we have seen, that pluralism, democracy, and free enterprise risk degenerating into new forms of tyranny without moral culture to restrain and shape them. It was John Paul's view that the Catholic Church and papal social teaching thus had a vital role to play in the new world order.

Yet the question arose: How should Catholics engage in the public arena of a pluralist society? How do Catholics in public life urge moral principles, vote, govern even, on issues such as the exploitation of human embryos for research, questions of war, deployment of nuclear weapons, abortion? Progressive Catholics, following the recommendations of Vatican II, favored dialogue with opinions that often seem hostile to Catholic values in order to seek common ground, or indeed to influence public decisions without compromising their basic principles.

John Paul, however, tended through the 1990s to exert a denunciatory approach on key issues, especially sexual morals, with a readiness to employ harsh "culture of death" language. At the same time, a constituency of Catholic thinkers and writers, some of them vociferous and influential in the Catholic media, was working determinedly to advance John Paul's confrontational style. The split between those Catholics who ignored papal social teaching, on the one hand, and those who aggressively promoted it, on the other, delineated one of the most serious and expanding fault lines on a matter of supreme importance between progressives and traditionalists within the Catholic Church. How does a Catholic live, vote, and represent political constituencies in a pluralist society?

Leading American conservatives and, it seems, John Paul himself assumed that pluralism in the twentieth and twenty-first centuries found its origin not in Christian traditions of universal respect but in the ideas of John Stuart Mill (see, for example, Father Richard John Neuhaus's "John Paul II and the Public Square" in *John Paul II: Witness to Truth,* edited by Kenneth Whitehead). In other words, pluralism derives from utilitarian, amoral intellectual origins that are easily exposed as equivalent to indifferentism (any belief is as good or as bad as any other) and "anything goes" moral relativism. If this were indeed the case, then the traditionalists and the Pope were surely right to confront rather than to attempt dialogue with beliefs and values that seemed opposed to Christian principles.

Yet there was a striking anomaly in the thinking of Father Neuhaus. For while he was prepared to grant that Christianity provided the basis of authentic respect and tolerance of others, he failed to see the connection between that respect and the origins of political pluralism in the modern period. Pluralism, in the British and American traditions, was in large measure inspired by John Locke and Thomas Jefferson, whose intellectual roots were nurtured, as were those of the American founding fathers, within a Christian rather than a utilitarian tradition. That Christian tradition allowed that individuals had a right to choose their values and beliefs because they deserved respect as children of God.

Yet John Paul's condemnatory, dogmatic tone discouraged the reception of this notion in the public sphere. He routinely presented concerns in black-and-white contrasts, focusing on single issues such as contraception. He encouraged snap judgments, rejected critical dissent from within his own Church, and excluded many who were struggling with individual circumstances in good faith and conscience.

The failure of John Paul to espouse pluralism as a crucial Christian legacy may well prove the greatest failing of his papacy. The antagonism between Islam and the West has become a confrontation between a fundamentalist foreclosed identity, on the one hand, and relativistic secular materialism on the other. John Paul might have led the religions of the Book toward religious pluralism based on mutual respect, and away from fundamentalism. While engaging in interfaith rhetoric, he has tended to undermine the concept of pluralism as a meeting point for differences in beliefs and values. It was a matter of deep sorrow to John Paul that he was unable to persuade the European Union to adopt a Christian dimension to its constitution. It can be argued that this failure stemmed from his inability to promote pluralism as a Christian legacy.

CHAPTER SIXTEEN

Women

As the decade of the 1990s progressed, John Paul turned his attention increasingly to the role of women in the Church and in the world. In June 1995, he addressed a special letter to women in the hope of influencing the upcoming World Conference on Women in Beijing. He apologized for the wrongs inflicted on women by men throughout the ages. He made a heartfelt appeal that everyone, and in a special way states and international institutions, should strive "to ensure that women regain full respect for their dignity and role." He added that "when one looks at the great process of women's liberation, it has been substantially positive. This journey must go on." But just a year earlier, he had definitively and for all time ensured that the Catholic Church would deny priesthood to women.

There can be no doubt that had John Paul encouraged a debate on the idea of ordaining women, immense splits might have occurred in the Church between emboldened progressives and outraged traditionalists. He decided to put the question beyond discussion for all time in order to forestall any such divisions. Yet, quite apart from the ordination issue, and despite his protestations that he and the Church honored women, John Paul had failed to convince an influential constituency of the women faithful that he genuinely respected the female sex. There had been times, in fact, when he came across as explicitly misogynistic and confrontational. He shared with Mother Teresa a perverse notion that feminism was equivalent to promoting abortion. Mother Teresa herself would send a message to the Beijing conference on women, saying that "those who want to make women and men the same are all in favour of abortion."

As with his writings on sexuality, John Paul's regard for women was imbued with an idealism drawn from his devotion to the Virgin Mary. In his *Familiaris Consortio* (*The Community of the Family,* 1981), John Paul made connections between womanhood, motherhood, and the family in terms that would become familiar throughout his reign:

> May the Virgin Mary, who is the Mother of the Church, also be the Mother in "the Church of the home." Thanks to her motherly aid, may each Christian family really become a "little Church" in which the mystery of the Church of Christ is mirrored and given new life. May she, the Handmaid of the Lord, be an example of the humble and generous acceptance of the will of God. May she, the Sorrowful Mother at the foot of the Cross, comfort the sufferings and dry the tears in distress because of the difficulties of the families.

The subtext is that women can resist the temptation to use contraceptives by emulating the Virgin Mary's submission and willingness to suffer—either by abstinence or by having more children. "Spouses are the permanent reminder to the Church of what happened on the Cross." Exclusion from the priesthood similarly should be borne with acquiescence and obedience.

Acquiescence had been the keynote of his 1988 exhortation *Mulieris Dignitatem* (*On the Dignity and Vocation of Women*), which contained what he characterized as his "new feminism." He congratulated women on the great revolution in their lives and opportunities. He approved of them working and praised their "special sensitivity." But they must accept, he wrote, their God-given role as mother (whether they have children or not), and they must not resist the "authenticity" of their God-given gender—namely, their divinely ordained acquiescence.

Many women who were party to the debates on population control in Cairo in 1994 were obviously concerned with family planning, but also with parallel issues of poverty, development, and combating male oppression. There were questions about spacing children in the family in impoverished regions of the world that could hardly be solved, either wholly or in part, by recourse to Marian submissiveness.

The issues of women and development had come to a head in 1994 as a result of President Clinton's determination to make safe and legal abortions available worldwide. In the ensuing debates, John Paul had a tendency to conflate women's rights in general and women's right to "choose."

In advance of the Cairo conference, John Paul had granted an audience to Mrs. Nafis Sadik, the Pakistani head of the UN Fund for Population Activities. He evidently feared that the United States was about to impose a "culture of death" agenda on the Third World, and he was determined to put across the position of the Catholic Church. However, she was intent on explaining to the Pope, and thereby to Catholics, the view of her UN team, which had studied the interests of women in many developing countries. She clearly objected to being characterized by the single issue of abortion. There can be no doubt, however, that she was urging legalized and medically safe abortions as opposed to self-abortions and backstreet abortions.

Dressed in a sari, she was shown into his library, where he spoke to her alone. There are two versions of the episode—hers and John Paul's. At the beginning of the meeting, according to John Paul, he handed her a lengthy memorandum on the Church's objections to the Cairo draft document and attempted to explain to her the Church's teaching. "She didn't want to discuss it," John Paul told the papal biographer George Weigel several years later in an interview.

Sadik, however, later wrote an extensive description of the meeting from her own perspective in a memorandum she gave to Politi and

Bernstein, authors of the 1996 biography of John Paul *His Holiness*. At one point, according to her, John Paul said, "Family planning can be practiced only in accordance with moral, spiritual, and natural laws."

She interposed: "But natural laws make for unreliable methods of family planning."

The discussion then turned to individual choice in family planning. "In this area," John Paul said, "there can be no individual rights and needs. There can only be the couple's rights and needs."

According to her memory, she responded: "But couples implies an equal relationship. In many societies and not just in the developing world, women don't have equal status with men. There's a lot of sexual violence within the family. Women are quite willing to practice natural methods and abstain, because they're the ones who get pregnant and don't want to be. But they can't abstain without the cooperation of their partners."

As Sadik recalled, "John Paul burst out angrily, 'Don't you think that the irresponsible behavior of men is caused by women?' "

George Weigel has suggested that Dr. Sadik did not give an accurate account of what happened, since she also, in his view, misrepresented the work of the agency she headed and the implications of the Cairo draft document. Weigel intends his readers to assume that the document was no more than a veiled attempt to foist abortion on the developing world, and that her refusal to accept this characterization of the issues was a deception.

I am convinced that John Paul, as his secretary attested, was normally of an even temperament. But having personally seen the Pope lose his temper at Castelgandolfo with a small crowd of youngsters who ignored his order to keep quiet during his homily one Sunday in June 2001, and taking into account scores of reports, private and public, of his occasional angry outbursts (of which his domineering treatment of Father Cardenal in Nicaragua was an example), I do not think that Sadik's account rings entirely false, given the importance to him of the issue of abortion.

John Paul, who had made some of the world's nastiest dictators quake, had rarely, if ever, in his pontificate been faced with a person who bandied words with him like this—and a woman at that. But we do not need to rely on Narif Sadik to conclude that John Paul's attitudes were deeply patriarchal on most issues relating to women.

In 1995, George Carey, Anglican Archbishop of Canterbury, spoke to John Paul on the matter of women priests. Carey asked John Paul, again in a private meeting, to state his objections to ordaining women, and the Pontiff, before changing the subject, gave a blunt answer: "Anthropology!"—by which Carey understood the Pope to mean that women could not be ordained simply and solely *because* they were women. Those who have studied papal statements on the question of women priests know that John Paul has some very sophisticated arguments on the question, central to which is the notion that man stands in relation to women as Christ the bridegroom to the Church as bride. Beautiful though such an ideal may be, it is hardly anthropology in the sense in which Carey was using the term.

Carey has commented on this papal response: "This was the very argument I had rebuffed before my installation as Archbishop, when I had stated that the idea that women cannot represent Christ at the altar was a great heresy." This was something extraordinary, that an Anglican archbishop should accuse the Supreme Pontiff of heresy. But while the Pope may well have believed that the issue was about "anthropology," as far as the Catholic Church at large was concerned it very soon came to be about John Paul II and papal authority.

In May 1994, John Paul issued his announcement declaring that the Church had no authority to confer priestly ordination on women, and that the judgment was to be held definitively by all the Church's faithful. It was of course a crushing blow to women who aspired to ordination, and indeed to acceptance, as many aspiring women ordinands saw it, of their full humanity. As I have commented above, it was clearly aimed at forestalling divisions in the Church. But it was also an astonishing display of unwarranted autocracy over his bishops, the Church's theologians, and his papal successors for all time.

Professor Francis Sullivan, S.J., who had for many years taught papal magisterium and infallibility to students at the Gregorian University in Rome, informed readers of *The Tablet* on June 18 that in his view it seemed "at least doubtful" that the Pope's statement constituted an infallible pronouncement. He was soon to be disabused by a *pronunciamento* from Cardinal Ratzinger insisting that the Pope's teaching on women's ordination "pertained to the deposit of faith" and that it had been "infallibly taught in the ordinary and universal teaching authority." In other words, theologians needed to shut up once and for all on the issue or face the consequences. This went back to a ruling by Pius XII, the wartime Pope, that where theologians are in dispute and the Pope steps in to settle the argument, no further discussion is to be countenanced, however competent the experts. The split between the theologians and the Vatican—or, more accurately, John Paul—was only beginning. What we had, in fact, was a Pope who had once urged that freedom was a characteristic of our humanity, telling the faithful that they should not even talk about an issue that was not a matter of settled doctrine. Clearly, when John Paul came from Poland to Rome he had brought a bit of the Iron Curtain with him. But as he also knew, or should have known, telling people that they can't talk about something only makes them talk all the more.

A broad constituency of Catholic feminists was inclined to respond to the Pope's attitudes and writings on women in 1994 and 1995 in a variety of ways. Their comments in some instances come close to accusing John Paul of the arrogance toward women that Mrs. Sadik claims he put into actual words. These women were neither bra-burning men-haters nor well-heeled liberals who routinely engage in pope-bashing.

Shirley Williams, a devout Catholic, a former senior minister in a British Labour government, and a professor of electoral politics at Harvard University, puts it this way: "For too long, women have been stereotyped in the Church, as saintly mothers or wicked temptresses. Their individual humanity has gone unrecognised. For too long the exploitation of women, their disproportionate suffering as victims of poverty, violence and sexual abuse, have been ignored by the Church. And even now, the Pope does not consider access to the priesthood."

For Jackie Hawkins, former executive editor of the Jesuit-sponsored journal of spirituality *The Way*, John Paul's initiatives on women illustrated a deep contradiction: a devious hybrid of flattery and patriarchalism. She starts with a comment that aptly describes what so many Catholic critics of John Paul have felt but rarely expressed so frankly in print: "Give me a self-confessed, fully-paid-up male chauvinist any day rather than a man who, with however much goodwill, mistakenly believes that he understands women—and feels bound to tell them so." Then she gets to the real issue:

> For a modern woman, the Pope's suit is pressed seductively in the idle section . . . then, presumably when we are meant to be totally disarmed and breathless with anticipation, the manacles snap shut. The final three paragraphs are the usual old story: only men can be icons of Christ, Mary is modelled, unrecognisable as a real woman . . . "in giving themselves to others each day, women fulfil their deepest vocation." Nothing has changed: we are, still, simply human props of various designs. Words of flattery and support have proved hollow.

Less directly antagonistic to John Paul, yet no less unresponsive to his appeal, was Pia Buxton, the British provincial of the worldwide congregation of missionary and teaching nuns known as the Institute of the Blessed Virgin Mary:

> I appreciate, and am grateful for, the particular gifts that God has given to women and I thank Pope John Paul II for reflecting on these and sharing his reflections with us. But I find that the structures of the Church frequently deny the fulfilment of these gifts and are not always congruent with my experience of praying the Gospel as a woman.

CHAPTER SEVENTEEN

Sexology and Life

As John Paul entered his mid-seventies, and the second decade of his pontificate, he was looking increasingly like an angry prophet, increasingly harsh, increasingly wintry. Age was beginning to tell, and he was suffering one physical affliction after another. In July 1992, he had a nonmalignant growth the size of an orange taken from his large intestine and stones removed from his gallbladder. In November 1993, he broke his shoulder in a fall. The following year, he fractured his femur slipping in the shower and was obliged to have an artificial hip replacement. He told the faithful that God was asking him to suffer in reparation for the sins against unborn children. In 1996, he had his appendix removed. During this period, moreover, the first symptoms of Parkinson's disease appeared: a tendency for his left hand to shake uncontrollably. As he traveled the world, he no longer kissed the ground: Instead, he was offered a tray of national soil to kiss without stooping.

I traveled with John Paul in March of 1993 when he visited Sicily. He preached one Sunday morning as storm clouds threatened against a rugged mountain backdrop. Looking disheveled and anguished, he inveighed against a catalogue of evils: greed, unrestrained capitalism, the degeneration of family life, poverty, violence, terrorism, the destruction of the environment. But nobody could accuse him of lacking hope. I saw him again in Denver later that year when he addressed a hundred thousand young people; this time he looked less troubled: The next generation gave him cause for optimism.

By the mid-1990s, the goals of John Paul's pontificate, and the means he was employing to achieve them, were abundantly clear. There were popes who evidently had a plan or an agenda from the beginning of their pontificates, while others spent their reigns reacting to the tide of events. Benedict XV, Pope of the First War, was reactive, tossed on the storms of a conflict that involved Catholics on both sides of the belligerent divide. Pius XII, Pope of an even more terrible World War and the Cold War, nevertheless had a shopping list of schemes: building works, liturgical reform, a resounding dogma in honor of the Virgin Mary, encouragement of scriptural studies. John XXIII, Pope for a mere five years, had one big grand slam: the Council, which reverberates to this day.

As he approached the midpoint of his second decade in office, John Paul appeared in a class all his own. He inhabited a papal eminence far above the mundane chores of administration and bureaucracy. He aimed to change the world—not with organizational initiatives but with missionary visits to every quarter of the globe, and with literary outpourings: a torrent of encyclicals, addresses, public letters, and commentaries. He was bent on creating a new vision of Christian humanism for the world. Having propelled communism toward oblivion, he was now bent on calling capitalism to order. He sought a moral restoration of the mind, the body, and man's stewardship of nature and society; a new feminism, a corrective to free enterprise and democracy, ecumenism, interfaith dialogue, evangelization to the ends of the earth; the correction of the course of the ship of the Second Vatican Council. His deepest concern by far, however, was the ethics of sexual morality, his determined denunciation of contraception, and his anguished concern for the protection of human life.

He saw the issues—contraception, divorce, illicit unions, homosexuality—as a dimension of the "culture of death" against which he taught and preached with increasing vehemence. He was inclined to draw a moral equivalence between contraception and abortion; at the same time, he expounded the notion that sins against sexual morals and the sanctity of life were intrinsically evil: There could be no mitigating circumstances, in terms of either intention or pleas for a sense of proportion—such as an appeal to the lesser of two evils.

John Paul had by now made his mark as a prodigious writer, and the texts continued to come thick and fast. It was clear that he would go down as the most prolific pope in history. The extent of his fascination for, and attention to, literary structure could now be seen in the pattern of structural relationships among his principal encyclicals, those great teaching letters addressed to the entire world. It was now clear that some had been consciously planned as trilogies before he put pen to paper. His very first encyclical, for example, was part of a triptych on the Trinity written over almost ten years. No pope had attempted such a sustained flourish.

His writings had the semblance of an enormous weighty tapestry woven and massively stitched from his readings of Scripture, encyclicals of previous popes, and frequent quotations from his own prodigious outpourings. His most sustained literary theme by far had been an extensive meditation on sex and love that in book form he titled *Theology of the Body*. The material was published separately, in four parts, during the 1980s. From that quarry he returned again and again to chip away at seams that provided themes and texts for scores of allocutions, addresses, and sermons on what he called "sexology." The material formed deep connections, moreover, with his concerns about "the culture of death" expressed in his encyclical *Evangelium Vitae* (*The Gospel of Life*), published on March 3, 1995, a document that was itself the third part of another triptych that included *Centesimus Annus* (*The Hundredth Year*) and *Veritatis Splendor* (*Splendor of the Truth*).

Theology of the Body: Human Love in the Divine Plan, finally published in 1997 as a single volume, was the fruit of a series of written addresses read out at his regular Wednesday-morning general audiences over a period of five years. At great length and in studied detail, John Paul had expounded the notion of man and woman as sexual partners; here, too, could be found deeper elaborations for the evils of contraception, second marriages, illicit unions, sex outside of marriage, masturbation, homosexuality, and of course abortion.

John Paul's aim was to go beyond Paul VI's encyclical on sexual morality, *Humanae Vitae,* and to provide a more "anthropological" and pastoral approach. Week after week, he enlarged on themes such as the human person as an image of God, Adam and Eve and the creation of sexual and gender difference, the meaning of marital love, sexual congress, and the creation of the family. During that early period in his papacy, many people, even theologians, found the addresses convoluted, dense, and repetitive. This work, which constitutes, in the view of some keen papal supporters, John Paul's vital legacy to the world, has been perhaps his least influential.

John Paul's ideas on marital love had matured over many years, from his early pastoral life as priest and bishop in Poland (when he wrote the disastrous study titled *Love and Responsibility),* to his contributions during the Second Vatican Council. As we have seen, at the heart of his thinking is the notion that love between man and woman is like the love between the persons of the Holy Trinity: a meeting of persons and wills open to transmission of new love. If we are made, as Christians believe, in the image of God, then we have been created to act as God does. When we fail to love as God does, in total self-giving, by the use of contraceptives, we deny our essential humanity, degrading ourselves and our partners.

Another recurring theme involves the difference between men and women in God's creative plan. John Paul would have us meditate on the loneliness of a sexually undifferentiated Adam in the Garden of Eden, a prelapserian human being who is neither male nor female but representing humanity itself. Out of this human being's "loneliness," God in his goodness, as John Paul declares, creates male and female, the female being essentially the "helper." Thus, he appeals to biblical narrative to make an anthropological and biological point about complementarity in gender difference. The notion is powerful in a theological sense, and it must be said: If a Pope cannot expound the theology of sexuality, then who can? Unfortunately, despite his efforts to enrich the idea of womanhood, his image of the male remains inescapably patriarchal. The male alone, it seems, is morally active, while the woman is morally passive.

Despite the biblical underpinning for his ideas about sexual relationships, he makes claims for his thesis as a "phenomenological" perspective. Phenomenology, to recapitulate, is a philosophical style indicating an onion-peeling approach to philosophical meditation, returning frequently to, and circling around, a given theme from a variety of perspectives, never neglecting personal, subjective experience.

Yet subjective experience is barely evident in John Paul's *Theology of the Body*. His commentaries are detached from the realities of sexual life. There is no attempt to describe the experience of love in terms of personal histories: emotion, financial and work stress, children, illness and age. Nor does he make the least reference to the vast range of literature, poetry, the novel, art, psychoanalysis, modern psychology, gender studies, neuroscience, and contemporary social anthropology. Nor is there a single reference in the vast six-hundred-page compendium to the enjoyment of sex, the delights, the disappointments, the suffering and loneliness of bereavement and desertion. He talks of the "ecstasy" of sex as a quasi-spiritual experience in terms that are detached from real life. The Pope who wished to make an original contribution to the "embodied" soul has produced a thesis about sex that is utterly disembodied. At the same time, he couches his thesis in a turgid, jargon-ridden prose. Here is John Paul's verdict on the evil of contraception:

> It can be said that in the case of an artificial separation of these two aspects, a real bodily union is carried out in the conjugal act, but it does not correspond to the interior truth and to the dignity of the personal communion—communion of persons.

This communion demands that the language of the body be expressed reciprocally in the integral truth of its meaning. If this truth be lacking, one cannot speak either of the truth of self-mastery, or of the truth of the reciprocal gift and of the reciprocal acceptance of self on the part of the person. Such a violation of the interior order of conjugal union, which is rooted in the very order of the person, constitutes the essential evil of the contraceptive act.

And while John Paul may have some valuable spiritual insights for those preparing for Christian marriage, his counsel is unrelentingly harsh and negative for those whose marriages have failed. A person who has divorced a spouse and remarried, according to John Paul, has now treated the first spouse as a "thing." The only way, according to John Paul, for people to retain dignity after their relationship has fallen apart is for their union to be dissolved, or annulled, by the Church. But without an annulment, separated marriage partners must not marry again; they must renounce sexual union for the rest of their lives. The discussion cries out for case histories involving real people: those who have had to learn through experience, often bitter, that dignity and integrity are often absent in first marriages, only to be rediscovered on entering a new, more mature, and mutually loving relationship.

Equally distant from experience are John Paul's comments on homosexuals, who can never aspire, he declares, to a relationship, or "familial" love, since it is impossible, he says, for two men (or two women) to give themselves physically to each other in genuine love. Hence any attempted union between them ceases to be a total self-donation, and such acts are "always and in every case sterile, not serving life." Thus, homosexuality can never become more than a way of two persons "using each other." This denunciatory reflection takes a very narrow and unrealistic view of the circumstances of many homosexual relationships. Nor can he accept that many religious homosexuals see themselves as part of the richness of God's creation.

Couples employing in vitro fertilization (IVF), moreover, are guilty of selfishness and disordered behavior, according to John Paul, and also of violating their dignity by manipulating and using their bodies. IVF, in John Paul's view, "reduces procreation to a merely biological laboratory act when it must be, by God's will, the fruit of a covenant, a communion of persons, as expressed in the conjugal embrace of a man and woman joined in marriage." Artificial conception thus divorces the life-giving potential of the body from the person. One wonders whether John Paul has ever met a child conceived as a result of IVF and noted the absence of life potential.

Reading through John Paul on sex and marriage, and considering his failure to communicate a pastoral message in an accessible fashion for ordinary people, one is struck by his disdain for those enthusiastic audiences who came before him week after week. He evidently did not care whether people understood, let alone accepted, his message. The material nevertheless has had its fans. The Catholic social scientist Michael Novak has written, "There will come a time when minds will be open, when women and men will begin to wonder: when God wrote Eros into our embodied selves, what did he intend? In the mountain passes of the soul, they will not find many guides as daring as Karol Wojtyla, climber in the snow-tipped Tatras." Some of us prefer our guides on matters of sexuality and marriage to have their feet placed on the ground rather than firmly up in the air.

In a different order of writing and thinking, and far more powerful and influential, was John Paul's encyclical *Evangelium Vitae* (*The Gospel of Life*), published in March 1995, a warning to the world that the value of human life is under threat. The encyclical had a long period of gestation. John Paul had been inspired by a plenary meeting of the College of Cardinals held in April 1991, when Cardinal Ratzinger delivered a stirring address on "freedom of indifference," drawing parallels between the nihilism and cultural chaos of 1920s Weimar Germany and the current circumstance of contemporary high culture in the West. Out of this period of "indifferentism" (the view that any belief or value system is as good or bad as any other, or indeed as none) arose, in Ratzinger's view, the tyranny of Nazism. Many might quarrel with Ratzinger's analysis of the negative aspects of the Weimar period, ignoring as he does the powerful economic pressures on Germany and the fragmentation created by the Versailles Treaty. John Paul, however, created a trajectory of his own in an exercise of authentic collegiality, by soliciting the views of all the bishops in the world and returning again and again to the Second Vatican Council.

He starts by declaring that his encyclical is "especially pressing because of the extraordinary increase and gravity of threats to the life of individuals and peoples, especially where life is weak and defenceless." In addition to the ancient scourges of poverty, hunger, endemic diseases, violence, and war, "new threats are emerging on an alarmingly vast scale." He cites prostitution, selling of women and children, disgraceful working conditions, euthanasia, capital punishment, experiments with human embryos, abortion, and the emergence of genocide and torture—he had in mind the Balkans and Rwanda. Quoting the Council, he declares that such practices "poison human society, and they do more harm to those who practise them than to those who suffer from the injury. Moreover they are a supreme dishonor to the Creator."

John Paul wrote *Evangelium Vitae* in the year following the Cairo conference (1994) on population, the same year as the Beijing conference on women. It was a powerful and timely reminder that the Catholic Church stood out against every form of abuse of life. It was greeted enthusiastically by a wide constituency of leaders of other faiths as well as secular commentators, but there were critics who believed that it was undermined by its close connection with an earlier, controversial encyclical, *Veritatis Splendor* (*Splendor of the Truth*, 1993), which was viewed in progressive circles as a veiled reiteration of John Paul's insistence that contraception was intrinsically, in all cases, a grievous sin. At 48,000 words, *Splendor Veritatis* condemned the notion that truth was relative and that conscience had primacy. Its target was not only what John Paul perceived to be a tendency in secular Western culture but fallacies within contemporary Catholic theology as well. There had been rumors that John Paul had hoped to apply infallibility to his views on contraception in the document but had been persuaded otherwise at the last moment.

Once again, John Paul had in his sights the error of relativism; once again, he was not inclined to make clear distinctions between pluralism and relativism. The central issue was how far certain acts can be defined always and everywhere as wrong, independently of intentions and consequences. In the view of many moral theologians, he was thus tending toward a rigid fundamentalism.

Certainly, as the decade of the nineties wore on and he approached his twentieth year in office, it seemed that as far as the papacy was concerned the issue of contraception was still at the forefront: The members of the Catholic faithful practicing contraception were being told loudly and clearly that their consciences could not be absolved; that there was no such thing as good conscience in relation to certain actions. Pastors were being told that they had no right to give absolution to those who made no firm purpose of amendment to avoid contraception. His intransigence on the question indicated looming problems for Catholic aid workers who believed that condoms should be part of their strategy in countries where they were battling HIV infection.

*

It revealed much about John Paul's pastoral attitudes toward sexual sin that late in the decade, on the very eve of the millennium, a religious sister and an American priest who had spent their lives ministering to homosexuals were forbidden by the Vatican to continue their work. Sister Jeanine Gramick and Bob Nugent, declared the Vatican, were "permanently prohibited from any pastoral work involving homosexual persons." According to Cardinal Ratzinger's Congregation for the Doctrine of the Faith, Father Nugent and Sister Gramick's "ambiguities and errors" had caused "confusion among the Catholic people" and had "harmed the community of the Church."

Above: Karol, age two, with his parents, Emilia and Karol Sr., 1922.
Viviane Riviere/SAOLA/eyevine

Left: Karol Wojtyla, age seven, celebrates his First Communion, 1927.
Bettmann/Corbis

Above: On stage in Wadowice, 1937. Couple on extreme right are Karol Wojtyla and Halina Kwiatowska.
Viviane Riviere/SAOLA/eyevine

Left: Karol Wojtyla with long hair as a student in Krakow. He studied Polish language, history, and drama and joined a theatre group.
Viviane Riviere/SAOLA/eyevine

Below: Karol Wojtyla, extreme right, age nineteen, resting during the construction of an army camp while on military training in eastern Poland in July 1939.
Adam Gatty-Kostyal/AP

Above: Father Karol with students,
Saint Florian's parish, Krakow, 1950.
Viviane Riviere/SAOLA/eyevine

Right: Father Karol shaves outdoors while
accompanying students on a vacation trip
in the Tatra Mountains.
Reuters

Below: Pope John Paul I greets Cardinal Karol Wojtyla,
Archbishop of Krakow. John Paul I was found dead
in bed on the morning of September 29, 1978.
Corbis Sygma

October 16, 1978: John Paul II appears for the first time on the balcony of St. Peter's, to tell the world, "Be not afraid!" **Vittoriano Rastelli/Corbis**

Pope John Paul collapses in his Popemobile after being shot by the Turkish gunman Mehmet Ali Agca, May 13, 1981.
Reuters

John Paul visits
Mehmet Ali Agca,
the would-be
assassin, in his cell
at Rebibbia jail.
Bettmann/Corbis

Poland's President
Lech Walesa kisses
the hand of John
Paul on the Pope's
visit to Poland in
June 1991. Walesa,
the former head
of the Polish union
Solidarity, had
worked with John
Paul through the
1980s to free Poland
from the Soviet
yoke.
**AP/Rainer
Klostermeier**

John Paul kisses the ground at Managua Airport, Nicaragua, March 4, 1983.
Bettmann/Corbis

Under a banner for peace, John Paul joins the Dalai Lama (on his left) and the
Archbishops of Thyateira and Canterbury at Assisi for the first Day of Prayer for
Peace in the World, October 27, 1986. **Corbis**

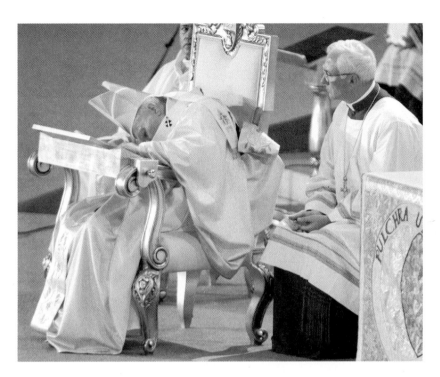

John Paul falls asleep during a canonization ceremony in the Basilica of Our Lady of Guadalupe, Mexico. **Erich Schlegel/*Dallas Morning News*/Corbis Sygma**

Right: John Paul greets pilgrims from his wheeled platform during an audience in the Paul VI Hall, Vatican City, September 18, 2002. **AP Photo/Massimo Sambucetti**

Top: John Paul greets German Cardinal Joseph Ratzinger (left) and his secretary, Archbishop Stanislaw Dziwisz (center), on October 16, 2003.
AP/Plinio Lepri

Above: U.S. President George W. Bush grasps Pope John Paul's hand during a meeting in the Clementine Hall at the Vatican on Friday, June 4, 2004. Bush had presented the Pope with the Medal of Freedom, America's highest civilian award.
AP/L'Osservatore Romano

The mentality that reigned in John Paul's Vatican in the late 1990s toward homosexuality had resonances that would have fascinated George Orwell. The two pastors, who believed that homosexuals required a ministry like any other Catholics, had been hounded by Vatican officials throughout the reign of John Paul. What happened in 1998, the year before they were banned, is instructive.

In August of that year, the two were required to make formal declarations to the Vatican on their positions with regard to homosexuality. Father Nugent declared that he had never "deliberately denied or placed in doubt any Catholic teaching which requires the assent of theological faith." He had never "publicly rejected or opposed any proposition" that was to be held definitively. He took "full responsibility" for any failure in his writings and asked pardon. Meanwhile, Sister Gramick, according to the Vatican, while expressing her loyalty to the Church, simply refused to express any assent whatsoever to the teaching of the Church on homosexuality.

In December, the Vatican told Father Nugent that his declaration did not express with enough clarity "internal adherence to the various aspects of the teaching of the Church on homosexuality." Father Nugent says that he was now pressed to state his "internal adherence" to what the Church teaches on homosexual acts—namely, that they are "intrinsically evil" and that the homosexual inclination was an "objective disorder." Again Father Nugent attempted to comply—after all, he wanted to continue ministering to people who he felt had been excluded. In his profession of faith, written under compulsion, he made some amendments, altering language that he believed was pastorally insensitive. He amended "intrinsically evil" to "objectively immoral."

By July 1999, Father Nugent was informed that the Vatican did not accept his profession of faith because his linguistic changes had obscured the meaning of the text, and because his arguments challenging the infallibility of the Pope's teaching on homosexuality had implied that the doctrine was "open to debate." He and Sister Gramick were therefore banned from continuing their ministry to homosexuals.

The Nugent and Gramick affair indicated just how domineering John Paul's Vatican had become as he prepared to usher in the new millennium. The insistence on the "internal adherence" of Father Nugent to the Church's teaching on homosexuality signaled a return to the bullying attitudes of the so-called anti-Modernist oath legislated by Pius X in the first decade of the century. The Vatican was demanding that Father Nugent publicly accept the same meaning of the teaching proposed by the Pope without any form of dissent, even within the depths of his conscience and soul—"internal adherence." This went against every norm of morality in Christian thinking, and was tantamount to a form of mind control.

Equally disturbing was the basis on which Father Nugent and Sister Gramick had been accused. The system of sneak "reporting" of "misdemeanors" committed by pastors, as well as bishops, particularly in relation to pastoral care of marginal groups, had become widespread within two years of the commencement of John Paul's reign and had grown apace. The term used within Vatican circles is "delation," which amounts to an anonymous denunciation. The delation does not have to be signed, nor is the Vatican official who takes up the case obliged to inform the denounced individual what precisely is contained in the accusation or who has brought it (if indeed it is known). Cardinal Ratzinger, who of course has John Paul's full confidence, has defended the practice on the grounds that his department is small and understaffed: He can hardly police the entire Catholic Church.

One of the favorite "misdemeanors" reported to Rome, and most often acted upon under John Paul, has been the pastoral care of homosexual Catholics.

PART TWO

IN PURSUIT OF
THE MILLENNIUM

2000–2004

No one with a head can fail to ask whether the Church is best served by the long infirmity of its chief pastor, or to wonder what weeds flourish round him as his energies and focus fail.

—EAMON DUFFY: *The Tablet,*

OCTOBER 18, 2003

CHAPTER EIGHTEEN

Millennium Fever

From the outset of his pontificate, John Paul had gazed gimlet-eyed on the coming of the third millennium. He had a weakness for synchronicities, predictions, anniversaries, red-letter feasts, hints that his life and times were not subject to coincidence, nor indeed to any earthly explanation. At that extraordinary Lent retreat, preached before the hair-shirted, discipline-spiked Paul VI in 1976, he had talked of a Second Advent, a springtime for the Church that would coincide with the beginning of the third millennium. But he had also spoken, in a most unorthodox manner, about a Second Fall to be redeemed by the coming of the Second Eve.

One of Christianity's more troublesome phenomena is its tendency to millennial fever: the expectation of a transformation of the world. And the millenarian narrative invariably tells of a period of trial followed by a climax: end-time, apocalypse, utopia, or rapture.

John Paul made it clear often enough that those seeking the clue to his life and times would find it in the coming third millennium. As early as 1994, in the Apostolic letter *Tertio Millennio Adveniente (Coming of the Third Millennium)*, John Paul had declared: "In fact, preparing for the Year 2000 has become as it were a hermeneutical key of my Pontificate." The statement was plain enough, despite the characteristic tease—"as it were." Within the coming millennium consisted the meaning of his pontificate, making connections, for those who could read the signs, with the Third Secret of Fatima.

"Despite appearances," he wrote, "humanity continues to await the revelation of the children of God, and lives by this hope, like a mother in labour." Quite what that revelation would be, in and around the year 2000, he was not as yet prepared to reveal. But he nonetheless appealed for preparation and expectation in the period of waiting in order to ensure "an increased sensitivity to all that the Spirit is saying to the Church and to the Churches."

The enticing, inchoate quality of the expectation is intriguing. So, too, is its striking correspondence with alternative post-Modernist millennial brooding. Consider a figure as distant from John Paul as could be imagined—the French feminist Luce Irigaray, whose hymnodic tropes form an uncanny parallel with John Paul's premillennial meditations: "Keeping the senses alert means being attentive in flesh and in spirit," she wrote just a year after the publication of John Paul's Advent encyclical. "The Third Era of the West might, at last, be the era of the couple: of the spirit and the bride. After the coming of the Father that is inscribed in the Old Testament, after the coming of the son in the New Testament, we would see the beginning of the era of the spirit and the bride."

When the third millennium of Jesus Christ dawned, the Jubilee Year 2000 had been preceded by a flurry of renovations and paint in the Eternal City. A vast underground car park was built within the Janiculum hill to take the thousands of coaches; Leonardo da Vinci Airport had a face-lift; hostels and lodgings for the hundreds of thousands of young people, the old, the sick, and every kind of pilgrim had been made ready in the city and throughout the seven hills. Special electric buses had been laid on to take pilgrims to the seven basilicas of Rome in pursuit of plenary indulgences (issued by John Paul in a special Papal Bull), the free pass straight from earth to heaven without stopping in purgatory.

John Paul's schedule was packed with back-to-back rituals and ceremonies. On Christmas Eve, dressed in a shimmering lightweight

Lurex-and-silk psychedelic cope, he opened the holy door in St. Peter's to a fanfare of ivory tusk horns. A congregation of some 8,000 worshipers looked on in eerie silence as if expecting a thunderclap such as that which shattered the windows at the definition of infallibility at the First Vatican Council in 1870. Christ, John Paul told the expectant assembly, was "the door of our salvation," but "people often seek the truth elsewhere." In a more festive mood, he greeted the crowds from his office window as the clocks struck midnight on New Year's Eve amid a deafening fireworks display. On New Year's Day itself, he opened another holy door at St. Mary Major's.

The first week of the millennium passed with little evidence of a transformation. In fact, it looked like business as usual. In China, six new bishops were consecrated by the government-controlled Chinese hierarchy without consultation with the Pope. In Indonesia, violence flared between Muslims and Christians, with firebombings and shootings; Muslims and Copts came to blows in an Egyptian village south of Cairo; and it was announced that in 1999 some thirty-one Catholic priests and religious had been murdered for their faith in Africa and South America.

John Paul had reached the millennium year like a man expending his last reserves. It was widely expected within the Vatican corridors that he would collapse exhausted, happy at last to be dismissed in peace. There had indeed been a sudden lapse, as if he had been coasting down a long gentle incline and suffered a sudden steep fall off the plateau. He could hardly walk, and talking was difficult, too.

In January, I attended one of the many celebrations in St. Peter's Square. More than 15,000 sick people and their caregivers were gathered around him on a bright chilly morning when he opted to preside at an outdoor Mass. He was deeply stooped, his powerful neck thrusting forward at ninety degrees like an ancient tortoise, his torso collapsing to one side, one eye virtually closed, his left hand shaking uncontrollably, an unmistakable trace of saliva at the sides of his mouth. A monsignor was assigned to take care of the stack of papal handkerchiefs held constantly at the ready to check his drooling. He was still on his feet for a short part of the service, but his speech was slurred, his text often garbled. The service stretched for two grueling hours. At the end, he looked like a prizefighter who had gone fifteen rounds in the ring; not for nothing had he carried those buckets of rocks from a yoke twelve hours at a stretch in that quarry in wartime Poland.

When he needed to go more than a few yards, he was transported on a trolley that had first made its appearance after Christmas. It was a kind of wheeled version of the *sedia gestatoria* of the old days, the litter in which popes were carried while being fanned by ostrich feathers. This contraption with parallel side bars and bars to the front, on which he could take a grip to steady himself, gave the impression that he was still moving upright on his feet: One could almost imagine that he was walking, or even floating on air through the crowds, the white-bow-tied papal gentleman-in-waiting discreetly guiding the wheeled zimmer frame from behind. Suggestions that his mobility was destined to go altogether, however, had been greeted with fury by the Vatican Press Office. When John Follain, the *Sunday Times* of London correspondent in Rome, predicted in a newspaper report (after consulting Parkinson's disease specialists) that John Paul might be in a wheelchair within two years, the Vatican rebuttal declared that his piece "lacked precise sources and information" and that the story "did not deserve consideration." Meanwhile, David Willey, the BBC correspondent in Rome, had been informed by a Curial cardinal that John Paul was often in bed by six o'clock in the evening, an item of information that was similarly greeted with outrage and scorn.

It would take several years for the more frank descriptions of John Paul's debilitation, even at this stage, to be admitted. Former Archbishop of Canterbury George Carey has stated in his memoirs (*Know the Truth*, 2004) that on meeting John Paul in 1997, he was shocked by how much the Parkinson's disease had taken its toll. In one of the most frank accounts of John Paul at this stage in his illness, he described the dramatic contrasts in John Paul's episodes of debility and his ability to function. According to Carey, the Pope spoke in a "low, expressionless voice and seemed almost uncomprehending at times." He had to be prompted by aides and looked "like a man at the end of his ministry." Carey writes that when he mentioned the encyclical on ecumenism *Ut Unum Sint* (*That They May Be One*, 1995), an attendant cardinal, Edward Cassidy, who was in charge of the Council for Christian Unity, had to remind the Pope that it was the encyclical he, John Paul, had written on unity.

Shortly after this encounter, Carey reported, John Paul was transformed, most likely owing to the regimen of drugs he had begun taking.

> Sitting opposite me, he was alert, focused and engaged. There was none of the "absence" I had felt earlier. We had a wide-ranging discussion about the mission of the Church and relations with Islam. . . . The contrast with his earlier exhaustion was staggering.

The reaction to John Follain's modest observations in the year 2000, however, was nothing compared with the furor that greeted suggestions that the Pontiff should perhaps resign. In the second week of January, Bishop Karl Lehmann of Mainz in Germany, a mere sixty-three years of age, said that it was possible that John Paul might retire. Lehmann had been president of the German Episcopal Conference for twelve years and was regarded as a responsible fellow. But within hours of the comment on German radio, the story was being reported the length and breadth of Europe as an episcopal call for the Pope's resignation. The posturing began at once, with Curial cardinals rushing to dissociate themselves from anything so preposterous. Their Eminences Vincenzo Fagiolo, Alfons Maria Stickler, and Ersilio Tonini instantly put their names to emphatic expostulatory denials of encroaching debility, as well they might: Fagiolo was eighty-two, Stickler ninety, Tonini eighty-six. Meanwhile, the Vatican Press Office, playing it cool, merely placed a translation of the broadcast on the wires without comment.

The bishop had by no means demanded the Holy Father's resignation. But he had shattered a papal taboo. Asked by an interviewer on Berlin's *Deutschfunk* whether the millennium might not be an appropriate juncture for the Pope to resign, the bishop replied that the Pope was "always attentive, following the discussions and grasping the questions," and that he was impressed by the Pope's "presence of spirit." A trifle patronizing, one might think. But then the bombshell. He said he was not qualified to judge "whether the evident Parkinson's disease had had repercussions on his capacity to lead the Church and to make decisions." For an institution that never admitted that a pope was ill until he was dead, this constituted a staggering affront to papal protocol. Then he said: "I personally believe that the Holy Father is capable of confessing with courage: 'I can no longer fulfill my role in an adequate way as is necessary.' I believe the Pope would be able to say this if he had the impression that he was no longer able to guide the Church in an authoritative way." Then he went for broke. "Slowly, slowly," opined the bishop, "the cycle of his life is drawing to a close." Bishop Lehmann's gentle reminder of the Holy Father's mortality was considered nothing short of sacrilegious, let alone premature. As Monsignor Dziwisz had pointed out with acidulous unction, most of those who had said such things in the past were "now themselves in heaven."

In any other walk of life, a stricken chief would consider resignation. In fact, there have been at least four resignations by popes, two who had been exiled by Roman emperors during the second millennium. Pope Celestine V resigned in 1294; a holy monk given to fasting and visions, he proved incapable of managing the complex business of the papacy. His successor, Cardinal Caetani, wrote out the abdication speech, then kept Celestine imprisoned until his death at age ninety.

Pope Gregory XII resigned in 1415 in order to end the Great Western Schism, in which there were two, and later three, claimants to the papal throne. Following this calamitous period, it became at least conceivable that the pope would be answerable to the Church in a general council. In theory, a heretical pope could be deposed by the cardinals or a council, although this has never happened. Nor has any pope ever resigned because of physical or mental illness.

But despite the denials and the posturing, the private talk in Rome among Curial old-timers was indeed of John Paul's competence. And a consequence of that consideration, among Vatican watchers, at least, was speculation about the weeds that were prospering as John Paul's capacities degenerated.

An early item of poor judgment, and the presumptuous influence of reactionary aides, was the announcement made by the Pope just before Christmas, and barely taken on board by Catholics at large, that Pius IX, Pio Nono, was to be beatified in the autumn of the Jubilee Year. Pio Nono was the longest-serving Pope in history, reigning from 1846 to 1878. He was chiefly famous for calling the First Vatican Council, which declared the dogma of papal infallibility and papal primacy, although he was also known for his infamous syllabus of errors that denounced democracy, pluralism, workers' unions, and newspapers. A fine exemplar for the twenty-first century, to be sure!

Less known by the faithful was his record in the realms of child abuse—his part in the conspiracy to kidnap a seven-year-old Jewish boy named Edgardo Mortara from his parents in Bologna. In 1856, a Christian servant, the equivalent of a caregiver, had secretly and illicitly, and probably invalidly, baptized the Mortara child. She happened to tell the local grocer what she had done, whereupon the shopkeeper's assistant reported the fact to the papal police (Bologna being within the Papal States), who turned up in the parents' absence and hauled the boy off to Rome to have him properly Christianized in the special "house of catechumens" against his own will and the wishes of his parents.

Pio Nono, an epileptic given to temper tantrums and a morbid, although occasionally justified, conviction that the whole world was against him, adopted the child and would play with him, hiding him under his cassock in a way that today would be described as "inappropriate." His mawkish and unlawful relationship with the boy continued over several years, while he ignored the pleas of the world, including no fewer than twenty editorials in the *New York Times,* to give the child back to his parents. Eventually, the boy was sent away to a monastery and ordained a priest at age twenty-one, alienated ever after from his inconsolable parents.

It was hard to see what virtues were being recommended by the decision to beatify Pio Nono. As the pedophile priest crisis mounted month by month, and was due to break explosively in the United States beyond anybody's expectations, the decision to beatify Pio Nono, who today, in any civil society, would have faced a jail sentence for child molestation and kidnap, was sending entirely the wrong signals. But saint-making under John Paul had become an out-of-control issue of internal Church politics rather than a religious project aimed at general edification. Within the Vatican, those who deplored the Pius IX decision, fearing that it brought the practice of saint-making into disrepute, had their own views. My favorite Vatican informant said: "It's a right-wing antidote to the planned simultaneous beatification of Pope John XXIII, whom everybody loved, and who was a progressive. Pius IX symbolizes a centralized and autocratic papacy and bureaucracy." It was widely rumored at this time, moreover, that Pius IX was in fact a sudden substitute for Pius XII, who had been earmarked for beatification along with John XXIII for many years but whose reputation had taken something of a bruising due to recent less-than-flattering biographical studies. In addition to all these considerations, it was noted that there had been no public cult of Pope Pius IX (a prerequisite of beatification). On the contrary, following his death a Roman crowd had attempted to throw his cadaver into the Tiber while it was being drawn to its final resting place.

Pius IX's papacy had suffered the ignominy common to pontificates that decay with age and ill health. Cardinal Manning of Westminster, staunch supporter of Pio Nono through the battles of the First Vatican Council and champion of the Infallibilists against the Inopportunists on the score of papal inerrancy, put it succinctly two years before the Pope's death: "darkness, confusion, depression . . . inactivity and illness." Longevity, Manning was convinced, lay at the root of all these problems.

CHAPTER NINETEEN

Ufficioso and *Ufficiale*

In the early weeks of the Jubilee Year 2000, despite the rejoicing and the ceremonial junketing, there was a distinct impression in and around the Vatican of malaise, an almost palpable sense of paralysis and stress. The gossip was increasingly about nervous breakdowns, Alzheimer's, prostate cancer, depression, aging, and imminent death. There was nothing new about this wave of gossip in the dying days of a pontificate. Hans Küng recollects how in December 1962 gossip went the rounds in the Vatican that John XXIII, the Pope of the Council, had stomach cancer. There was also maliciously pious talk of this being the work of the "hand of God," to prevent his doing more damage to the Church.

In 2000, there was a pervasive sense of depression, especially among prelates who had once fancied their chances of taking the Church either decisively to the left or to the right, following the new broom of a future pontificate. Instead, they had seen their hopes founder as they, too, grew old and were left grieving over their vanishing prospects and hardening arteries. Just before Christmas, Cardinal Camillo Ruini, Vicar General of the Diocese of Rome, and considered by many, not least himself (as evidenced by the manner in which he graciously postured in public), to be a conservative successor to John Paul, underwent a quadruple heart bypass at sixty-seven, putting the triple tiara forever beyond his reach. The great Cardinal Carlo Maria Martini of Milan, moreover, considered eminently papabile for years by the progressives, was suffering from Parkinson's himself and had made arrangements to withdraw to Jerusalem to spend his twilight years absorbed in scriptural scholarship.

Early in my days as a reporter on Vatican affairs, I was warned by a Curial official of two different kinds of gossip: *ufficiale* and *ufficioso*. *Ufficiale,* as the word suggests, means that the source is authentic. *Ufficioso,* however, indicates that the information might well be reliable but that the source, for whatever reason, is not coming right out and putting an official stamp on it. The chronicling of Vatican affairs with unattributable tittle-tattle has severe limitations. And yet, to ignore the ebb and flow of Vatican gossip is to neglect the essential white-noise background of the Vatican experience and its levels of morale. Rome is a city of trattorias and restaurants: Eating, drinking, smoking, and talking are the principal pastimes. One gets more of a feel for the state of Vatican morale in a quiet corner of a restaurant with an indignant monsignor than from a thousand Vatican press releases. In an interview in 1987 with Archbishop Marckinkus, head of the Vatican Bank, who had been the target of rumors—emanating from his colleagues—that he had murdered John Paul I, Roberto Calvi, and Yuri Andropov, the prelate said to me:

> In this place of all places . . . You can get caught up in this exaggerated bureaucracy where all the bad elements of being a person can come out. This is what happens in this place and that's the whole problem . . . You get a little bit here, a little bit there; that's what creates confusion. This is a village, excuse me if I say this, a village of washerwomen. You know, they get down in the river, wash clothes, punch 'em, squeezing all the old dirt out. In normal life people get away and have other interests, but here— what else is there to talk about . . . when you're in an enclosed place like this there's nothing else to do, nowhere to go, nothing else to talk about . . .

On a wintry evening in January 2000, I sat in a trattoria near the Campo di Fiori in the old city, giving dinner to a member of the Vatican Curia, my Monsignor Sotto Voce (Deep Throat), who had aged since he first began plying me, thirteen years earlier, with unattributable indiscretions over his favorite dishes: double-egged fettucine, roast suckling pig, two bottles of Villa Antinori, and a glass or two of chilled Prosecco "to clear the head."

We talked that evening about the function of the Vatican Curia, its denizens, and the atmosphere at the outset of the third millennium of Christianity. The Vatican Curia is involved with the wide-ranging management of the Church universal: relations with governments of the world, regulation of theological orthodoxy, nomination of bishops, education of priests, discipline of priests and nuns, commissions for the laity, for ecumenism, for life issues, for the missions, institutes of canon law, and of diplomacy, of music and liturgy, even of the Pope's bank. The whole highly centralized operation is run by fewer than 3,000 workers, including laity and nuns; but the clergy, numbering under 1,000, occupy all the senior posts.

Vatican employees take just a month's leave a year, usually during August. They work a six-day week, from 9 A.M. to 1:30 P.M., when they take lunch and a siesta, and from 4 P.M. to 7:30 P.M. Often they are required to work on Sunday, too, and frequently take papers back to their lodgings. Salaries, my monsignor told me, ranged from $1,000 to $1,600 per month, tax-free and payable in euros; incomes could be supplemented with Mass stipends (averaging one hundred a year at about $30 a service) sent to the Vatican from all over the world. Some legitimately boosted their incomes by becoming chaplains to communities of nuns. Retirement age was seventy, and the pension was about two-thirds of salary.

In a city pulsing with nightlife, *dolce vita*, and the expenditure of money mainly earned elsewhere, most of the Vatican officials, he told me, lead miserable existences. "They take the office back with them to a tiny garret somewhere in the city. If they meet up in a cheap trattoria occasionally with colleagues, it is to talk shop: back-biting, office gossip, who offended them, who they did down."

The greatest prize is to become a bishop, an archbishop, a "prince" of the church. Then they get an apartment and a car, and can have a cousin or an aunt live in to take care of them. The majority will be disappointed, of course. In consequence, many lose heart and take to secular extracurricular pursuits: journalism, teaching, tourism, working as consultants for governments and international agencies. The moonlighters can afford a more lavish lifestyle—golf, travel, eating out—which creates another source of envy and gossip.

As he worked his way through the second bottle of Villa Antinori, I felt that something drastic had occurred in the past year or two to this typical middle manager in the Vatican institution. I got a sense of frustration and fear, boredom and fin de siècle. He talked of the scandal that had erupted in the previous year when a member of the Curia published a book titled *Via col Vento I Vaticano*, which translates into English as *Gone with the Wind in the Vatican*. It spoke of increasing nepotism, homosexual scandals, corruption, and "clientism." In its introduction, the author declares: "The time has come for the Church to ask pardon of Christ for the many betrayals of its ministers, especially those within the pyramidal authority of the ecclesiastic hierarchy."

A hapless prelate, Monsignor Luigi Marinelli, a seventy-three-year-old former official of the Congregation for Oriental Churches, was accused of being the perpetrator of this anonymous work, packed with juicy scandals. He was being "processed" by a Vatican court. In fact, it was a joint effort by a number of officials—who called themselves the Millenari or Millenarians. The material in the book carried no more weight than gossip, of course; but the mere fact of its publication and its huge popularity (some 100,000 copies had sold by the turn of the millennium) said something about the climate in the Vatican.

A key source of stress, according to my monsignor, was the overlaps of competence and authority as a result of deliberate divisions of power. An example was the long-standing conflict between the Holy See's media organizations. The Council for Social Communications, supposedly responsible for all media policy, overlapped at many points with the Vatican Press Office, prompting antagonisms and feuding. The head of the Press Office, the Spaniard and Opus Dei official Dr. Navarro-Valls (a former bullfighter and medical doctor), was said to be "out of favor" (although others said that he had merely given up interest since he was tired). At the same time, exacerbating the internal rivalries, there was the daily Vatican newspaper *L'Osservatore Romano*: a law in and unto itself, its direct executive, in principle, the Pope. Vatican Radio (which Opus Dei made an unsuccessful bid to control, or so went the persistent rumors) was still dominated by the Jesuits, who reported to yet another organization known as the Information Office, which was part of the Secretariat of State, the equivalent of a government foreign secretariat.

Laywomen, who might have exerted a civilizing influence, were present in the Vatican in pitifully small numbers. The contemptuous way in which they were treated revealed the misogynist culture that prevailed. A former secretary, now living in Switzerland, reported that she was treated more like a slave than a human being and that she was literally locked in her office each day by her boss, a distinguished Dominican priest-theologian, and had to knock to be allowed to go to the bathroom. Another told me that after she was appointed personal assistant to an archbishop, officials were in the habit of opening the door to her office and staring at her in sullen silence. When she went to the Vatican cafeteria, male bureaucrats would move away if she sat close to them.

Monsignor Sotto Voce spoke of the system of "delation," of those anonymous denunciations of erroneous nuns and clerics throughout the world. "Any ignorant sneak, bearing a grudge on account of an individual's liberal views, will be listened to," he said. "As a result, the perpetrator must agree to swear loyalty to the Pope and eat dirt. He risks losing his post as well as his reputation and future prospects." Even first-year students at the Pontifical Gregorian University, he said, had been known to report on their lecturers.

Control of the Catholic media had become an essential feature of the current power vacuum. Reverence for the mystical role of the papacy was a crucial component of conservative information management. There was consequently a psychological barrier against speaking in critical terms about any of the Pope's policies, declarations, or actions. Conservative Catholic journalists and spokespersons, drawing an equivalence between Catholicism and reverence for the papacy, had assumed the right to openly insult anyone who criticized the Pope or the Curia.

But there was a seamier theme of innuendo during my evening with Monsignor Sotto Voce as a result of two unresolved Vatican-linked scandals. In the previous year, a young Swiss guard had shot dead the colonel of the corps and his wife in the heart of the apostolic palace. Then he committed suicide. There were stories of gay grudges and affairs. Several lay Italian forensic sociologists linked the incident with a combination of Vatican workplace stress and sexual intrigue. Monsignor Sotto Voce recalled that five months earlier, a papal flunky named Enrico Sini Luzi was found strangled in his apartment—the victim, it appears, of a grudge killing. The incidents had brought an atmosphere of gay-bar bathos to the sacred precincts of the Vatican. During the investigation it emerged that, by day, Luzi piously attended the Pope in white gloves and evening dress, and by night consorted with rent boys in the scruffy parkland of the Villa Borghesi. As for the Swiss guard killings, which still remained unsolved, was it an inexplicable act of madness, as the Pope's spokesman had announced to the world's press? Or was it a token of something rotten within the Pope's ancient city-state? As the Romans on the streets were putting it, "*Qualche cosa bolliva nella pentola!*" ("Something was boiling in that pot!").

Clearly, the Vatican had been for generations an unhappy community of seething tensions. But now there was an added ingredient in the volatile mix: the malaise of a sclerotic pontificate as well as the growing senility of the College of Cardinals. Many of the Curial cardinals resident in the Vatican were well into their seventies and eighties. According to the Vatican pharmacy, the most popular prescription for members of the Curia was Valium.

Then there was the Pope himself. Evidence that John Paul was neurologically ill started as early as 1994, when the distinguished Vaticanologist Peter Hebblethwaite commented in his book *The Next Pope* that John Paul, then aged seventy-four, was often listless and that his left hand was constantly trembling. By that stage of his life, John Paul had suffered from the severe gunshot wound during the May 13 attack in St. Peter's Square, he had undergone the operation for an intestinal tumor the size of an orange, and he had shattered his femur in a bathroom fall. In addition to Parkinson's, moreover, he was suffering from other ailments of old age, including severe arthritis. Nor should it be forgotten that despite the health of his early manhood he had been almost killed in a road accident involving a truck.

The Pope's aides derived much comfort from the Pope's defiance of the doomsayers. Peter Hebblethwaite himself died in 1994 after declaring that John Paul's papacy was now "a lame duck." The issue in January 2000, however, was not so much the Pope's imminent death but his ability to think. The current administration of the Vatican and the inner clique of the papal court were understandably reluctant to admit that a pontificate was lame or at its end, since that would prompt discussion of new policies and new personnel at the top. When a pope dies, his appointments die with him. Every papal household factotum, boon companion, and papal favorite is set to be dismissed. The same would apply in the event of a papal resignation.

My Monsignor Sotto Voce commented: "He won't resign, because you can't have two popes"—by which he meant that if John Paul were to abdicate, and his successor were to take a firm stand on either side of the Church's liberal-traditionalist divide, the "losers" might attempt to focus loyalty on the still-living abdicated pope.

There was, however, according to one onlooker, a more mystical dimension to John Paul's dogged determination to keep going come what may. The insistent reminder that heaven had made known its wishes on the issue of the Pope's resignation had been argued by the Pope's closest friend: Cardinal Andrzej Maria Deskur. A stroke victim since the beginning of the conclave in October 1978, he remained, at seventy-six years of age in 2000, the Pope's closest confidant.

Back in 1987, I had been invited to take tea with Cardinal Deskur in his Vatican apartment. He sat in a wheelchair close to a battery of buttons and telephones. He could speak perfectly well, but there were long periods of silence. At one point, he said to me: "The Pope lives in a gilded cage." I tried this way and that to get a conversation going, but all my ploys and gambits were gobbled up along with glittering shovelfuls of buttery, sugary cakes. And all the time his large, suffering eyes behind the schoolboy spectacles never left my face.

Now, more than a decade later, Deskur had intervened in a curious manner on the question of John Paul's resigning. Giving a rare interview to a trusted journalist, Lucio Brunelli, from the Rome daily *Il Tempo,* he said: "The motto *totus tuus* is not an empty expression for John Paul. He took the vow to the Madonna and it is part of his vow to entrust to the Madonna the hour and circumstance of his own death." He went on to say that when Paul VI was tormented by the decision of whether to resign or not, he got a "very clear admonition from heaven."

The French mystic Marthe Robin, he continued, had a vison: "Our Lady told her that the pope was tempted to resign and that this would be a very serious mistake." The mystic, he said, was a recipient of the stigmata who died in 1981 but still somehow "found a way to inform Paul VI" from beyond the grave. Now, he went on, several years back when John Paul was returning from a trip to India, there was a fierce snowstorm around Rome and the papal airplane had to land in Naples, from where the Pope had to take a train to Rome. "During that train ride, the Pope had in his hands a book by Jean Guitton. Can you guess which one?" To which the interviewer, Brunelli, promptly responded: "A book that recounts the life of that French mystic?" "Exactly," said Deskur. "That was precisely the book he was reading."

Such was the basis on which John Paul's closest confidant came to the firm conclusion that there were mystical reasons for the Pope's refusal to resign.

CHAPTER TWENTY

The Patient Pope

Whatever messages the supernatural realms had to impart, the question of John Paul's competence was now being openly discussed in light of the inexorable nature of his illness: Parkinson's disease. The desperate reality was its crablike progress: It moved a little forward while first one symptom, then another became prominent. At times the symptoms appeared to be in retreat before inching forward again to claim more of the body's motor controls.

Parkinson's is caused by the loss of a small number of cells in a deep region of the brain known as the substantia nigra (so called because of the cells' dark coloration under a microscope). These cells produce a natural brain chemical called dopamine that regulates the operation of speech and movement. An individual in good health can exist with few or no symptoms until some eighty percent of the cells have been depleted. At first there is loss of normal mobility: Many patients suffer a symptom known as festination, involving the tendency to run forward with short steps in order to keep upright. This might explain a story Sotto Voce told me about John Paul "running to the lift" in the previous year.

There are periods of remission, followed by further impairment of the ability to move, speak, breathe, and swallow. Every benefit from his medication has to be paid for by deficits and problems in other parts of his brain and nervous system. The principal antidote is levadopa, a man-made chemical that acts as a substitute for the body's dopamine, thus reducing the symptoms. Administering the right level of levadopa requires constant monitoring and modification. Eventually, levadopa begins to fail as the neuronal connections in the brain weaken, disrupting the effective transmission of the drug to the essential cortical regions. At the turn of the millennium, John Paul appeared to be on a plateau in this stage of reduced effectiveness of the drug.

Neurological specialists had been working for two decades on surgical procedures aimed at alleviating the condition. None would meet papal approval. One, favored by neurosurgeons under Professor Anders Bjorkland in Lund, Sweden, involves the insertion by canula of fetal postabortion brain tissue into the patient's brain. Some six fresh fetal brains are used in the operation for each side of the brain. Another strategy, still at the research stage, is to exploit stem cells from human embryos, a research activity and therapy condemned by the Pope. Yet another involves the implanting of two electrodes deep on the two halves of the brain attached to a pacemaker or pulse generator sewn under the skin, usually beneath the collarbone. The procedure does not cure the Parkinson's disease, but it can reduce rigidity and tremor. When I asked Britain's leading implant surgeon and Parkinson's expert, Professor Tipu Aziz of the Radcliffe Infirmary, Oxford, about the possibility of treating the Pope, it was evident that he had been consulted about the Pontiff. "The problem is that I would have to examine him, which I haven't been invited to do. But there is no reason why he shouldn't respond to this treatment." The theory behind the procedure is that Parkinson's affects the normal firing patterns of neurons in areas of the brain crucial to movement. By stimulating the patterns with artificial pulses, one would expect to see a measurable reduction of symptoms.

With the final stages of the disease comes the possibility of the most alarming symptoms of all: acute depression and psychosis—

notably in the form of expanding phases of paranoia. A close aide told me that his advisers encourage his trips abroad because he "gets depressed if he does not have something to look forward to." There had been no indication by the year 2000 that the Pope was suffering from paranoia, but he had a short fuse, according to Sotto Voce. He has seen him "banging the table" with his good fist when he was frustrated or thwarted.

The Pope's physician, Renato Buzzonetti, a septuagenarian who cared for Paul VI and John Paul I, was being advised, I discovered, by a network of world-class neurologists, none of whom was Italian and whose identities were kept a closely guarded secret. It was inconceivable that the Pope had not been informed of the final danger and indignity of his illness. The most likely antidote for depression would be fluoxetine hydrochloride (Prozac), which increases the action of serotonin in the brain, whereas psychotropic drugs for paranoia are likely to exacerbate the motor-control symptoms affected by Parkinson's. So what provisions had he himself made for a lapse into psychosis?

Paul VI, it was revealed after his death by his private secretary, Monsignor Pasquale Macchi, left a single-line instruction that if ever he should become non compos mentis, the papacy should be considered vacant and a conclave accordingly called. But who was to decide that the Pope was incapacitated? And in the case of paranoia, who would decide that the Pope was psychotic rather than the victim of a genuine conspiracy to oust him?

There were no clear precedents for John Paul's predicament, although there had been plenty of conspiracies to remove popes down the centuries. Benedict XI was said to have died of powdered glass in his figs. In 1503, Alexander VI, the notorious Borgia Pope, probably died from arsenic poisoning: His body was so swollen after death that the undertakers had to jump on his stomach in order to close the coffin lid. A case of clear paranoia occurred in the eighteenth century when Clement XIV became convinced that the Jesuits were planning to kill him. As a result, he refused to even kiss the feet of crucifixes in the Vatican, believing them to be tainted with poison. He died of natural causes.

There have been no precedents in modern times, moreover, for an illness quite like that of John Paul's, with its increasing loss of mental function and even delusional episodes. Leo XIII, who died in 1903 at the age of ninety-three, was elected as a stopgap in 1878 but took an unconscionably long time dying. After what appeared to be his last dying gasp, a week before he died, he called for pens and papers and with a clear head started to work again. Pius X died suddenly in 1914, allegedly of a "broken heart" following the outbreak of World War I. Pius XI suffered for ten years from diabetes and heart disease. He was an invalid through the period of the rise of Hitler, but he remained highly focused until his death in 1939. Pius XII was one of the great hypochondriacs of twentieth-century history. He had teams of specialists and was much given to unconventional medications, including a dangerous chemical used in leather tanning that he used as an antidote to soft gums. He received treatment at the hands of Paul Niehans, the bogus Swiss physician who administered monkey gland cells for longevity, sexual potency, and other complaints. Pius XII suffered hiccoughs for about five years as a result of the tanning chemical, but was compos mentis when he died at the age of eighty-two in 1958. John XXIII had stomach cancer but died in full possession of his faculties in 1963. Paul VI suffered from prostate disease and continued his duties with a catheter until undergoing an operation inside the Vatican. He died of a massive heart attack in 1978, clear of mind till the very end. John Paul I, the current Pope's predecessor, died of a pulmonary embolism, aged sixty-six, after a pontificate of only thirty-three days.

Bishop Lehmann's reasonable, if ill-advised, opinion that John Paul would resign if he felt it was all too much had not taken paranoia into account. More important, he had not taken into account John Paul's "mystical" view of his papacy and the history of the world, with its bearings on providence and guarantees that the good Lord, with Mary's intercession, would not let him down in the final stages of his pontificate.

In the meantime, it appeared increasingly obvious that the papal court was becoming ever smaller, ever drawn in on itself. A Jesuit professor friend at the Gregorian University assured me: "He is not capable of having the sort of conversations he once had. He does not listen, he does not communicate." This opinion, along with the report that he was often in bed early, was vehemently challenged by Father Richard John Neuhaus, the American Lutheran convert priest and editor of *First Things*. In the pages of his journal he averred that "when the Pope was not working at a pace that would exhaust a person twenty years his junior," he was in the company of none other than Father Neuhaus. "Over the years and in recent months," attested Neuhaus, "I have spent many hours with the Pope, during the day and over meals in the evenings." The curious aspect of the Neuhaus outburst was not simply that it contradicted the abundance of reliable eyewitness reports. It was clear to the entire world that the Pope was severely debilitated, precluding the absurd impression of late-night intellectual revels around the dinner table with journalist boon companions. Neuhaus's story, however, drew attention to the entente that had developed in the dying years of Wojtyla's papacy between papal authority and conservative media apologists. I did some checking, only to find that according to reliable Vatican sources John Paul—chronically disabled as he was, and with the entire Catholic world on his shoulders—had been favoring Father Neuhaus with his company to an extent that had excited no little astonishment among the Vatican monsignori. Small wonder that segments of the conservative Catholic media were claiming to speak exclusively for and on behalf of the papacy.

To the Holy Land

If there was any truth in the assertion of his Curial aides that travel, in this late stage of his pontificate, brought John Paul out of his tendency to low spirits, his first and principal trip of the Jubilee Year stood to give him an unparalleled boost. During the last week of March, in the run-up to Holy Week and Eastertide, he realized one of his most cherished ambitions—to spend time in the Holy Land in this year of all years.

He arrived on Wednesday, March 22, after several weeks of jaundiced reaction in the Israeli media and expressions of reckless optimism on the part of Palestinian Muslims and Christians. *The Tablet* Middle East correspondent, Trevor Mostyn, for example, reported that ordinary people were saying, "Something wonderful will happen when the Pope comes." They were seeing a parallel between this visit and his trip to Poland before the collapse of communism. There was more than a hint of millenarianism in the air. But there were hostile opinions, too, from those who saw John Paul as a representative of the West and therefore part of the problem rather than its solution.

The visit was an act of personal devotion and pilgrimage in keeping with John Paul's mystical vision of his purpose and the narrative of his papacy, but it was also an opportunity to make the right noises about hopes for reconciliation between Israelis and Palestinians. Even more important, it was an occasion, yet again, to attempt to mend fences between Catholicism and Judaism. There had been continuous rumors since the autumn of the previous year that Pius XII, the Pope who had remained silent during the Holocaust, was about to be beatified. The announcement that Pio Nono had been nominated as a substitute had done nothing to quash rumors that Pius XII would be raised to the altar before the year was out. Jewish opinion was restless on the issue.

Not surprisingly, the trip presented an opportunity for Palestinians and Israelis to exploit the papal visit to their own ends. Flying into Bethlehem by helicopter, Yasser Arafat greeted John Paul formally as he alighted: "Welcome, Your Holiness, to Palestine, Bethlehem, and to Jerusalem, the eternal capital of Palestine." The Palestinian leader went on to say that he appreciated the Pope's "just positions in support of the Palestinian cause."

When he finally spoke, John Paul commiserated with Palestinian suffering: "Your torment is before the eyes of the world. And it has gone on too long." There would be no end to the conflict in the "Holy Land," as he guardedly put it, "without stable guarantees for the rights of all peoples involved, on the basis of international law and the relevant United Nations resolutions and declarations."

The reactions on both sides of the divide were quick to translate his message to their own advantage. Yasser Arafat's wife told assembled journalists that the Pope's speech sent a "a clear message for an independent Palestinian state." The Israeli authorities dismissed the speech, saying that it represented "nothing new."

Next he presided at Mass in the church of the Basilica of the Nativity. During a rendering of the "Ave Maria" by a twelve-year-old girl, John Paul seemed to fall asleep. An attendant Franciscan friar assured the journalists that the Pope was a great mystic and that he had been "deep in meditation."

John Paul was now transported in his Popemobile to the Deheisha Palestinian camp, where some 100,000 refugees had lived since 1948 in an area surrounded by Israeli settlements. Beneath a banner that proclaimed "Palestinians have the right of return," he delivered a strongly worded speech showing sympathy for their poor quality of life: "You have been deprived of many things that represent the basic needs of human persons: proper housing, health care, education, and work." He spoke of their "degrading conditions," of their separation from loved ones, "their barely tolerable" circumstances. Unfortunately, the Palestinian authorities had made no provision for translating the speech into Arabic. No sooner had he finished than a PLO representative launched into a high-octane rabble-rousing response.

The next day, he was greeted by Israeli prime minister Ehud Barak at a ceremony attended by a besuited and restrained audience at the Yad Vashem Holocaust Museum in West Jerusalem. John Paul relit the eternal flame there and prayed in silence. If the Israelis thought they were going to get a confession of specific Catholic guilt for the Holocaust, they were disappointed. But he said feelingly: "As Bishop of Rome and successor of the apostle Peter, I assure the Jewish people that the Catholic Church is deeply saddened by the hatred, acts of persecution, and displays of anti-Semitism directed against Jews by Christians at any time and in any place." It was no more than a repetition of his familiar declaration of sorrow for the sins of the children of the Church rather than the Church or the papacy itself. He went on to tell them that he paid "homage to the millions of Jewish people who, stripped of everything, especially their human dignity, were murdered in the Holocaust." Then Edith Tszierer, whom he had carried on his back for three kilometers after her release from a labor camp, came forward to thank him for his act of mercy.

The trip was not without tensions and sadness. The Christian population of Jerusalem had declined from 20 percent of the population to 1.7 percent, about 10,000 in all. The churches and shrines were mostly empty. There was resentment from the Greek Orthodox Patriarch of Jerusalem, Diodorus I, because of the Pope's tendency to speak on behalf of all Christians. When they met, the Patriarch criticized the Roman Catholic Church for trying to increase its numbers by exploiting unemployment, education, and other social needs in the region. The Pope responded peaceably enough that he was "greatly encouraged" that they were trying to get to know each other better.

Then came the planned, predictably tense, interfaith meeting at the Pontifical Institute of Notre Dame of Jerusalem. The idea was to get the leading Jews, Christians, and Muslims around the table, but the Grand Mufti of Jerusalem turned down the invitation at the last minute, stating as his reason that Rabbi Yisrael Lau had publicly supported the Israeli occupation of East Jerusalem. His place was taken by Sheikh Taisiir Al Tamini, Chief Justice of the Palestinian Authority, but this did not prevent an outbreak of unpleasantness. When the Chief Rabbi spoke, he said he was grateful to the Pope for recognizing the state of Israel and "for your recognition of Jerusalem as our eternal and undivided capital." This caused a rumpus in the audience as the words were translated and understood. A man shouted out: "The Pope has given no such recognition!"

The Pope, following the exchanges through interpreters, kept his counsel. But in his reply he managed to displease all sides of the argument one way or another by stating that Jerusalem was a city for all three religions of the Book. Nobody disagreed, however, with his conclusion that "not everything has been or will be easy in this coexistence."

On Friday, he celebrated Mass for 100,000 young people on the Mount of Beatitudes, which was deemed to be the largest congregation of Christians in the Holy Land of all time. The gathering was organized by a Catholic militant lay group, the Neo-Catechumenates. His homily came as a shock as he denounced the secular standards of the world for creating a negation of Christ's Sermon on the Mount. "Blessed are the proud and violent," he thundered sarcastically, "those who are unscrupulous, pitiless, devious, those who make war not peace, and those who persecute those who stand

in their way. Yes, says the voice of evil, they are the ones who win!"
The Neo-Cat youngsters loved it.

On his last day, Sunday, John Paul paid a visit to the Grand Mufti,
Sheikh Ikrimah Sabri, in the garden of the Al Aqsa Mosque, the
holiest Islamic shrine in Jerusalem. Above the gathering a balloon
carried the Palestinian flag in defiance of an Israeli ban on the flag in
Jerusalem. Then he went to the Wailing Wall, which was festooned
with Israel flags, where a rabbi spoke discomfortingly for Catholic
ears of Jewish suffering in the "dungeons of the Inquisition" and in
the cattle trains headed for Auschwitz. "God's presence," he went
on, "has never budged from the Western Wall."

In response, John Paul recited Psalm 122. Then he put a trembling hand up to the wall and prayed. After a time, he went as if to
shuffle away but returned, as if he had forgotten to do something
important. Taking a piece of paper from Stanislaw Dziwisz, he put
it in a crack in the wall and blessed it. The text was already available
to the journalists: "God of our fathers, you chose Abraham and his
descendants to bring your name to the nations. We are deeply saddened by the behavior of those who in the course of history have
caused these children of yours to suffer, and, asking your forgiveness, we wish to commit ourselves to genuine brotherhood with the
people of the Covenant." The text was later taken to the Holocaust
memorial at Yad Vashem.

That afternoon he departed for Rome on an Alitalia aircraft
named *Jerusalem*. When he arrived at Leonardo da Vinci Airport, he
said: "These have been days of intense emotion. A time when our
soul has been stirred not only by the memory of what God has done
but his very presence, walking with us once again in the land of
Christ's birth, death, and resurrection."

CHAPTER TWENTY-TWO

Third Secret of Fatima

As we saw, on the Feast of Our Lady of Fatima in 1982, John Paul traveled to Fatima to place the bullet that had nearly killed him in the crown of the Virgin. He told the faithful that one hand guided the gun, but it was another, "a motherly hand, which guided the bullet millimeters away from vital blood vessels, also halted him at the threshold of death."

John Paul's long-held conviction about the interventionist role of the Virgin Mary in the history of the world had thus been revealed to him in a personal, revelatory way. She had intervened to save his life that day in St. Peter's Square. He gave the impression that he was inclined to believe that he was saved for a divine purpose. He came to realize that great events of history of the late 1980s were linked to the messages the Virgin had imparted to the three Portuguese peasant children. Following the assassination attempt and his deeply felt convictions about the role of the Fatima Virgin, John Paul took steps in 1984 to dedicate Russia, although by implication rather than specific name, to the Immaculate Heart of Mary. The most powerful expression of his mystical understanding of history, the fall of communism, and the Virgin of Fatima was expressed in the autobiographical *Crossing the Threshold of Hope*, published in 1994. He wrote: "And thus we come to May 13, 1981, when I was wounded by gunshots fired in St. Peter's Square. At first, I did not pay attention to the fact that the assassination attempt had occurred on the exact anniversary of the day Mary appeared to the three children at Fatima in Portugal and spoke to them the words that now, at the end of this century, seem to be close to their fulfillment." The words, of course, he now intimated related to the Virgin's prophecy that Russia would cease to spread its errors and become converted to Christianity. By the year 1994 Soviet communism had fallen, but by 2000 the devout hope of Russia's conversion appeared as far from realization as it ever had been. John Paul, however, had not repined. There was other business to attend to, which was the significance of the Third Secret of Fatima as it applied to *him*.

On the Feast of Our Lady of Fatima, Saturday, May 13, 2000, there occurred in Portugal a great event. On the previous day, the Pope had arrived at the shrine with Cardinal Sodano, his Secretary of State. That evening he prayed in the Chapel of the Apparitions and left a small red box at the foot of the statue of Our Lady of Fatima. The box contained a ring given to him by Cardinal Stefan Wyszynski, former primate of all Poland when John Paul was elected Pope.

The next day, before a crowd of a million faithful, John Paul presided at the beatification Mass of the two seers of Fatima, Francisco and Jacinta Marto. The two had died at the ages of eleven and ten, respectively, not long after the last apparitions on October 13, 1917. Sister Lucia dos Santos, the surviving seer, now ninety-three years old, joined the Pope and various cardinals and archbishops for the beatification ceremony.

The vast congregation that usually collects on the Fatima Feast was stunned when Cardinal Sodano announced that he had been given permission by the Pope to divulge the secret fifty-six years after its delivery. It is to be remembered that the seer had told the reigning Pope, Pope Pius XII, a devotee of the cult, that it should not be opened until 1960. Both the intervening Popes (not counting John Paul I, who was Pope for only three weeks) had declined to announce the secret. The decision of John Paul II to announce it in the millennium year would tell the world much about his state of mind.

The cardinal told the assembled crowds that the secret contained a "prophetic vision" similar to prophecies found in Scripture. He went on to explain that the elements of the secret were not to be interpreted with "photographic clarity," anticipating any objections that the prophetic vision was not an accurate description of what the cardinal (or, more accurately, the Pope) thought it described. Sodano went on to say that the vision "synthesized and condensed against a unified background events spread out over time in an unspecified succession and duration."

He averred that the content of the vision should be interpreted in a symbolic way but that the primary message was about "the war waged by atheist systems against the Church and Christians." It was also about the "immense suffering endured by witnesses to faith in the last century of the second millennium." Then he came to the actual words of the Third Secret. The seer, he said, declared that "a bishop, clothed in white, makes his way with great effort towards the Cross amid the corpses of martyred bishops, priests, men and women religious, and many laypeople. He, too, falls to the ground, apparently dead, under a burst of gunfire." This rendering of the Third Secret was highly edited, for the original, as it turned out, spoke of the bishop in white being "killed by a group of soldiers who fired bullets and arrows at him." Sister Lucia and the other seers, according to the Cardinal, had understood the figure in white to be a pope.

Here is the Third Secret in full, retaining her odd punctuation, in which quotation marks substitute for parentheses:

> And we saw in an immense light that is God: "something similar to how people appear in a mirror when they pass in front of it" a Bishop dressed in White "we had the impression that it was the Holy Father." Other Bishops, Priests, men and women Religious going up a steep mountain, at the top of which there was a big Cross of rough-hewn trunks as of a cork-tree with the bark; before reaching there the Holy father passed through a big city half in ruins and half trembling with halting step, afflicted with pain and sorrow, he prayed for the souls of the corpses he

met on his way; having reached the top of the mountain, on his knees at the foot of the big Cross he was killed by a group of soldiers who fired bullets and arrows at him, and in the same way there died one after another the other Bishops, Priests, men and women Religious, and various lay people of different ranks and positions. Beneath the two arms of the Cross there were two Angels each with a crystal aspersorium in his hand, in which they gathered up the blood of the martyrs and with it sprinkled the souls that were making their way to God.

A month after this revelation, which was greeted with near delirium in Fatima by devotees of the cult, Cardinal Ratzinger, the senior figure of doctrinal orthodoxy in the world, published a commentary confirming that the prophecy was indeed about John Paul II himself. He wrote: "When, after the attempted assassination on 13 May 1981, the Holy Father had the text of the third part of the secret brought to him, was it not inevitable that he should see in it his own fate?"

It was precisely to anticipate secular skeptics that Sodano had warned against the expectation of "photographic clarity." Ratzinger pointed out that there was naturally "a margin of error" when interpreting visions. Sure enough, one skeptical writer, the estimable Catholic American professor and author Gary Wills, would fail Ratzinger's test by seeking photographic literalness. Writing in the *New York Review of Books* on August 10, 2000, he commented: "The Turkish assassin Agca was not a group, not a soldier, not shooting arrows, and he did not kill his man in white. Nor had the Pope been stepping over corpses when he was shot, nor going up a hill, nor 'half trembling with halting step.' He was being acclaimed as he rode in his Popemobile, a white Jeep. Either the Virgin's crystal ball was clouded in 1917 or Lucia's imagination was overstimulated in 1944." Oh, Gary Wills. Ye of little faith!

*

For a religion as ancient as the Catholic Church, secrecy, multifaceted and with so many dimensions, has been from time to time an essential aspect of faith. St. Augustine of Hippo, the great sixth-century Father of the Church, emphasized the essentially ineffable and hidden nature of belief. The Eucharist, that central mystery of Catholicism, is, according to Thomas Aquinas, the medieval theologian and philosopher, *latens deitas,* "the hidden Godhead." And from early Christianity, secrecy was a condition of survival for Christians. They hid out in the catacombs, those secret places of the dead beneath Rome, to evade their persecutors. Christians recognized one another by clandestine signs. The fish, *ikthous* in Greek, was a secret sign for the acronym for Jesus Christ Son of God.

In later epochs, when Christendom was powerful enough to threaten its opponents, notably Islam, cabals and secret societies like the Knights Templar thrived, as jealous of their special privileges and interior knowledge as the modern-day Freemasonry. And as if in mirror image of its former persecutors, the Church's inquisitors readily ascribed secret practices to Catholicism's perceived enemies; the infamous blood libel against the Jews involved the accusation that Christian children were spirited away to be sacrificed in secret Jewish rituals in the dead of night.

In time, the Holy See's secretive network of papal nuncios and missionary Jesuits, pitched against Protestant enemies such as Queen Elizabeth of England, was the envy of the diplomatic world. The earliest extant cryptographic keys, dating from the fourteenth century, are stored in the Vatican. In the sixteenth century, Giovanni and Mateo Argenti, cipher secretaries to six popes, were the first to use a mnemonic aid to mix a cipher alphabet.

Papal secrecy as an instrument of influence, mostly now for the good, has persisted into modern times. The Vatican pressed into service sophisticated techniques of espionage during the Second World War when the Vatican was threatened on all sides and dependent on Mussolini's Italy even for light and water. Pius XII kept his diplomatic channels open by employing a sophisticated secret code, known as "Green," which has never been divulged to this day. In 1940, he secretly warned the Belgians and the Dutch that Hitler was on the verge of invading their countries. The lives of many Jews (athough not enough, in the view of some) and other displaced persons were saved by secret Vatican initiatives. During the Cold War, the Catholic Church in Eastern Europe managed to survive, despite Stalin's brutal persecutions, through age-old disciplines of courageous concealment.

But what does the Third Secret tell us about the direction of John Paul's Church and his papacy in the new millennium of Christianity? Secrets remain secret, even after their contents have been divulged to the widest number of people: Secrets invariably contain metaphors requiring further interpretation. What is the inner secret of the Third Secret, and who has the authority to crack the code?

John Paul believes that the Third Secret is about him. The vision speaks of both John Paul's status as an honorary martyr and that the decision was taken in heaven that he should survive for a divine purpose—the fulfillment of his agenda. Divulging the secret now, at the beginning of the new millennium of Christianity, guaranteed the maximum impact of the secret prophecy that has come to pass.

Religious secrets are about religious power. And by the mere fact of rescuing the Third Secret from oblivion (most of us, after all, had more or less forgotten about it), John Paul in one swoop encouraged an enthusiasm for the paranormal in Catholic popular piety and blurred the margins between private (or secret) and public revelation.

He who holds the power to make public revelation out of secrets received in private visions exerts a vastly unequal power relationship over the rest of the Catholic community. During the Cold War, many Catholics, fearing an imminent apocalypse, quaked at the prospect of the release of the Third Secret. Now that it had been divulged and officially interpreted, there was much to disturb Catholics, especially in the United States, where a rift between traditionalists and liberals continued to widen. Indeed, Catholic liberals might well have wished that John Paul had followed the example of his predecessor, John XXIII, and allowed the Third Secret to molder in a dark Vatican vault. Some secrets, after all, are best kept hidden forever.

As if to allay any such liberal-traditionalist interpretation, Joaquin Navarro-Valls announced that the Third Secret implied "no papal support for traditionalists opposed to ecumenism." Some traditionalist groups, he said, had "wrongly appropriated some aspects of the Fatima message, speculating in a millenarian fashion about the assumed, but false, contents of the message." He went on to say: "The decision to publish the secret obeys the conviction that Fatima cannot be kidnapped by any particular party position."

A palpable point was being made here. The beatification of the young seers of Fatima on May 13 had bestowed a decisive legitimacy on the message of the visions, despite any disclaimers from the Vatican. There were web sites on Fatima already urging the belief that the message was "synonymous with an orthodox adherence to the doctrines, rites and traditional practices and teaching of the Roman Catholic Church." The propagandizing continued, claiming that the world was "convulsed by a series of deepening crises . . . beyond the capacity of human beings to alleviate or solve." This, indeed, was the interpretation of the message that John Paul had urged all along.

On May 18, a week after the Feast of Our Lady of Fatima, John Paul celebrated his eightieth birthday. He concelebrated Mass in St. Peter's Square with seventy-eight cardinals from six continents; in his homily he mentioned those "who are sick, alone, or in difficulty." He added an extra thought for those who "for various reasons no longer exercise the ministry" but who continue "to bear within them the configuration to Christ which is in the indelible character of holy orders." For those who were at this stage considering the status of priests who had molested children and young people, the comment came as a surprise.

That day, Cardinal Ratzinger gave an interview to *La Repubblica* emphatically denying that the Pope would ever resign. "In the most absolute way, I do not believe in such an eventuality," he said. He could not see how the Pope could imagine retiring, even in the distant future, he went on. The Pope was carrying out his pastoral mission, and "his presence is vital to the Church today." The Third Secret of Fatima reverberating across the previous century was sufficient endorsement that John Paul had been singled out by providence to survive.

CHAPTER TWENTY-THREE

Jubilee Theatricals

Amid the nonstop papal theatre of the millennium year were many remarkable rallies in honor of the Jubilee and John Paul that revealed some intriguing dimensions of the pontificate. Typical of the more frivolous and Italianate was the Giublieo Pizzaoli, or Jubilee of pizza chefs. John Paul welcomed at an audience in St. Peter's Square 2,000 pizza chefs from places as far-flung as Australia, Spain, and the United States. They made giant pizzas in the papal colors and distributed some 50,000 slices to pilgrims and beggars around Rome.

Not least of the religious get-togethers was the interdenominational ceremony that took place in the first week of May at the Coliseum, the site of early Christian martyrdom. John Paul had convened the celebration in order to remember the martyrs of various Christian denominations killed during the twentieth century. According to the Vatican, some 12,962 had been killed for their faith: Nobody could fault the imagination of John Paul for such a millennial opportunity. Having opened the ceremony inside the Coliseum, John Paul moved out to a space facing the Palatine Hill where he stood amid fanfares of trumpets beneath a cross painted by a Bulgarian Orthodox artist. Addressing a 10,000-strong congregation, he drew a parallel between Ancient Rome and recent history, speaking of the "countless numbers" who "refused to yield to the cult of the false gods of the twentieth century and were sacrificed by communism, Nazism, and the idolatry of race." It was a hot and muggy day, and the recital of the "witnesses to the faith" became tediously drawn out, grouped as they were in eight different categories: victims of different persecutions, by different ideologies, in different parts of the world, each of which had citations attended by prayers and a ceremony involving the lighting of lamps. John Paul, despite evident discomfort and debility, soldiered on as if gaining stamina from the sheer tedium of the proceedings. To the surprise of many, amid the martyrs of the Americas, Archbishop Oscar Romero was mentioned just by name (according to Vatican reporters, his name was introduced at the last moment by John Paul, as if a grudging gesture—after all, it *was* the millennium). This mention of Archbishop Romero, the martyr of El Salvador, was nevertheless a reminder of John Paul's neglect of a man many millions of Catholics would have liked to see formally beatified.

The Coliseum also became the scene of another extreme kind of theatre that was to provoke the Holy Father's righteous anger and his declaration that the Jubilee Year had been besmirched and desecrated. For the weekend of July 8, gay-rights groups had called a World Gay Pride Week march, which threatened to pass the borders of St. Peter's Square and venture down the Via della Conciliazione. There was consternation at the highest levels of national and local government, not to mention the Vatican.

First the socialist mayor of Rome, Francesco Rutelli, promised to attend the march, then he withdrew his offer while still allowing a grant of $150,000 to be disbursed and the festival to go ahead. Allegations and counterallegations flew. A center-right MP, Marco Taradash, said Rutelli and his supporters were looking "increasingly like minions of the Vatican." Some liberal Catholic organizations came out in support of the gays. Pax Christi, a Catholic peace group, declared that it was deplorable that nobody, including the Pope, had protested against a military parade marking a national armed forces day on the weekend previous to the scheduled march. Such hypocrisy "was not in tune with the climate of the Jubilee, which speaks of reconciliation and peace" while accepting an event based on a "macabre pride in arms." The prime minister of Italy, in a classic *compromesso,* said that the timing of the festival was "inopportune" but insisted that the government had no power to stop it.

After much negotiation and posturing, some 200,000 gays and lesbians and their supporters gathered in the Eternal City from many parts of the world for what promised to be the most extravagant strut and flaunt ever witnessed in this city of extravagant parades. In temperatures over ninety degrees, the participants, mostly highly painted, posed in various states of undress and outrageous transvestite costumes. Barred from areas close to the Vatican City, the demonstrators paraded around the pagan environs of the Circus Maximus. An assortment of antigay groups, including a mass of traditionalist Polish pilgrims bent on defending the Pope's honor, had threatened to break up the parade. In the end, the clashes did not materialize, and the bizarre procession went off without violence. There were a number of figures from Italian public life present, including the Italian minister for equal opportunities, Katia Elillo. One of the marchers wore a tall white paper mitre, in emulation of the Pope, which declared: "God also loves me." A Catholic priest from Avellino gave a speech in which he "outed" certain well-known high-ranking members of the Curia.

I was in the Eternal City that weekend and mentioned the demonstration to the taxi driver as I was being driven from the airport. "So they had a gay pride parade," he said with a frozen shrug. "Why should the Pope complain? If you want to see a gay parade, just drop into St. Peter's any day of the week." These incorrigible Romans!

The next day, the Pope had his turn as he spoke to massed crowds in St. Peter's Square. He spoke of his "bitterness" at the gay demonstration. He said it was "an affront to the great Jubilee." It was "an offense to the Christian values of a city so dear to the hearts of Catholics worldwide." The Pope went on to quote at length from the section on homosexuality in the *Catechism of the Catholic Church*. He described homosexual acts as contrary to the natural law but acknowledged that the "number of men and women who have homosexual tendencies is not negligible." They do not choose their homosexual condition, he told the bemused crowds, and "for most of them it is a trial." He emphasized that, according to the *Catechism*, homosexuals "must be accepted with respect, compassion, and sensitivity" and that "every sign of unjust discrimination in their regard should be avoided." They were called to "fulfill God's will in their lives" and, if they were Christians, "to unite to the sacrifice of the Lord's Cross the difficulties they may encounter from their condition." In other words, gays might not be able to help the way they are, but they should not express themselves sexually. The crowd in St. Peter's Square cheered him on as he reached the end, but throughout Italy and many parts of the world, his words prompted criticism and controversy among Catholics, gay and straight alike.

Of all the theatrical mass demonstrations of the Jubilee, however, the most impressive, and worrying for some, was the rally on August 20, described as the finale of the World Youth Day 2000, when an estimated two million young people gathered, starting at 3 A.M., at the Tor Vergata field on a university campus on the outskirts of Rome. John Paul had shown his rapport with mass rallies of young people on previous occasions: Denver in 1993, Manila in 1995, and Paris in 1997. He wanted one every two years, but he delayed this Rome gathering so that it would fall during the Jubilee.

There had been four days of activities as the young people were flown in from all over the world. How this great crowd came together is of some interest: Many of the world's 4,000 bishops had made a concerted effort to recruit young people through their parish priests, who raised money and organized the travel. One diocese, Denver in the United States, raised enough money to send three hundred young people to Rome. The larger Catholic movements and groups also had a hand in bringing in delegations: Communion and Liberation, Focolare, and Opus Dei. The organizers insisted that it was John Paul's charisma that brought them in; but from another perspective, it was a mammoth Jubilee present for John Paul, as he so liked to wow vast crowds of the young.

There were mass confessions—hundreds of priests listening to tens of thousands of individual confessing kids in the Circus Maximus in Rome, scene of that dastardly gay pride march. The confessions went on nonstop for twenty-four hours, and it was claimed that some 300,000 kids eventually confessed their sins and received absolution.

The day of the rally itself was blistering hot, but as the young people continued to wait hour after hour in considerable discomfort for John Paul's arrival, they entertained themselves with live music and dancing and chanting, among which was the phrase "John Paul, the closest to God on earth!"

John Paul eventually descended in their midst in a helicopter to cheers and chants. The many delays and false expectations had built the atmosphere to pressure-cooker exploding point, prompting resonances for an older generation of the mass hysteria of rallies of a different nature.

As the evening wore on, the meeting grew increasingly emotional, with the young taking it in turn to be "witnesses to faith" in the style of evangelicals, followed by a group "profession of baptismal faith" renouncing "Satan and all his works and pomps." Then John Paul began to impart his message: He wanted them to consider not so much what they were as what they should be. They were called to "go against the tide" to the point of a new martyrdom. He agreed that it was difficult "for engaged couples to be faithful to purity before marriage," but they had to work and struggle. It was a struggle that "so many of you are winning through God's grace," he said. Whether it was from sheer exuberance or boredom with the length of his homily and its topic, which was repeated in various languages, the kids continuously interrupted with "John Paul Two, we love you." Eventually, frustrated by the interruptions, he said laconically: "Perhaps I have talked too much." But they refused to take the hint and kept up the rowdy interruptions, chants, and football-fan-type bursts into song. "I'm not finished yet," said the old boy a little testily now, "this lesson is not yet over!" The young people roared all the louder—two million of them buoyed up on a tide of near hysteria. At one point, his talk was interrupted so often that he said wryly: "Thanks for the dialogue!" Then he managed to get this much out: "In the course of the last century, young people like you were summoned to large gatherings to learn the ways of hatred." John Paul had evidently got a whiff of something less than sacred in the proceedings. "Today you have come together to declare that in the new century you will not let yourselves be made into tools of violence and destruction."

With this his helicopter appeared, and he departed for the Vatican.

The crowds stayed on through the night, awaiting the Mass that would follow on the morning of the next day, to be celebrated by John Paul.

And so he returned in the morning to a rather more restrained reception after a night of revelry. They got a little festive again during his homily when he told them that only Jesus could satisfy the longings of the human heart and that they would get closest to him in the Eucharist. At his peroration he called for vocations to the priesthood, an appeal that was met with applause, mainly led by the bishops and clergy who were present around the altar in large numbers. His last message to the prodigious crowd of young was that they should "carry the proclamation of the Christ into the new millennium" and that they should keep the spirit of World Youth Day alive when they returned home.

That, of course, was the key concern. In many countries, as John Paul well knew, young people were not going to church. In France, notionally a Catholic country, only seven percent of young people under sixteen go to church even once a year. The Pope evidently took much pleasure from the sight of some two million Catholic youngsters. But did the emotion and excitement of "worship" en masse indicate commitment? Their presence revealed perhaps that there was a hunger for religion, but the statistics showed that the parish-based religion of their parents did not stir them.

When the Tor Vergata arena was cleaned up, the workers, it is reported, found drifts of condoms outside one of the larger tents.

CHAPTER TWENTY-FOUR

Contrition and the Jews

It was a piece of theatre unprecedented in the long history of the Catholic Church. In the second week of March 2000, at a ceremony specially choreographed for the occasion in St. Peter's, John Paul publicly sought pardon from God for the sins committed by "the sons and daughters of the Church" down the centuries; at the same time, he forgave all the wrongs committed against the Church by others.

The ceremony started with a Mass concelebrated by 30 cardinals. There were some 200 bishops besides, amid a throng of 8,000 souls. In violet vestments, the liturgical color for penance, John Paul first prayed on his knees before the famous Michelangelo Pietà to the right of the entrance to the basilica, then, on board his special mobile platform, was pushed up to the high altar as the Sistine Choir sang the Litany of the Saints.

He told the gathering that the Church was "to kneel before God and beg pardon for the past and present sins of her children" so as to gain "purification of memory." The wording was all-important: John Paul was not about to confess, explicitly, that the Church—the spotless Bride of Christ—had herself done wrong, or that the papacy was in any way in error. But there were those, and cardinals among them, who doubted both the wisdom and the legitimacy of the Pope seeking even a qualified forgiveness, and indeed forgiving others for sins committed against the Catholic Church in the past. Hitler? Stalin? Nero? Who has the right, other than the victims themselves, to forgive?

Not the least of the theological problems was the spectacle of the third-millennium Pope setting himself up as judge over the Church of the entire past. The Crusades and the Inquisition, for example, were approved by the Church for centuries: popes and saints spoke out in favor of them. Did this mean that this Pope had assumed a magisterial authority greater than that of the popes down the ages? The papal theologian, a rather bumbling French Dominican named Father Georges Cottier, speaking at a press conference, denied that the Pope was doing any such thing—but it was difficult to resist such a conclusion.

"We must recognize," John Paul said, "that certain of our brothers" were unfaithful to the Gospel, especially in the last millennium. So "we ask pardon," he said, "for the divisions among Christians; for the violence which some of them used in the service of the truth; and for attitudes of diffidence and hostility adopted towards followers of other religions." He also indicted Christians for a share of responsibility for the "evils of today." The list was special to John Paul's agenda, and there was more than a hint of the sins of Catholic theological dissidents—the liberals and the progressives—for religious indifference, secularism, ethical relativism (in other words, the sins of pluralism), then the violations of the right to life (the "culture of death"), contraception, abortion, homosexual acts. By the same token, he declared that the Church forgave the wrongs done by others "to us."

In a piece of new liturgy devised for the occasion, John Paul asked forgiveness for seven different sorts of sins. As each sin was invoked—one at a time—candles were lit, one by one, seven in all, each by a leading cardinal. And seven times John Paul made a show of repeating *"mea culpa"*—"through my fault." Cardinal Gantin, the black African seventy-eight-year-old from Benin, started by asking

for the aid of the Holy Spirit. Next came Cardinal Ratzinger, orthodoxy watchdog, confessing "sins committed in the service of the
truth," at which, lo and behold, just as the good prince of the
Church lit his candle, whether by contrivance or coincidence, a dove
flew over and around the confessional of St. Peter right in front
of the Supreme Pontiff, then retreated whence it had come high
up in an aisle of the basilica. At least one cardinal in the gathering,
the Frenchman Paul Poupard, later intimated that it was a miraculous event—he had rubbed his eyes to make sure that he had not
been dreaming.

Cardinal Etchegaray, the French head of the Council for Justice
and Peace, now confessed sins against the unity of the "Body of
Christ and wounded fraternal charity." Cardinal Cassidy, the Aus-
tralian responsible for Vatican relations with Jews, confessed sins
committed against Judaism, the Pope adding: "We are deeply saddened by the behavior of those who in the course of history have
caused these children of yours to suffer." So it went on: confessions
for sins against peace, against women "who are too often humiliated
and marginalized," against the poor, the disadvantaged, and unborn
killed in the womb.

Then John Paul, in an affecting gesture, clung to the tall crucifix
on the altar, leaning his head against it in sorrow. A deep silence
filled the basilica. Never had St. Peter's seen such papal pathos, made
all the more emotional by his stricken state.

It was only to be expected that there would be abstentions, wry
comments, and questions about this unusual event. Some journalists
who do the Vatican beat were quick to point out that several days
earlier the Pope had held an international symposium to review
developments since the Second Vatican Council—and that women
and journalists had been excluded. Like two earlier sessions of
review, one dealing with anti-Semitism and another with the Inquisition, the symposia organizers managed to disappoint expectations
and offer insult. Some 250 "experts" were welcomed at the Vatican
II review, but only two women observers out of forty were invited.

Also excluded were scholars considered to be "untrustworthy" or "out of line." Journalists were given no opportunity to follow the proceedings.

The most widespread focus of criticism of the ceremony of pardon in St. Peter's, however, related to the failure to be more specific about the Church's offenses against Jews—papal culpability in particular. In Germany, the religious communities were divided on the matter. Bishop Karl Lehmann of Mainz and several leading Lutheran bishops hailed the initiative, but the vice president of the country's Jewish council condemned it as "halfhearted and disappointing."

In this Jubilee Year 2000, the controversy over the diplomacy of Eugenio Pacelli as Cardinal Secretary of State in the 1930s, and Pacelli as Pius XII during the war, had grown to fever pitch. In the meantime, it seemed clear that preparations to beatify the wartime Pope were still going ahead. There had been many papal initiatives in the previous forty years aimed at healing the breach between Judaism and Catholicism: John XXIII's general acknowledgment of religious anti-Judaism through the centuries, Paul VI's visit to Israel, John Paul II's two synagogue visits and his "Remembrance" statement in the spring of 1998 on the history of offenses against the Jews. The cumulative impact of John Paul's work for Jewish-Christian relations was considerable, as was his influence, largely unknown in the West, on catachetics in schools and seminaries designed to eradicate residual anti-Semitism in Eastern Europe. But despite all this, John Paul had used the occasion of the "Remembrance" document specifically to exonerate Pius XII's wartime conduct, proclaiming in an extended footnote that the wartime Pope had nothing for which to apologize and everything to be proud of. "The wisdom of Pope Pius XII's diplomacy was publicly acknowledged on a number of occasions by representative Jewish organisations and personalities," John Paul wrote in a footnote.

While it had been generally accepted that John Paul had done more to repair relations between Jews and Catholics than any other Pope in modern times, many Jews continued to believe that there was still a shadow over these relations. In an essay published in *The Tablet*, Professor David Cesarini, who held the chair of modern Jewish history at Southampton University in Britain, put it like this one week after the "pardon" ceremony:

> Jews remain puzzled why he was not able to [apologize for Pius XII]. What they perceive as his evasiveness fuels suspicion about his agenda and that of the Church more generally. It leads some Jews to interpret papal policy in such a way as to undermine what John Paul II is striving to achieve.

Questions had been raised, for example, about John Paul's visit to Auschwitz in 1979 during that first great papal trip to his homeland a year after his election, when to the shock of many Jews he drew an equivalence between the Jewish and non-Jewish victims of the Nazi persecution. Jewish sensitivities were further offended when in 1984 a community of Carmelite nuns set up a convent adjacent to the walls of Auschwitz. They wanted to pray for the expiation of crimes committed at the camp and to display solidarity with the Jewish victims of the place. In Jewish tradition, however, a place of martyrdom is left desolate; it is never created into a sacred space. Next there was a dispute over an eight-meter-high cross erected in the garden of the convent, marking the spot where 140 Polish resistance fighters were murdered. But it looked, again, like Christian triumphalism—an attempt to Christianize the Holocaust. Then there was the dispute over Edith Stein. Was the philosopher murdered by Nazis because she was a Jew or because she was a Catholic? The citations at her beatification referred to her as a Catholic victim of the Holocaust, to the distress of many Jews. It was noted, moreover, that in the remembrance document endorsed by John Paul, anti-Semitism was deemed a feature of neopagan hatred without reference to hundreds of years of Christian-inspired hatred of Judaism. At the same time, the document focused on Jewish persecution of Christians as a kind of counterbalancing mitigation.

By the beginning of 2000, the year in which it was confidently expected that Pius XII would be beatified along with John XXIII, Pius IX was substituted. As we have seen, Pius IX's reputation was linked with the modern tradition of papal centralism, which seemed to be invoked in order to balance John XXIII's quest for collegiality. Unfortunately, Pius IX was also linked with the scandalous story of the kidnapping of Edgardo Mortara, a seven-year-old Jewish boy who was forcibly Christianized and never returned to his parents.

As Professor Cesarini has put it: "[John Paul] failed to act in such a way as to counter a trend in Vatican policy which was perceived as negative, even hostile. We are left asking, what is going on? Just who is in charge of 'Jewish policy' in the Holy See? Will the real Wojtyla please stand up? Although few are privy to the details, there are clearly factions at play in papal policy-making."

According to Cesarini and other Jewish commentators on the issue, there is no way to cut the Gordian knot of the Holocaust, and Catholic association with it, without the blade of an apology for Pius XII.

I would now argue, in light of the debates and evidence following *Hitler's Pope,* that Pius XII had so little scope of action that it is impossible to judge the motives for his silence during the war, while Rome was under the heel of Mussolini and later occupied by the Germans. He left no private diaries or correspondence with clues as to what was going on in his heart. But even if his prevarications and silences were performed with the best of intentions, he had an obligation in the postwar period to explain those actions. Ambiguous, diplomatic language (such as that Pius XII employed in his famous Christmas broadcast in 1942) is understandable when an individual's conscience is under huge pressure. Even if Pacelli's famous Christmas 1942 broadcast, in which he failed to name the Jews as victims and the Nazis as perpetrators, can be defended on account of his fear of prompting further atrocities, he was not entitled to remain silent indefinitely. He owed an explanation to the world. The duty to denounce the Final Solution should have been fulfilled when he was no longer under pressure. As it was, he not only failed to explain and apologize for his reticence but he claimed retrospective moral superiority for having spoken candidly.

Speaking to delegates of the Supreme Council of the Arab People of Palestine on August 3, 1946, he said: "It is superfluous for me to tell you that we disapprove of all recourse to force and violence, from whosoever it comes, just as we condemned on various occasions in the past the persecutions that a fanatical anti-Semitism inflicted on the Hebrew people." And so his failure to explain his wartime ambiguities was finally compounded with a retrospective attempt to portray himself as an outspoken defender of the Jewish people against the Nazis. With all the evidence that we have now to hand, we know he was no such thing.

On April 1, 2000, Professor David Cesarini wrote the following:

Maybe the Gordian knot will be sliced by a papal incumbent who is younger, or from the Third World, and so able to take a more objective view of the church's record during the Nazi period. Then it may be possible to work out a formula that permits an acknowledgment of the link between anti-Jewish actions and Catholic doctrine, and the institutional anti-Semitism in the Church that helped to foster the misjudgements of Pius XII, without invalidating the message of Catholicism or undermining the authority of the Holy See.

In October 1999, the Vatican established a commission of six scholars, three of them Jewish specialists, to study the wartime record of Pius XII. Unfortunately, the Vatican saw fit to do no more than hand each member a set of the printed volumes of documents published mainly during the reign of Paul VI. These volumes had been available for sale in Roman bookshops for almost two decades. By October of 2000, the commission was demanding proper access to the original archives and presented the Vatican with forty-seven questions relating to how Pius XII responded to detailed intelligence about Jewish suffering. They also pointed out that important pieces of evidence were missing from the published volumes.

These requests immediately drew harsh criticism from the man in charge of the cause for Pius XII's canonization, Fr. Peter Gumpel, S.J., for exceeding, in his view, its brief. The Jewish scholars accordingly withdrew from the commission, complaining that the Vatican was unwilling to reveal the truth about its role in the Holocaust. Father Gumpel accused the Jewish historians of unleashing "a violent attack on the Catholic Church." As is well known, decisions relating to papal archives are in the final resort a decision of the pope alone.

Meanwhile, John Paul showed a mixture of obstinacy and perversity by going ahead with his decision to receive in private audience Jörg Haider, the extreme right-wing Austrian politician who had been accused of links with the neo-Nazis and xenophobia. Israeli diplomats had begged John Paul not to meet Haider, and several Italian newspapers reported increasing tension in Rome. Some Jewish shops had been smeared with anti-Semitic slogans and Italian right-wing parties such as Fiamma Tricolore and Forza Nuova were jubilant at Haider's meeting with the Pope, but left-wing organizations and the Greens organized peaceful demonstrations against the visit.

Once again, John Paul had revealed his talent for making a theatrical gesture of outreach to the Jews while maintaining a determined course in what looked like the opposite direction. And it was to be the same with proclamations of friendship toward all other faiths and non-Catholic Christian denominations.

Are You Saved?

The issue had been controversial within the Catholic Church since Vatican II, and it was becoming more so with every passing year. How did John Paul profess himself Supreme Pontiff of the one true Church, infallible in matters of faith and morals, and yet genuinely respect other religions and Christian Churches?

The question as to whether Catholics should believe that their religion was the only means to salvation was an ancient and vexed one. In the great Jubilee Year, John Paul sent out contradictory signals, giving the impression that Catholics could have it both ways.

A historical note is in order. In 1953, an enthusiastic American Jesuit priest named Father Leonard Feeney (founder of a new order called Slaves of the Immaculate Heart of Mary) was excommunicated for refusing to withdraw his accusation that Pius XII, the Pope of the day, was a heretic for suggesting that salvation could be achieved outside the Catholic faith. Feeney had studied the question obsessively for years, ransacking Church councils and papal documents, and found a clear statement in the Fourth Lateran Council of 1215 that there is only one universal Church of the faithful, "outside of which none at all is saved." Pope Pius XII, apart from objecting to being called a heretic by an American Jesuit, thoroughly rejected the view, pointing out that there was a distinction between those who belong to the Church by faith and baptism and those who belong to it by a form of unconscious "desire." But did this mean that other religions were to be valued merely as subconsciously attached to the one, true Catholic faith? Had they had no intrinsic merit? Paul VI retracted the excommunication prior to Father Feeney's death, but Father Feeney nevertheless went to his grave with the words "Outside the Church: No Salvation" chiseled on his headstone.

Vatican II had stated in the document *Nostra Aetate* that "the Catholic Church rejects nothing which is true and holy in these [other] religions. She has a sincere respect for those ways of acting and living, those moral and doctrinal teachings which may differ in many respects from what she holds and teaches, but which none the less often reflect the brightness of that Truth, which is the light of all men."

Since the mid-1960s, there had been many Vatican initiatives for interreligious dialogue. In 1986, John Paul had invited representatives of the world's religions to pray with him at Assisi, the birthplace of St. Francis in Italy, a gesture that drew criticism from some Catholic conservatives. In 1991, he again appealed for respect for other religions in his encyclical on the Church's missionary role, *Redemptoris Missio*.

There had been various attempts since the Second World War to work out a Catholic theological *modus vivendi* with other faiths, if not an outright solution. One approach, by the German theologian Karl Rahner, proposed that all good people of other faiths, or none, could be described as "anonymous Christians," in that they recognized the Trinitarian God on the horizon of their consciousness. The formula was rejected by most non-Catholics interested in genuine dialogue as impossibly patronizing. Then, in the approach to the millennium year, came a proposition that seemed unexceptionable. Professor Jacques Dupuis, S.J., a Belgian scholar teaching at the Gregorian University in Rome, published his book *Toward a Christian Theology of Religious Pluralism*. It was described by Cardinal Franz König as "masterly," and by Gerald O'Collins, S.J., professor of fundamental theology at the Gregorian, as a "major contribution to present-day interreligious dialogue." A Curial interfaith expert within the Vatican, Bishop Michael FitzGerald, had said that it was "terrific."

Dupuis, taking Christianity as opposed to Catholicism as his starting point, proposed that the fullness of truth is not revealed until the end of the world and the Second Coming. So while not denying the uniqueness of Christian revelation, he suggested that other religions were traveling, like Christians, toward that fullness, and that all were united in the humility of their lack of full knowledge. He was not saying that all religions are equal, nor that the Catholic faith cannot make claims to being the one true faith, but he was certainly saying that Christians, Catholics included, did not yet enjoy the completion of revelation. Dupuis and his colleagues insisted that theirs was an orthodox view based on Scripture. "It is at our peril," wrote Professor O'Collins, "that we fail to follow the lead of John and Paul and acknowledge that in one, very significant, sense we do not yet have the fullness or completion of the divine revelation."

But this had proved most unsatisfactory to John Paul. In fact, it led to the temporary suspension of Father Dupuis's right to teach and a hostile cross-examination of the professor in Cardinal Ratzinger's offices. At one point, Dupuis was accused of asking "erroneous questions." Commenting on this charge, Professor O'Collins said: "St. Thomas's *Summa* is full of erroneous questions: That is how theologians proceed." Dupuis became so upset with the investigations that he ended up in a Rome hospital with a perforated duodenal ulcer.

Then came the public rebuttal at the very outset of the millennium year. On January 28, 2000, John Paul read out a statement in the presence of Cardinal Ratzinger on a special occasion to celebrate the work of the Congregation for the Doctrine of the Faith, the Vatican department that protects doctrinal orthodoxy. The Revelation of Jesus Christ, said the Pope, is "definitive and complete." Then he went on to insist that all other faiths are deficient compared with "those that have the fullness of the salvic means in the Church." He meant, of course, the Catholic Church. Members of the Jesuit staff at the Gregorian responded by alerting religious journalists to the fact that the Pope's statement was "rank heresy," that it had been written out for the Holy Father by Cardinal Ratzinger's department as part of a campaign to quash the views of Father Dupuis.

The next volley in the unseemly theological spat was a resounding "declaration," dated August 6, titled *Dominus Jesus*. It was signed by Cardinal Joseph Ratzinger but shortly afterward publicly endorsed, purposefully and very clearly, by John Paul. The subject was error involved in "relativistic theories" that seek to justify religious pluralism. The errors were spelled out as:

> relativistic attitudes toward truth itself, according to which what is true for some would not be true for others; the radical opposition posited between the logical mentality of the West and the symbolic mentality of the East; the subjectivism which, by regarding reason as the only source of knowledge, becomes incapable of raising its "gaze to the heights, not daring to rise to the truth of being."

At the same time, the Pope was making it clear that Christian churches deemed not to be apostolic (since they had not "preserved the valid Episcopate and the genuine and integral substance of the Eucharistic mystery") are not proper churches. This would include Anglicans, since the Pope had argued often enough that Catholic teaching on the invalidity of Anglican ordination is de facto infallible. The Archbishop of Canterbury, by this reckoning, was a layman of dubious religious affiliations and by no means head of an authentic church.

Back in England, on reading the declaration, George Carey, Anglican Archbishop of Canterbury, was dumbfounded. "Dominus Jesus appeared to me," he wrote, "to deny much of what had previously been affirmed about the ecclesial reality of other Churches." Carey immediately issued a press statement stating that the Anglican Communion "believes itself to be part of the One, Holy, Catholic and Apostolic church of Jesus Christ," and that he regretted the negative tones of *Dominus Jesus*. Cardinal Cassidy, the head of the Unity Commission in the Vatican, telephoned Archbishop Carey to let him know that he had nothing whatsoever to do with the document, an action Carey viewed as "crass in the extreme."

The storm that broke over *Dominus Jesus* within the Catholic Church was different from most earlier reactions to tough doctrinal statements. Tom Reese, the editor of the Jesuit weekly *America* and a pastor in New York, commented to me during the height of the resulting polemic: "This is a Vatican statement that has made ordinary parishioners furious. A lot of the arguments about doctrine involve academics. But *Dominus Jesus* seemed to them to insult people they loved and with whom they work every day of their lives. They won't put up with it."

The *National Catholic Reporter* excelled itself in its October 13, 2000, edition by carrying four pages of letters on the topic. There were, to be sure, two letters in support of the declaration, of which this, from a priest, exposed the deeply disturbing way in which the document could be read:

> Having read *Dominus Jesus* I whole heartedly agree that the "theology of religious pluralism" needs to be nipped in the bud. This new ideology of religious tolerance, begun in 1950, has created a growing confusion in the minds of not only the gullible laity, but also the intelligentsia in theological circles.

It sounded like stirrings from Father Feeney's grave. No doubt a conservative paper could have rallied many more letters in favor of the declaration, but the rest of the letters by ordinary Catholics expressed an angst and frustration indicative of what one takes to be the pluralist majority of Catholics in America. "Such political posturing in a cyber-knit world implies that the Roman Church is rushing headlong into the fourteenth century," wrote one. "Sounds to me like Jesus is a little more tactful, hopeful and loving than *Dominus Jesus*," wrote another.

It was only to be expected that the reactionary Catholic quarterly *First Things* would plunge in, calling the media to task for exaggeration and malign inaccuracy. "Yes," opined Father Neuhaus, "much of the misunderstanding was wilful. But the fact is that the media coverage . . .

was uniformly negative, as was the reaction of the several communities engaged in ecumenical dialogue with the Catholic Church."

Yet the source of the controversy was not so much the media but a profound internal contradiction in the text that led to resentment, and thence to a public relations disaster for John Paul that the media could hardly avoid reporting.

The Jewish faith, the parent religion of Christianity, had a powerfully legitimate grievance. The text of *Dominus Jesus* accepts that the treasures of spirituality in non-Christian world religions are God's work and come from the divine initiative. But this is only after it had defined them clearly as resulting from a purely human quest for God. The Vatican document is blatantly inconsistent. If God takes these initiatives in regard to the other religions, why talk about them as holding merely human beliefs? For God's initiative is always primary, and whenever human beings respond to God's initiatives there is faith.

Those who had taken offense at the document were by no means "wilfully" failing to understand. The long-term partners in interreligious dialogue with Catholics, Jews especially, were rightly protesting that the Pope had set back interfaith understanding decades by repeating the view that non-Catholics are in a "gravely deficient" situation.

Apart from the huge contradiction involved in a Jubilee Year when John Paul was encouraging all people of goodwill to join hands, another effect of the *Dominus Jesus* debacle was to prompt speculation about the performance of the Pope himself. Overnight his ecumenism and religious pluralism appeared disingenuous. Edward Kessler, executive director of the Center for Jewish-Christian Relations in Cambridge, said, "It may be that we are just witnessing conservative figures in the Church battling for the Pope's ear during the twilight of this papacy." Either way, it was more evidence that John Paul was at best only partly in control, either of his own mind or the decisions of his close associates.

But there were immediate and practical consequences besides. Following a ski train disaster at Kaprun, Protestants in the locality of

Salzburg had been infuriated at the insistence of Archbishop Georg Eder, the Catholic bishop, on holding a requiem for the victims rather than an ecumenical service. It was soon revealed that the requiem issue was only the tip of the iceberg. Protestants were complaining about "Catholic arrogance." A prominent Protestant minister in Salzburg declared that ecumenism for the Pope meant that all other Churches should come back into the Roman fold. Even the Catholic auxiliary bishop of Vienna, Helmut Kratzl, blamed the dispute on the mood created by *Dominus Jesus,* and Cardinal Franz König complained that *Dominus Jesus* "could perhaps have been expressed more politely and could have reflected a greater eagerness for dialogue." König was to go much further in his criticism of the Vatican's attacks on Professor Dupuis, calling them "discourteous and negative" and "not only impersonal but withering, as if they had been taken from a sixteenth-century catechism." In a rebuke that applied as much to John Paul as to Cardinal Ratzinger, König accused the Holy See of neglecting "the human aspect, ignoring the deep hurt it has caused . . . No one loses authority just because they are courteous." Cardinal Carlo Maria Martini of Milan was equally outspoken, saying that he felt that the document was "too strong," that it needed to be seen alongside the many other statements on the same topic made over the previous three decades. Hans Küng, not to be left out, wrote that *Dominus Jesus* was one more example of "Vatican megalomania."

There were, to be sure, Catholic bishops even in Austria who took an opposite view, demonstrating the polarizing effect of the document. Take Bishop Krenn of St. Pölten. Calling for a "pause" in ecumenical dialogue, Krenn declared that ecumenism was "sadly abused"; there was an "unfortunate" tendency, he said, to level down the differences between the Churches.

But there were tragic consequences in an area where many people had worked long and hard to speak across the fence, conscious of terrible memories of the past. In September 2000, the Vatican was forced to cancel a Jubilee meeting for "dialogue between Christians and Jews" after two Italian rabbis withdrew in protest over the document. The Chief Rabbi of Rome, Elio Toaff, and another Italian, Rabbi Piatelli, were due to speak at a symposium at the Lateran University. The rabbis issued a declaration saying that they could no longer participate because of the "the climate created" by *Dominus Jesus*. Rabbi Toaff, who welcomed John Paul to the Rome synagogue in 1996, had also canceled an interreligious meeting organized by the Sant'Egidio Community at Lisbon.

Few commentators spoke with such authority on the contradiction between papal arrogance and papal displays of tolerance as Tullia Zevi, former president of Italy's Jewish community and currently in charge of interfaith relations for the European Jewish Congress. She insisted that the rabbis had not come to their decision suddenly or emotively, nor was it a decision taken in isolation: It was one "widely supported by Italian Jews," she said, "who felt great unease at the contradictions in the heart of the Catholic Church between the opening to dialogue and a return of triumphalism."

Meanwhile, George Carey, Archbishop of Canterbury, recollects that he became aware at this time that the Pope's health was having a profound influence on the governance of the Church. "It inevitably meant," he has written, "that others in the Curia, notably Cardinal Ratzinger . . . and Cardinal Sodano . . . took on more responsibilities."

This, he went on, was causing alarm among Roman Catholic scholars and bishops around the world who felt that it "represented a hardening at the centre which worked against the personal mission of Pope John Paul." The alarm had been felt for some time. Carey comments that at a meeting as early as 1996 with Cardinal Joseph Bernardin of Chicago, one of the greatest American Catholic leaders of the twentieth century, the prelate had "voiced his concern to me about the encroaching power of the Curia." Bernardin had said that this encroachment went directly against the policy of Vatican II to strengthen the authority and power of national Churches and the local bishop "in communion with the Holy See."

CHAPTER TWENTY-SIX

Who Runs the Church?

On a day of pale sunlight in St. Peter's Square, John Paul looked out over a host of prelates resplendent in scarlet. The glorious color, cardinal red, signifies not so much triumphalism and ostentation as the blood of martyrdom, which cardinals swear they will willingly shed in defense of the Faith.

It was mid-February 2001, and John Paul was introducing forty-four new cardinals from every quarter of the globe. The ceremony, known as a consistory (which means "standing together"), was unusual as he had never nominated so many before in one go. They sat, these new-boys, surrounded by scores of existing cardinals, and in the congregation there were thousands of onlookers—the new appointees' flocks from back home, relatives, and friends. Sitting amid the sea of red, most likely, was a future pope. A thousand-strong group of Hondurans were convinced that their man had it in the bag. He was Archbishop Madriaga Rodriguez. As his name was read out, a great cheer went up from his effervescent supporters.

John Paul had now been Pope for almost 23 years, and 125 of the 135 cardinals (including the new ones) had been chosen by him. In truth, John Paul had shaped the composition of these powerful ecclesiastics who would choose the next pope.

Pope of surprises, he had also done something unprecedented.

At first he announced thirty-seven of the new appointees, then a full week later a further seven. Had he wished to gauge how the local Churches and the Curia would react to some obvious gaps in the list—only to catch everybody out by including them after a pause? One of the extra seven was Bishop Karl Lehmann of Mainz, chairman of the German Catholic Bishops Conference, he who, a year before, had talked openly of the Pope resigning. Nobody was more surprised, according to the Vatican gossips, than Lehmann himself, for Lehmann had fought the Pope, and lost, to keep open Catholic pregnancy-counseling centers in Germany that John Paul had seen as a form of collusion with abortion.

John Paul, so evidently ailing and yet buoyed up by the magnificence of the occasion, began to speak. He welcomed the new cardinals, defining as he did the significance of their office. He said: "We are calling some of our brothers to be part of the College of Cardinals that they might be united more strongly to the See of Peter, becoming members of the clergy of Rome." Each cardinal is assigned one of the many hundreds of parish churches in Rome and usually appointed to senior-level membership of several of the many congregations and departments that manage the Church—known collectively as the Curia.

Then one of the leading existing cardinals, Giovanni Battista Re, prefect of the Congregation for Bishops, the Vatican department that chooses bishops, greeted John Paul, declaring, to vociferous applause, that the world depended on his continued survival as never before.

During Mass, John Paul delivered a homily likening the complement of cardinals to a ship, a "mystical" ship that was about to "put out to sea, raising its sails to catch the wind of the Holy Spirit." He spoke of the enormously complex modern world, with its rapidly proliferating scientific and technological advances and its ever-swifter and more penetrating means of communication, which could be pressed into service by the Church to hold dialogue with "everybody of every class in order to bring them the hope that we treasure in our hearts." Then he quoted John Henry Newman, the great nineteenth-century English theologian and convert from Anglicanism to Catholicism. When Pius IX made him a cardinal, Newman had said: "The Church should do nothing other than pursue its mission, in faithfulness and peace, to remain always calm and firm, waiting on the salvation of God." Poor Newman was no stranger to storms and disruption. He had his upsets with ecclesiastical authority, as well as conflicts with secular critics like Charles Kingsley, who had accused him of promoting "lying on a system."

Some of those men in scarlet, including Cardinal Bernard Law of Boston, may well have been considering how they should face with calm and firmness the mounting pedophile crises back home, and the plight of those bishops and indeed cardinals who had encouraged them by conniving at their behavior.

But the talk in Rome that week was also about drastic reform in the management of the Church. John Paul had spoken in the past of the need for collegiality, although invariably on his own autocratic terms. Now, a year into the new millennium, he was talking of new initiatives for real collegiality. But how genuine was his aspiration?

As far back as 1995, John Paul had written his ecumenical document *Ut Unum Sint (That They May Be One)*, inviting theologians and even members of other Christian Churches (some of which would later be termed not proper Churches) to "engage with me in a patient and fraternal dialogue" in order to seek "forms in which this [papal] ministry may accomplish a service of love." It did not take long to discover that John Paul had been merely playing his old tactic—portraying himself as the collegial Pope while gathering the reins of authority ever more tightly into his own infirm hands.

The invitation for dialogue and criticism had looked particularly promising that year—until a few brave souls began to take him at his word. First there was *Papal Power,* published by Father Paul Collins in 1997. Collins, a priest and well-known religious broadcaster in Australia, was particularly critical of the growth of papal centrism through the medium of canon law, starting with the domineering methods of Pius X's anti-Modernist campaign in the first decade of the twentieth century. Then John Quinn, emeritus archbishop of San Francisco, published in 1999 a book of crystal clarity and patent humility titled *Reform of the Papacy: The Costly Call to Christian Unity*. Rightly, Quinn pointed out that if the Pope was serious on the issue of Christian unity, he could not behave like a chief executive of a multinational company. He must treat his bishops as local Church leaders in their own right instead of branch managers of a head office. Both men were doing no more than John Paul had suggested—"engaging in fraternal dialogue." But their views were immediately attacked as disloyalty and, in the case of Collins, heresy. Avery Dulles, S.J., for good measure, accused Archbishop Quinn of guile, of being interested only in undermining the Church's views on contraception (later, Dulles would receive the red hat, whereas Quinn, who eminently deserved one, did not). Paul Collins, a fine priest and brilliant religious affairs communicator, was investigated by the Congregation for the Doctrine of the Faith for heresy and hounded out of the priesthood.

As it was, on this February day in 2001, John Paul appeared to be as much in control as he had ever been. Open a Catholic paper or check into a Catholic news service or the Vatican web site, and you would find on any day of the week that the Pope had met world leaders, appointed bishops, presided over councils and commissions, written new directives, delivered homilies, and generally addressed himself on any and every topic under the sun. The unspoken fact was that in recent years he had increasingly been secretly delegating more and more to his Secretary of State, Cardinal Angelo Sodano, and Cardinal Joseph Ratzinger. Later, the extraordinary power of Stanislaw Dziwisz would become apparent. In the meantime, it was also apparent that the power of the bishops in their dioceses around the world was drastically decreasing. Bishops were complaining that when they came to Rome for their "consultations" with the Holy Father, there was little or no consultation but plenty of directives as to what they should be doing. When bishops retired, or died, or were moved, it was taking longer and longer for new appointments to be made. Each and every nomination had to go through the Pope, whose workload had been drastically lowered, although the publicity machine about him insisted that he was still doing the work of a man twenty years his junior.

But here he was on the day of this magnificent consistory, suggesting once again that it was due time to give back to his bishops more authority and involvement. In his homily he quoted from the apostolic letter he wrote in the previous month, titled *Novo Millennio Ineunte,* announcing that the Church should "start afresh from Christ." In the wake of the Jubilee Year, he declared, the Church must develop "forums and structures which serve to safeguard communion both in the Petrine ministry and Episcopal collegiality." He had gone on to assert that there was "certainly much more to be done to realise the potential of these instruments of communion."

✳

No sooner had the cardinals flown off home than John Paul announced that he was going to call them all back in May for the first "extraordinary consistory" in seven years. He was signaling that something sensational, historic, was about happen. Indeed, the papal spokesman, Joaquin Navarro-Valls, declared in a press release that the theme of the consistory was going to be the "study of the Church's prospects for the third millennium, in the light of the Holy Father's recent apostolic letter"—in other words, decision-making powers among bishops. The corridors of the Vatican and the trattorias frequented by the monsignori were buzzing with excited talk about a new "collegial" era in prospect.

The focus of many heated discussions was that cardinal's hat for Karl Lehmann. Something strange had happened. Among the first batch of cardinal nominations was Walter Kasper, who may well have prompted second thoughts about Lehmann's absence from the first list. Kasper had gone on the radio the day after his own nomination to say that he deeply regretted Lehmann's absence. Then it was noticed and much commented on that during the consistory ceremony Cardinal Sodano had greeted Lehmann with shows of joy and affection at the kiss of peace, while Ratzinger, when imparting his congratulations to his countryman Lehmann, had done it with obvious ill grace. Had Kasper and Lehmann won an important battle against Ratzinger? Was Ratzinger, approaching his eightieth year, at last a yesterday's man?

The nub of the internal struggle between the Germans went to the heart of Church governance and the bishops' quarrel with John Paul from the beginning of his reign. The struggle had been exposed in the prestigious German weekly *Die Zeit* by its distinguished former editor Robert Leicht.

In 1999, the then Bishop Kasper had written an essay on collegiality in a *festschrift* that prompted widespread speculation and argument in the corridors of the Vatican. Kasper had opined that "the progressive interpretation of Vatican II as a criticism and overturning of the centralism of Vatican I is being thwarted." In a clear indictment of John Paul II and Ratzinger, he went on to declare that "an attempt at restoration is working to restore the centralism which the majority at the Second Vatican Council clearly wanted to overcome." Then he cited a document written by Ratzinger in 1992, titled *The Church as Communion*, asserting that the text was "more or less in effect a reversal" of Vatican II. Kasper now argued that the true meaning of Church and Universal Church was to be found in the Acts of the Apostles. There, Kasper insisted, St. Luke "presents this Church as both universal and local. This is his perspective, though historically there were presumably several communities from the beginning: besides the one in Jerusalem, there were several in Galilee. The one Church therefore consisted of local Churches from the beginning." Ratzinger, Kasper argued, believes that the Universal Church precedes the local Church, which becomes "really problematic when the one universal Church is stealthily identified with Roman Church, and *de facto* with the Pope and the Roman Curia. When this happens, the CDF document must be understood not as a clarification of Vatican II's doctrine of the Church as communion but as a departure from it and as an attempt to restore Roman centralism."

Ratzinger hit back in an equally heavyweight German newspaper—the *Frankfurter Allgemeine Zeitung* (December 22, 2000). He started with the snide observation that "self respecting" theologians thought it their duty to hit out at the Vatican. He then quibbled with Kasper's interpretation of Acts, to defend once again the primacy of the universal over the local. Which prompted yet another thrust from Kasper, this time in the Jesuit journal *Stimmen der Zeit*, simply repeating his point and determined not to budge one tittle or jot in his argument.

This ecclesiastical brouhaha, which went largely unnoticed except by those who were carefully monitoring, with approval or dismay, the direction in which John Paul had been taking the Church, had huge significance for diocesan pastoral care. Should bishops be allowed to come to their own conclusions about how to resolve major pastoral problems? In the case of Germany, three bishops wanted to allow remarried divorcées, with certain qualifications, to be able to receive communion. But John Paul had emphatically said no. In another crucial area, at a point when Catholics and Lutherans were hoping and praying for increasing unity, Ratzinger, with the approval of John Paul, had published the document *Dominus Jesus,* informing the world that many Christian denominations, including the Lutherans, were "not Churches in the proper sense."

This was a devastating reflection, since it indicated that progress on Christian unity depended on the recognition of the local Church. As Kasper wrote: "The ultimate ecumenical aim is not a uniform united church, but one Church in reconciled diversity."

However, those who thought in 2001 that Ratzinger's days were done, and that Kasper and Lehmann were the coming men who would make a new beginning, would soon be disabused of that notion. Ratzinger was to stay in place, powerful as ever, as head of the Congregation for the Doctrine of the Faith, holding in tension the younger reforming Kasper, head of the Council for Promoting Christian Unity. Did John Paul thereby hope to tame the German firebrand, or was he genuinely hoping for a new beginning at the end of his papacy?

John Paul called an extraordinary consistory of cardinals for May 21 to discuss Church governance and the need for reform. The meeting ended on May 24 without any clear decisions or agenda for the future. As long as the Pope survived, it seemed, it would be more of the same. Few of those cardinals present had faced the issue of governance head-on. Cardinal Murphy-O'Connor, Archbishop of Westminster, suggested there should be more debate—all the time and not just every three years when the bishops met in Rome. Cardinal Daneels of Brussels said much the same: It was Catholic doctrine, he said, that the Church should be governed by the bishops with the Pope. His criticism of the synods was devastating: He suggested that the deliberation and summing-up processes were inadequate to the point of deceit. But in the crucial segment of the consistory earmarked for discussion of governance, few cardinals spoke, and the meeting moved on to other, less incendiary issues. At the end of the consistory, from which the media was barred, none would speak to the press about what had taken place. The cardinals had been ordered to remain silent. One Latin American cardinal said: "They told us everything that was said in the hall is property of the consistory."

9/11

On September 11, 2001, John Paul was resting at his summer palace above Lake Albano when the news arrived that finally dashed any hopes he had entertained of a period of a millennial springtime of the spirit in prospect. The news portended, rather, a period of terrible travail.

Like the rest of the world, John Paul learned that thousands of people had died when two hijacked planes with their passengers on board crashed into the World Trade Center in New York. Within two hours, the towers had collapsed. By that time, another hijacked plane had crashed into the Pentagon, killing 125 people, and a plane headed for an unknown destination crashed in Pennsylvania not far from the presidential retreat Camp David. It soon emerged that the attacks were the work of Islamic extremists; it would take a while longer to establish that the dark organizer of these atrocities was Osama bin Laden and his Al Qaeda terrorist group.

The Pope went immediately to his chapel to pray, "to beg for the Lord an end to such fratricidal violence." At times such as this, he was an obvious focus of attention for Catholics and non-Catholics alike, and he more than lived up to his stature as a great and unique religious leader, offering comfort as well as a plea for constraint in poised and powerful language made all the more authentic by the depth of his compassion.

He passed the message to his secretary of state, Cardinal Angelo Sodano, to broadcast to the world that he was horrified at the "inhuman terrorist attacks," that he was offering prayers for the victims and all Americans in what he called "this dark and tragic moment."

Later, he sent a telegram to President George W. Bush. "Shocked by the unspeakable horror of today's inhuman terrorist attacks against innocent people in different parts of the United States," John Paul wrote, "I hurry to express to you and your fellow citizens my profound sorrow and my closeness in prayer for the nation at this dark and tragic moment."

He was taken by helicopter back to the Vatican in the mid-morning of Wednesday the twelfth, to conduct his general audience in St. Peter's Square, where the people were asked not to applaud and to be prayerful. He told the crowds that he was deeply disturbed by this "dark day in the history of humanity, this terrible affront to human dignity." Expanding on his theme, he said, "The human heart has depths from which schemes of unheard-of ferocity sometimes emerge, that are capable of destroying in a moment the normal daily life of a people." But "faith comes to our aid at these times when words seem to fail." He went on to say:

> Christ's word is the only one that can give response to the questions which trouble our spirit. Even if the forces of darkness appear to prevail, those who believe in God know that evil and death do not have the final say. Christian hope is based on this truth. At this time, our prayerful trust draws strength from it.

His final prayer was for "the leaders of nations, that they not be overtaken by hatred and a spirit of vengeance."

Monsignor Sotto Voce told me later that the Vatican officials were terrified that the next target was going to be St. Peter's Basilica, John Paul being regarded as the Chaplain of the Western World—which, of course, he was not. The rumors would fly of an imminent attack for some months to come. From time to time, the Italian government would make the Vatican City a nonflyover zone.

In the meantime John Paul, by a prior arrangement, celebrated his first public Sunday Mass at the hill town of Frosinone some forty miles southeast of Rome. About 40,000 people turned up for the outdoor Mass, at which he told them that he was "heartbroken." Turning, as was his habit in times of crisis, to Mary, he said: "May the Virgin Mary help all not to give in to the temptation of hate and violence but to commit themselves to the service of justice and peace."

Back in Rome, through the appropriate channel of the Vatican council for inter-religious dialogue, it was noted at the highest level that Muslim leaders in Pakistan, Lebanon, Afghanistan, and the Palestinian Authority had sent condolences to the American president but that "not all the voices have been in condemnation. Some people have rejoiced at this blow to the USA, but the general mood would seem to be one of revulsion." The statement, which was very *ufficiale*, appeared designed as much to discourage attacks or threats against specific Islamic peoples, Arafat in particular, as to rebuke those who had failed to offer commiserations.

Two further reflections had been made by the end of that first weekend, clearly *ufficiale*, intimating that as far as the Pope was concerned, the world was dealing with undercurrents that required deep analysis and long-term solutions. Cardinal Walter Kasper, new head of the Council for Christian Unity, was saying Mass at Santa Maria in Trastevere; speaking to the Sant'Egidio community, which is charged by the Pope with peacemaking, he said that the "deeper reasons behind the calamity should be sought." For Christians, he said, the "response cannot simply be a matter for military measures or those of precaution and security. The Christian response must be to start an intensive and committed dialogue between cultures and religions, and this dialogue must be inspired and driven by a dialogue with God, who alone can heal wounds and reconcile hearts."

On Vatican Radio, Cardinal Roberto Tucci, organizer of papal visits, said that "the danger now is to fail to articulate clearly defined objectives." He said that it would be wrong to attack "entire populations, simply because Muslim fundamentalists are among them." It was clear that John Paul and some of his like-minded aides were sensing that the world was facing a bloodbath, and John Paul was preparing himself to set his face implacably against military action.

Tucci was responsible for the Pope's upcoming visit to the Central Asian country Kazakhstan, formerly part of the Soviet Union, which had been planned many months earlier and was due to commence the following Saturday. Many voices, in the Vatican and Kazakhstan, counseled cancellation, but John Paul would not hear of it. Between President Bush's declaration of a war on terror to Congress and anticipated military action, John Paul saw his trip as an opportunity to be heard and to be seen as active and engaged in world affairs. Besides, the visit would bring him a little closer to one of the last great ambitions of his papacy—to visit Russia itself. Kazakhstan had been a place of exile from Russia ever since the days of the czars; the population included Poles, Germans, and Ukrainians deported by Stalin in the 1930s and 1940s, as well as Muslims. Now Kazakhstan stood to be destabilized by Islamic terrorists trained in Afghanistan who had already attacked two southern neighbors, Uzbekistan and Kyrgyzstan, in the previous year. Most ethnic Kazakhs, 44 percent of the total population of sixteen million, are Sunni Muslims, while most of the 36 percent who are native Russians are Russian Orthodox. Through the previous decade, missionaries from a number of faiths and confessions, including evangelical Protestants, had flown into the country to evangelize. The government consequently attempted to impose an amendment to the law on freedom of conscience, banning faiths that were "nontraditional"—which might have included Catholicism. The measure was dropped a few days before John Paul's arrival.

On the six-hour flight from Rome, John Paul spent most of the time studying Bush's speech to Congress and its declaration of a long-term war on terror. Then he began to write an addition to the sermon he had prepared for the following day. He was met at the airport by the president, Nursultan Nazarbayev, who said he was grateful that the Pope had come "in spite of the very alarming situation in the world." Then he said that the tragedy carried the threat of "split and confrontation between civilizations and religions."

The next day, John Paul celebrated Mass in Motherland Square in Astana, the capital, against the striking blue backdrop of a traditional tent in which the formerly nomadic Kazakhs made their homes. He started by saying in Russian: "I know your history. I know the sufferings to which many of you have been subjected when the previous regime took you from your lands of origin and deported you here in a situation of distress and deprivation." Then he switched to English to say: "Religion must never be used as a reason for conflict."

Through the rest of his visit, he repeatedly stressed that the Catholic Church reaffirmed its respect for authentic Islam, "the Islam that prays and is concerned for those in need." At the same time, John Paul reiterated the need for a nonviolent response to the attacks. The night before his departure from Astana for Armenia, however, as the rumors flew about possible American strikes against training camps and suspected Osama bin Laden hideouts in Afghanistan, confusing *ufficiose* signals began to emanate from the papal party. On the flight from Kazakhstan, the Pope's spokesman, Navarro-Valls, told the Rome correspondent for Reuters that the Pope would understand if the United States had to resort to force to protect its citizens from future threats. This contradicted John Paul's statements calling for peaceful solutions, as well as the *ufficiale* comments of Kasper and Tucci at the weekend. Questioned later, Navarro-Valls refused to admit that there was any contradiction involved. He deflected further questions by saying: "I only said what's written about just wars in the catechism."

The debate over precisely what John Paul was teaching about just war, and what others thought he ought to be teaching, was only just beginning.

*

On Sunday, October 7, a week after John Paul's return to the Vatican, the United States and Britain launched an attack called Enduring Freedom on Taliban military sites in Afghanistan, employing Tomahawk missiles and long-range bombers. At five o'clock Greenwich Mean Time, President Bush addressed the American people and confirmed that British forces were assisting the U.S. military action. In the preceding weeks, a substantial fleet of carriers, submarines, and other vessels had been assembled in the Indian Ocean, and various countries in the Mediterranean and the Middle East had made their airbases and ports available. Italy's prime minister, Mr. Silvio Berlusconi, was a staunch supporter of the War on Terror and had pledged Italian troops. The Italian people immediately divided on the issue, prompting protests and demonstrations, although it is to be noted that Berlusconi controlled some 90 percent of the Italian broadcast media.

A debate was flaring on the issue of war, both within the Vatican and among various individuals outside who believed they had the authority, or the license, to interpret John Paul's mind on the issue. The Pope's secretary for relations with other states, Jean-Louis Tauran, said in an interview with the French Catholic newspaper *La Croix,* "We all recognize that Washington has the right to legitimate defense, because it has the mission to guarantee the security of its citizens." In the meantime, the remarks attributed to Navarro-Valls on the way from Kazakhstan had been interpreted by the news network CNN as a papal blessing on the air strikes on Afghanistan. Given the reach of CNN, especially in the Middle East and Asia, this was nothing short of a disastrous circumstance. Would Navarro-Valls have been so presumptuous in John Paul's younger, more focused days? Like Navarro-Valls, Tauran defended his statement by appealing to the catechism. He repeated, as many would in the coming months, the need for "defined objectives," "protection of the innocent," "proportionality." He also mentioned the need to reach a just settlement in the Middle East. But as if to rap Tauran over the knuckles, the head of the German Bishops Conference, Karl Lehmann (who had talked of the Pope resigning in the previous year), responded that he did not want to hear of "just wars" but of "a just peace."

Just as firmly, however, the papal biographer George Weigel argued for military action in an interview he gave to the Rome-based news agency Zenit. He had by now become a self-appointed interpreter of the papal mind, and at times, like Michael Novak and Richard John Neuhaus, a self-appointed stage prompter for John Paul's gaps and garbled lines. He believed, he said, that the 9/11 attacks were an act of war and not just a criminal act. He said that the attacks "cannot be properly understood by analogy to the criminal justice system," since it was clear that they were aimed at the destruction of the United States government. "I am quite convinced," he went on, "that preemptive military action against terrorists is morally legitimate under the principles of the Just War tradition." Weigel, like his colleagues Novak and Neuhaus, had clearly ceased to be a mere reporter of the papal mind and had become a Catholic mover and shaker in his own right, a role that he would continue to exercise vigorously on the issue of war and the Catholic Church in the coming months and years.

That same day, however, the head of the Nigerian Bishops Conference, Archbishop John Olorunfemi Onaijekan, pointed out that the cost of just one missile currently being sent into Afghanistan could build twenty hospitals in Nigeria. He spoke of the anger and hopelessness bred by poverty and oppression, which meant that "there will always be a suicide bomber who says 'I have nothing to lose.'" He added that it would be more effective to hunt down and capture bin Laden "by building dozens of hospitals in Afghanistan rather than dropping hundreds of bombs in the desert."

The official position of the Catholic Church in the eyes of the world, and especially the Islamic world, was of immediate and continuing consequence. That week four masked gunmen broke into St. Dominic's Catholic Church in the southern Pakistan town of Bahawalpur and opened fire, killing eighteen people and wounding many more as they worshiped. Eight of the dead were women and children. The worshipers were in fact a federate body of several Christian denominations. A Pakistan Catholic missionary priest said in an interview that Christians had been preparing themselves for a backlash against the bombing in Afghanistan. It was, he said, "Pakistani Christians' worst nightmare come true."

Meanwhile, outside the walls of the Vatican, the streets of Rome were scenes of rival demonstrations for and against the war. At one rally in support of America's military action, Sophia Loren, Luciano Pavarotti, and New York mayor Rudolph Giuliani spoke via video link to the Italian people. The Italian tenor Andrea Bocelli sang live on stage, and Silvio Berlusconi, waving an American flag, delivered a rousing closing speech in support of military action.

In the last week of October, Osama bin Laden was reported to have named Italy as an enemy of the Islamic nations, and rumors of an imminent strike against St. Peter's Basilica increased. Metal detectors were in position at the entrance points to St. Peter's Square and large numbers of police were in evidence surveying the pilgrim crowds. Vatican officials, moreover, continued to assert that John Paul was a friend of the Palestinian people, and of Yasser Arafat in particular, and that he had strongly criticized the U.S. actions against Iraq in the Gulf War. Since those confusing signals, mainly on the part of others, at the end of his Kazakhstan visit, John Paul had been mute on the issue, except for repeated requests for the faithful to say the rosary—the message of Our Lady of Fatima.

Strange, however, that protests and demonstrations for peace could prompt such unholy rows, even in association with the Pope. In early October, John Paul's own newspaper, *L'Osservatore Romano*, became embroiled in a spat over a fifteen-mile mass peace march from Perugia to Assisi involving 250,000 people. The march, which normally occurred every year, had begun back in the autumn of 1961 during the Cuban missile crisis and attracted a mixture of political and religious groups who normally were not on speaking terms. The 2001 march included Franciscan friars, the Latin Patriarch of Jerusalem, and various justice and peace groups. *L'Osservatore*, however, criticized the march as an "unworthy spectacle" since there had been participants openly supporting the attacks on Afghanistan. The paper stated that the consequent abuse and bickering between the marchers was tantamount to "blasphemy." Youngsters in Catholic Action had boycotted the march in disgust and organized their own protests in more than a hundred different town squares across Italy. Meanwhile, John Paul led a group rosary in St. John Lateran along with the bishops who were in synod, followed by joint prayers with religious representatives of Judaism, Islam, and Christianity and an assortment of Italian political leaders and ambassadors. The event was ring-fenced by unprecedented police and military security.

John Paul's initiatives to encourage interfaith prayer meetings, however, provoked some of the more xenophobic elements in Italian religious and public life, suggesting that John Paul's failure to set an example as an interfaith leader (the *Dominus Jesus* debacle, for example) had led to predictable consequences in this time of crisis. As John Paul called on the world to begin a fast for peace in order to coincide with the Muslim month of Ramadan, many non-Catholics in Italy, including Communists and Buddhists, enthusiastically took part, led by the Cardinal Archbishop of Milan, Carlo Maria Martini. But a number of reactionary Catholic bishops instantly and vehemently objected. For example, Bishop Alessandro Maggiolini of Como pointed out to the Italian public that this was no thing for a Catholic to do "because my faith is true; Islam is not." Which was more or less the message that had emanated from the *Dominus Jesus* document, which John Paul had so recently and publicly endorsed. Silvio Berlusconi, who had declared in the heat of the 9/11 crisis that Islam was an inferior culture to that of Christianity, had Father Gianni Baget Bozzo, his personal spiritual director, speak for him. "There's risk of confusing people with a different God," he opined, "that is not the God of Jesus Christ."

As autumn deepened, John Paul also came under fire for a fund the Vatican had established for the victims of terrorism. The Comboni Missionaries complained in their journal, *Nigrizia,* that the Pope had chosen the Banco di Roma to handle the charitable contributions, whereas, as was well known, the said bank was a major financier of the arms trade.

Small wonder, as the weeks passed, that John Paul became increasingly discreet on the crisis and the military action and ever more melancholy and apocalyptic. At an open-air ceremony in the Piazza di Spagna, he said: "Dense clouds are gathering on the world's horizon. Humanity, which greeted the dawn of the third millennium with hope, now feels weighed down by the threat of new, terrifying conflicts. Peace in the world is at risk." At another Mass, he said that the world had entered the new millennium hoping for peace, but the events of 9/11 had "jarringly dashed these longed-for aspirations." One of his devoutly wished hopes was for peace in the "Holy Lands." He had been particularly affected by recent reports of running battles in the Holy Places in Israel and in the Palestinian Territories.

Grasping at the example he had given in St. Peter's when he had asked forgiveness for all the sins of the Church committed through the ages, John Paul was ending the *annus horribilis* of 2001 convinced that the only answer was forgiveness. In a sixteen-page document issued as a peace-day message to the world, John Paul urged that while self-defense is legitimate, forgiveness "always involves an apparent short-term loss for a real long-term gain. But violence is the exact opposite. Opting as it does for an apparent short-term gain, it involves a real and permanent loss." John Paul appeared, as he himself had said at Frosinone in the week of 9/11, "heart-broken." He appeared, moreover, broken in health. However, his message, against the background of the speedy military successes in Afghanistan, came across as unrealistic, the message perhaps of an old man whose eyes were set on the next world rather than this one. Who, after all, seriously considered that formally forgiving Osama bin Laden would bring an end to the spasmodic mass-murder terrorism such as had occurred in New York? But his woes in this new millennium were only just beginning. He was about to encounter a species of sin, committed by the sons of the Church, that would tax his policy of forgiveness to the limit.

CHAPTER TWENTY-EIGHT

The Sexual Abuse Scandal

As the Church entered the new millennium, which John Paul had longingly anticipated as an era of spiritual springtime, he found himself and the Catholic Church embattled on a single issue: the pedophile priest scandal. The analysis and management of this crisis by John Paul, his close advisers, and Curial aides has proved one of the most crucial challenges of his pontificate.

It is necessary at the outset to note that most of the thousands of priestly abuse cases involved pubescent or postpubescent, early-teenage boys rather than infants. Noting this fact, some traditionalist Catholic commentators conclude that the crisis stems from homosexuality in the priesthood. The root of the problem, however, in the judgment of many qualified experts, is personal and sexual immaturity on the part of the perpetrator. Priestly abuse is invariably about unequal power relationships rather than sexual hedonism. The problem is also about the weakness of Catholic bishops and the enfeeblement of the local Church for which John Paul bears a measure of responsibility.

The eye of the storm was in the United States, although the problem was more widespread. In the previous six to seven years, some 120 priests had been investigated in the United Kingdom for abuse of minors, with twenty-one convictions; in France during the same period, some 20 priests had been convicted of rape and molestation of children; in Catholic Ireland, some 150 priests were similarly convicted, and there were cases in Italy, Austria, Spain, Mexico, Australia, Canada, and parts of Africa.

Accusations and liability went to the highest levels. In Belgium, Cardinal Godfried Daneels, tough, progressive, considered papabile by many, was reproached in court for making light of the behavior of an abusing priest under his jurisdiction. The late Hans Groër, former Cardinal Archbishop of Vienna, once a Benedictine abbot, was accused of sexual abuse of young novices. In 1995, a former monastic student came forward to claim that Groër had abused him some years earlier. That same year, Bishop Johan Weber of Austria had sought a commission to investigate Groër, as the scandal was pushing the Austrian Church into its worse crisis since World War II; but John Paul refused to countenance it. Weber offered to take early retirement in 2001, and the Pope promptly accepted. In Honduras, Rodriguez Maradiaga, the youngest cardinal in the world and also considered papabile, has been accused of sending a pedophile priest abroad to work again in a parish, and also to escape justice.

But the United States was the focus and the chief anxiety. In the early months of the year 2000, the Catholic Church in America was being sued in Federal Court as a criminal organization. One of seven abused former seminarians of the diocesan seminary in Palm Beach, Florida, had filed an action against the entire American Catholic Church under legislation aimed at the Mafia. The RICO (Racketeer-Influenced and Corrupt Organizations) Act combats groups and institutions with a "pattern" of illegal behavior. The seminarian claimed that the Catholic Church was just such a body, and all its bishops part of the conspiracy.

It was a bad Lent in 2002 for Catholic Boston—a city whose Catholics had generously supported the Holy See for more than a century and a half. The Catholic, Boston-based writer James Keenan commented: "The scandals are enough to place us all in sackcloth and ashes. If Lent cultivates a communal sense of shame, then this has been the most fertile Lent in my 50 years; no other disposition captures what we Catholics feel about our Church and its leadership in this revolting and disgraceful tragedy." Hardly a day passed through Lent of that year without a priest being arrested somewhere in the United States. More than fifty-five priests had been removed since the New Year. The reported liability settlements had reached $500 million, and some eighty-nine priests in Boston alone had been indicted. And now diocese after diocese was being scrutinized, revealing time and again that bishops, perhaps 50 percent of them, had systematically covered up their priests' pedophile abuse. Keenan recorded that even as he was writing his piece for a Catholic weekly, he heard on the radio about three new incidents involving a bishop in another diocese, a high-ranking Boston priest, and a local religious priest. The *New York Times* on March 20 attempted to sum up the catastrophe: "The accounts that have come out of the Roman Catholic Church's sexual abuse scandal could hardly be more horrific—altar boys lured into bed by priests; children entrusted to the Church's care forced to perform oral sex."

It was the sheer extent of the crisis, as much as the fact of it, that appalled people. Pedophile abuse in the priesthood was nothing new in the Church's long history—in either the early or the late modern periods. Karen Liebreich's scholarly book *Fallen Order* reveals how sexual abuse of children was practiced routinely in the seventeenth century by members of the Piarist Order, a congregation dedicated to education of the children of the poor. She also revealed how Jose de Calasanz, the founder of the Piarists and later canonized a saint, knew of the scandal and attempted to cover it up. Nor were popes blameless. Liebreich's study shows how Pope Innocent X appointed a man known to be a practicing pedophile to take charge of the order. During the immediate period of the Counter-Reformation, when priests were being encouraged toward ever-greater self-discipline, the Piarist scandal reveals a scarcely credible undergrowth of corruption and abuse. The central villain was Stefano Cherubini, principal of a Piarist school in Naples, who threatened to bring down the order if accusations of his abuse were made public. We find the saintly founder of the Piarists writing to a colleague, advising that he "cover up this great shame in order that it does not come to the notice of our superiors."

Nor is priestly pedophile practice new in the long-term past of the Church. In the year 1050, a future saint, Peter Damian, addressed a report to Pope Leo IX on the widespread practice of clerical pedophilia, excoriating not only those who perpetrated such deeds but the "do nothing superiors" who were "partners in the guilt of others." Back in the eleventh century, the Pope and Rome bridled at the forthright criticism.

If clerical sexual abuse comes in waves, the Vatican had early warning of what was in store when a case in Lafayette, Louisana, was reported to the Vatican's Congregation for the Clergy (responsible for, among other things, the discipline of the clergy) as far back as September 1982. A Father Gilbert Gauthe had been indicted by a grand jury on thirty-four counts of sexual abuse involving nine boys; one charge included rape, which carries the death sentence in that state. The diocesan lawyers were bracing themselves for damages of $4 million, but that level of settlement for such crimes would soon become woefully inadequate; in 1986, the same diocese was destined to pay a $600,000 settlement to the family of a boy who was sexually attacked on one occasion by a senior seminarian. There were some aggravating details, to be sure: It was Good Friday, and the seminarian had softened up his victim by plying him with liquor. But what was unusual, in fact alarming, about the Gauthe litigation was the appearance of Pope John Paul II's name on the list of defendants as one relieved of liability for damages. It turns out that this was a slip more canonical than Freudian. The Pope's name was speedily dropped. But the question remained, in principle if not in law: To what extent did John Paul II take a measure of responsibility?

Following the Gauthe case, news of the wider scandal, leading to a full-blown crisis, would take years to come to light. And when it did, everybody who read a newspaper or listened to a broadcast anywhere in the world could not have failed to get the drift. One aspect of the crisis that concerned Catholic laity, and for obvious reasons the Holy See, even in the early stages, was the ballooning financial liability. Driving the judicial processes in the United States was not so much criminal prosecution as tort law, which involves the financial liability of organizations that fail to observe a duty of care to clients and employees. As the Church faced astronomical damages, the faithful began to question the sense of giving to the diocese when the proceeds were being spent not on schools and hospitals but on payouts for erring priests. At the height of the scandal, in April 2002, *BusinessWeek* published a Gallup poll, dated March 27, indicating that some 80 percent of Catholics were thinking of cutting off charitable contributions to the Church.

The full sordid picture in the United States was not to emerge until February 2004, when a wide-ranging investigation was published by the College of Criminal Justice at John Jay University in New York. In the meantime, the Holy See tended to dismiss or to minimize the crisis. In 2002, when the serial atrocities of Fathers Geoghan, Shanley, and Birmingham of Boston were being exposed, Cardinal Ratzinger, who discusses the problems of the Church in the world every Friday with John Paul, confidently averred that less than 1 percent of priests had been the targets of complaints (his use of the word "targets" in no way acknowledged actual guilt in that estimate). The true figure, as would come to light two years later in the John Jay report, was that 4 percent of all priests serving in ministries in the United States had been plausibly accused of sexual abuse with minors in the second half of the twentieth century. During the lifetime of a fifty-two-year-old individual born in 1950, some 4,400 Catholic priests in the United States had been credibly accused of sexually attacking some 11,000 minors. That represents virtually half of the period of John Paul II's papal watch.

It was to emerge that 80 percent of the victims were boys, typically age thirteen and upward. Two-thirds of these children were attacked more than once. Some 3 percent of priests abused ten victims or more. About 90 percent of the attacks were explicitly and directly genital, as opposed to inappropriate stroking and kissing, with a quarter of that number involving penetration. A typical perpetrator was in his thirties and had been involved in abuse for about a year. Typically, too, only 14 percent of cases brought to the attention of the perpetrators' dioceses were reported by the bishops to the police. And yet half of those reported to the police were convicted. Damages paid to victims' families stood at $572 million in 2002 and would increase to $700 million by the summer of 2004; legal costs and loss of donations made matters worse.

The statistics would reveal a steeply rising curve of incidence that began in the mid-1960s and began to decline in the mid-1980s, although the abuse continued through the 1990s, suggesting that there was something about the post–Vatican II era, and indeed the Church of John Paul II, that created an ambit hospitable to clerical abuse of minors. That same period saw the defection of some 100,000 priests (20,000 in the United States) and 200,000 nuns. At the same time, it appeared from many reports that the seminaries were filling up with gay men. According to Donald B. Cozzens, a former rector of an American seminary writing in 2002 (*The Changing Face of Priesthood*), some seminaries in the United States had gay populations as high as 75 percent. In January 2000, moreover, a survey collected and published by the *Kansas City Star* suggested that the AIDS death rate among Catholic priests was at least four times that of the general population. The Vatican declined to comment, but Bishop Raymond Boland of Kansas City–St. Joseph said: "Much as we would regret it, it shows that human nature is human nature."

The media conflagration, made all the worse by lack of timelines, distinctions between infant and teenage victims, distinctions between allegations and actual convictions, and incendiary mixes of reporting and commentary, exploded into something even greater than the extensive details of the scandal itself. As Peter Steinfels of the *New York Times* noted, "untethered to precise knowledge," it was expending itself in "general alienation from the Church" as well as agendas for reform. Catholics on either side of the conservative-liberal divide were hurling abuse at each other, attempting to convince the faithful at large that their opposite wing in the Church was to blame. The conservatives were blaming the era of post–Vatican II permissiveness, hedonism, widespread laxity, and the infiltration of homosexuals into the priesthood. The progressives or liberals were arguing that the decisions of Vatican II had not been applied; that the bishops and the laity had been rendered immature and irresponsible by an authoritarian, highly centralized Holy See; this, in turn, they charged, had encouraged a generation of clerics in arrested development at a time when permissiveness was pervasive in society at large.

But what had John Paul thought?

As the media chorus rose to a crescendo in the early months of the Boston crisis, baying for the resignation of Cardinal Bernard Law for covering up for perpetrators, John Paul ordered Cardinal Law to remain at his post. Then, in the midst of the Boston media frenzy in the early months of 2002, John Paul took the opportunity of his customary Maundy Thursday letter to priests to declare his view of the crisis. It was timed to be read throughout the world at the Mass of the Chrism, when priests gather in their local cathedrals to confirm themselves in their vocations and renew their ordination vows before their bishops. This is what the Pope wrote:

> We are personally and profoundly afflicted by the sins of some of our brothers who have betrayed the grace of ordination in succumbing even to the most grievous forms of the "mysterium iniquitatis" at work in the world . . . A dark shadow of suspicion is cast over all the fine priests who perform their ministry with honesty and integrity . . . the church shows her concern for the victims and strives to respond in truth and justice to each of these painful situations.

John Paul's first thoughts, then, were not for the victims but for the image of the Catholic priesthood and the effect of the repercussions of this abuse on "fine priests." And while he was "afflicted" by the sins of his brother priests, he was merely "concerned" for the victims. Although it was no doubt true that his "brothers" had betrayed the grace of ordination, there was no acknowledgment of deeper betrayals: of trust, of parents, of all who addressed them as "Father." If ever the priesthood had been revealed as the measure of an individual's maturity, as opposed to a mystical state that had descended from above, it was the crisis of the priestly sexual abuse.

Then we come to the nature of the crime. John Paul character-ized sexual abuse of minors by priests as *"mysterium iniquitatis"*: the mystery of the iniquity, or sin. The phrase, culled from the Latin of the Vulgate edition of the Catholic Bible, specifically and exclusively from 2 Thessalonians 7, occurs in a striking passage that speaks of the end-time and the coming of the "wicked one." As in the allu-sions to a Second Fall in his 1976 Lenten homilies, the chapter seems, through its inchoate language and images, to refer again to the wickedness that will spread before the Second Coming. "For the mystery of iniquity already worketh; only that he who now holdeth, do hold, until he be taken out of the way. And then that wicked one shall be revealed whom the Lord Jesus shall kill with the spirit of his mouth." The obscurity is not a result of sloppy translation.

Describing priestly sexual abuse in terms of a dense, apocalyptic passage in an epistle of Saint Paul only served to obfuscate insultingly the crimes committed against young individuals and their families, dis-tancing the perpetrators, and indeed the Church, from responsibility. It also removed John Paul from a context in which spades are called spades, and abusers abusers. Importantly, it gave the impression that these men did not set out to abuse and deprave the young, but that they were enticed by this *"mysterium iniquitatis"* in the realms of the powers of darkness, which had been given large scope and sway by God in anticipation of the end-time. Responsibility was thereby partly shifted from the individual to the presence of Satan in the world.

The letter was read out at a news conference at the Vatican's Press Office by Cardinal Castrillon Hoyos, the seventy-three-year-old Colombian who had been made a cardinal in 1998 and now headed the Congregation for the Clergy. The cardinal sat for a full fifteen minutes taking notes as Navarro-Valls collected questions from the journalists present. When the cardinal finally rose to the podium, he set the questions very deliberately to one side with a flourish and a smile. There was an atmosphere of acute anticipation as the correspondents braced themselves to receive the fruit of his thoughts, which, his audience understood, were those not merely of the cardinal but of Pope John Paul himself—the full application of his philosophical, theological, and mystical meditations on the priestly abuse problem.

"The language used is interesting," Cardinal Hoyos started enigmatically. Then, raising the level of mystification, he said: "This by itself is an X-ray of the problem." Quite what "this" referred to was not made apparent. Then he read out a prepared statement.

This pedophile crisis, he told the assembled journalists, was a problem of "pan-sexuality and sexual licentiousness." It was well known, he went on, that 3 percent of American priests had "tendencies towards pedophile behavior but only 0.3 percent were actual pedophiles." (The John Jay figures of the 2004 investigation would soon show these to be shot-in-the-dark figures.)

Then, to the amazement of the assembly, raising his voice, he took a swing at all those other abusers who did not happen to be Catholic priests: "I would like to know the statistics," he said carpingly, "from other groups, and the penalties others have received, and the money others have paid to victims." It was as if he was saying this was not just about pedophiles but about Catholic-bashing. We don't hear the media telling us, he was implying, about the Anglicans, and the Boy Scouts, and the Greek Orthodox. Nor do we hear of hundreds of millions being paid out by them! So it was also about money-grubbing lawyers in America to whom the Church had responded exorbitantly—and obviously foolishly.

He finished by declaring in an expansive fashion that nonetheless the Church was taking this problem seriously. "We have never ignored the problem of sexual abuse, above all among its sacred ministers, even before it was on the front pages." The innuendo was inescapable: that the sensationalist media, as opposed to the "sacred ministers," had a lot to answer for. Canon law, he pointed out to the press conference, had been altered to allow a victim to bring a case ten years beyond a victim's eighteenth birthday. But he wanted to get across a clear message: The Church was going to continue to deal with internal matters in an internal way. The Church would maintain its "secret canonical norms" so as to avoid a "culture of suspicion." So the less transparent the Vatican was going to be, the fewer suspicions would be raised! Then he departed from the meeting, having failed to answer a single specific question put to him by the correspondents.

Before leaving this discussion of the Holy Thursday message to priests, it is important to note the point the Holy Father made about the effect on the good clergy. "A dark shadow of suspicion is cast over all those fine priests who perform their ministry with honesty and integrity." There was, of course, a measure of truth in this. The abusers had made life difficult for decent priests. On the other hand, commiserations with the damaged image of the clerical caste was part of the problem, according to many progressive commentators, one of whom was the redoubtable Father Thomas Doyle, a kind of clerical Michael Moore, who had commented in the *Irish Times*: "Something is wrong and that wrong can't be sandpapered away by emotional expressions of personal hurt or self-righteous expressions of rage at the abusers. It is *precisely* this clerical narcissism that produced the crisis in the first place."

Members of the Curia tended to blame, even at this late stage, gay priests—or "homosexualists," as they preferred to call them. Joaquin Navarro-Valls, papal spokesperson, invited an equivalence between pedophilia and homosexuality when asked about the crisis. He said: "People with these inclinations," meaning homosexuality, "just cannot be ordained." A strange statement, in view of the fact that an NBC report in 2000 put the number of gay priests in America at anywhere between 23 and 58 percent. There was also a view, hardly accepted by the Anglophones in the Curia, that the problem had to do with "English-speaking" countries, where secularism was deemed to be rife, rather than the Latin countries, where children were loved and cherished. It was widely overlooked in Rome that the reason English-speaking countries had more cases than the rest of the world was that legal systems in North America, Britain, and its Commonwealth favored a rigorous and open discovery process as well as a mania for tort law.

As for the papal biographer George Weigel, he was moved to comment that "anyone who has watched this man for 23 years cannot but understand that his heart is breaking." He went on to defend John Paul's emphasis on the sinfulness of sexual abuse, rather than its criminal, social, or psychological character. By sinfulness, he clearly meant that reference to *mysterium iniquitatis*. But other commentators, such as David Clohessy, director of the Survivors Network of Those Abused by Priests, deplored the focus on the "bad apples" rather than the guilt of bishops who covered up the crimes. Richard Sipe, an ex-priest and psychiatrist who has become a specialist on the phenomenon, complained that the Church was still refusing to look at the fundamental cause of the problem, which, in his view, was a tendency to arrested development among priests owing to inadequate recruitment and seminary formation.

Given that a pope, in his "gilded cage" (as Deskur once put it), has his knowledge of the world filtered for him, one wonders just how real the problem appeared to him. Most people in the real world seem to know a priest, or a victim, who has been involved. As it happened, John Paul knew just such a priest personally. He was Juliusz Paetz, emeritus archbishop of Poznan, Poland, whom Cardinal Sodano forced to resign from his diocese on March 28, exactly one week after the Pope's Maunday letter and in the midst of the Boston catastrophe.

Paetz, at the time of this writing sixty-nine years of age, had been part of John Paul's Polish household in the 1990s. But after he was consecrated archbishop, reports filtered back to the Vatican that he was sexually abusing seminarians in his diocese. There were allegations that he used an underground tunnel to visit his victims, a detail straight out of the nineteenth-century fantasies of the novel *Maria Monk*—although in this case apparently true. Vatican investigators looked into the accusations and confirmed them by November 2001. He exculpated himself, saying: "Not everyone understood my genuine openness and spontaneity toward people." Robert Kaiser, the Vaticanologist, has commented in his e-mail column "Rome Diary" that he talked to a Vatican official who had been propositioned twice by Paetz. "Paetz," he has written, "was finally banned by the rector of his own seminary for making continual advances on the young men there who were training for the priesthood." Kaiser continued: "'And we cannot tell the Holy Father about Paetz today,' said one source of mine inside the Vatican. 'The news would kill him.'"

On the other hand, we cannot doubt that John Paul was well apprised of every aspect of the predicament of Cardinal Bernard Law of Boston. Law was a central figure in the sex-abuse scandals that swept America. He was accused of moving priests who had sexually abused minors from parish to parish without notifying the police or even subjecting these pastors to church discipline. With much reluctance, after a year's prevarication, John Paul accepted Law's resignation in 2003, by which time the cardinal's position was untenable in his diocese. The cardinal retired to the chaplaincy of a community of nuns in Clinton, Maryland, where he would remain until June 2004, when John Paul honored him by appointing him archpriest of the Rome Basilica of St. Mary Major. The post is one of considerable status, and from this vantage point he will play an important role in the Holy See as a member of some seven congregations and two councils; in other words, he is on the board of crucial departments that run the universal Church. Catholics in America may well wonder why Law currently (2004) sits on the board of the Congregation for the Clergy (one of the duties of which is the "discipline" of priests) and also on the board of the Congregation for Bishops (which has powers over appointing diocesan bishops). The St. Mary Major appointment coincided with the news that some 357 parishes were to close under the direction of Boston's new arch-bishop, Sean O'Malley. Commenting in the *Boston Globe*, Eileen McNamarra observed: "The Vatican had to choose the same week to install the chief architect of their disaster in a Roman Basilica? Set aside the fundamental depravity of rewarding a co-conspirator in serial child rape with a plush posting to the Eternal City. How much clearer a signal could the Roman Catholic Church send to the faith-ful that it administers justice in two tiers, one for the laity and another for its clerics?"

*

The question remains: To what extent has John Paul been responsi-ble, even in part, for the scandal? There can be no doubt that he deplored the behavior of these priests and that, indeed, it has bro-ken his heart. But he bears a measure of responsibility insofar as the crisis became visible in the early 1980s and he failed to judge the nature and the extent of the crisis and act decisively. If John Paul did nothing else within the Catholic communities during his papacy, he should have focused on this crisis in the priesthood and how it related to the status and morale of the bishops who had a duty to care for the faithful in their diocese and were responsible for the dis-cipline of priests.

Through the early part of John Paul's papacy, men were leaving the priesthood in the tens of thousands to get married. Under Paul VI, these men were speedily released from their priestly vows. Not only did John Paul attempt to exclude these men from the sacra-ments by refusing to release them from their vows, a bullying and uncompassionate reaction, but he failed to recognize clear signals that the priesthood was under intense and widespread pressure due to cultural shifts in sexual mores, the huge impact of sexual permis-siveness in the media, and altering views on sexuality and gender. The era of the 1960s and 1970s saw a gigantic clash of cultures between sexual permissiveness and the traditional disciplines of the clerical caste; and the more priests who absconded, the more difficult the predicament of the priests who remained—many of them increasingly isolated and demoralized. During this period, John Paul shut his ears to pleas from the local Church to consider a married priesthood, and calls for a woman priesthood. These calls were symptomatic of deep undercurrents that needed to be studied and understood, not merely quashed. He also shut his ears to repeated warnings that priestly formation, which continued to be monastic in style, was hopelessly inadequate for the sort of world in which a priest was now required to work.

John Paul has expounded throughout his reign an idealistic, elevated notion of priesthood that harks back in spirit to the Council of Trent and the belief that special graces and charisms descend on the priest the day he is ordained. However, the Trent document on priestly grace, taken from Timothy, makes it clear that such graces are like "embers" that have to be "fanned." But John Paul was a priest of the era of Pius XII, when it was believed that ordination raised the recipient to a pinnacle higher than the angels. He fed his imagination on the ascetical, self-sacrificial models of St. Vincent de Paul and the Curé d'Ars. He belonged to a generation and a tradition that believed that the sacrament of ordination endowed the ordained minister with an "ontological" character, meaning an indelible and unalterable mark upon the soul. The danger of such a model of priesthood, without severe qualifications and vigilance, is that it can appear attractive to men who are weak and fragmented, who see priesthood as a means of acquiring unearned status, authority, and respect.

At the same time, while bishops knew full well the growing extent of the abuse problem, they had grown so used to waiting for Rome to act on local crises that they failed to take the initiative. John Paul's pontificate weakened the status, the authority, and the role of the bishops rather than confirmed them as the local teachers, governors, and sanctifiers.

The bishops have acted in precisely the way disempowered employees behave. They did their best to keep the problem out of the media; they covered up, moving erring priests from place to place (where they invariably offended again); they failed to address the impact on the victims; they failed to reform the clerical caste, the regimes in their seminaries, their methods of recruiting priests. They did not act decisively, by laicizing erring priests and turning them over to the civil authorities, because they did not believe that they had the authority to do so. Bishops did not fail because they were weak and venal men; they failed because of generations of increasing enfeeblement of their office by Rome, further undermined by a Pope who acted as both universal and local pastor. Treat bishops like branch managers of a multinational company and they will act like them. They did not fail to act simply because they were craven but because they did not believe that they had the power to act.

Even after the worst of the scandals had come to light and the bishops had determined on rigorous action, John Paul and the Vatican undermined the autonomy of the American bishops. The U.S. Conference of Catholic Bishops met between June 13 and 15, 2002, at Dallas, Texas, in order to draw up guidelines for dealing with past, present, and future cases of priestly sexual abuse. The bishops voted, with a few exceptions, for a "zero option" policy of "one-strike-and-you're-out." There were differences among them (some hoped for leniency for the less serious cases in the distant past), but the majority of the bishops present realized that they needed to draw a line under the crisis and make a new beginning. They realized that for the Church to come through the crisis they would have to convince both the faithful and the American public of their resolve. At the end of the three days, a detailed charter of tough measures was passed, 239–13.

To the astonishment of the world, however, the American bishops were not allowed to pass the charter into Church law. They were obliged to wait for the Pope's ratification of their decisions. A Vatican official told the Catholic News Service that the Vatican decision would take up to three months. In fact, it took six months for the final sanction, or *recognitio*, to be passed, and for significant changes to be made by Rome. The alterations involved bringing the charter into line with the Code of Canon Law, a Napoleonic-style instrument of Church law (dating, with revisions in 1983, only to 1917; originally, Canon Law involved extensive local discretion). Under the Vatican qualifications, accused priests would be given more protection than the charter had allowed, and laicization (defrocking) procedures would be attended by "pontifical secrecy." The charter had provided for authoritative tribunals composed of lay Catholics, but the Vatican had ruled this out: The laity were to have only an "advisory" role in the process. As the *National Catholic Reporter* correspondent John Allen commented: "How will the requirement of 'pontifical secrecy' affect cooperation with civil and criminal authorities? Will both victims and accused priests be left in the dark for long periods of time as the legal machinery grinds on? Will a lack of transparency undermine public confidence in the process?" But the biggest issue was the Vatican's, and the Pope's, insistence that such a major decision involving a grievous crisis in a major local Church should be centralized. The message this sent to the bishops of America, once again, was that they did not have full authority to cope with urgent matters of discipline.

A final and terrible irony of the priestly abuse crisis, and its corresponding crisis among the bishops, is the catastrophic undermining of diocesan authority as a result of bankruptcy law in the United States. In July 2004, Portland, Oregon, became the first diocese in America to seek the "Chapter 11" haven from creditors after the diocese went broke. Portland, which is a diocese of no more than 350,000 souls, has assets worth between $10 and $50 million, but its liabilities amount to claims for $340 million in abuse damages. The diocese will be protected against its creditors while its finances and assets are reorganized. This means, however, that the local bishop, in this case Archbishop John Vlazny, surrenders his independence and authority in all manner of Church business to a local circuit judge. There has been nothing quite like this capitulation of a diocese to secular authority in the modern period outside China and the Iron Curtain countries. Other dioceses in America are contemplating the same route out of bankruptcy.

For many other reasons, the priestly abuse crisis will have repercussions in the Church for decades to come. In Europe and North America, recruitment into the seminaries has plummeted. Young men are even more reluctant to consider a priestly vocation than they were before the crisis broke. Not surprisingly, Catholic mothers are not inclined to nurture a priestly vocation as they once did. And this comes at a time when the average age of the current generation of priests indicates a massive shortfall of active priests in a few years' time.

The American situation has tended to overshadow other scandals throughout the world. In Austria, the Church has been in a state of upheaval as a result of the behavior of Bishop Kurt Krenn, who has sought to make light of a sex scandal in his seminary. In July 2004, some 40,000 pornographic images were found on the seminarians' computers. There were instant calls from both faithful and his brother bishops for Krenn to resign, but the Vatican insisted that only the Pope had the power to withdraw him, and the Pope vacillated. Krenn was a deeply conservative bishop who had been nominated by John Paul in 1985 despite widespread objections. He is known to be a supporter of the Neo-Nazi Austrian politician Jörg Haider, and more recently refused to adhere to the guidelines on abuse of minors proposed by his brother bishops. When four of his colleague bishops denounced the sexual abuse perpetrated by the late Archbishop of Vienna, Hans Groër, Krenn reportedly went on television to say that they would "roast in hell."

Inevitably, the history of this period will note that the crisis erupted during John Paul's watch, a period in which he presided over an increase in Rome's authority and a decrease in diocesan authority. He should not escape censure for his failure to see the early signs of the crisis and to act appropriately. This past quarter century, the period of his pontificate, will be remembered above all for the priestly sexual abuse scandal and its far-reaching consequences.

CHAPTER TWENTY-NINE

John Paul and AIDS

I t had been confidently expected that John Paul would win the Nobel Peace Prize in the year 2000—and if not then, perhaps by the end of the second year of the new millennium. On August 21, 2001, the Lutheran bishop Gunnar Stallseth, a member of the Nobel Peace Prize committee, had made it clear why John Paul had been turned down yet again. "I challenge the Vatican to redefine its attitude to condoms," he told reporters who had gathered to interview UN Secretary General Kofi Annan, who was on a visit to Oslo. "The current Roman Catholic theology is one that favors death rather than life."

By the beginning of the third millennium, and two decades after AIDS emerged as a major killer disease, some 43 million people, according to the United Nations, had been infected with HIV, and more than 23 million had died. Among the infected, there were 19 million women and 3.2 million children under the age of fifteen. In 2002, 5 million people became infected. By the end of the twentieth century, AIDS had become the second-worst epidemic in history, surpassed only by the Black Death. In sub-Saharan Africa, AIDS is the biggest killer by far: Some 3 million died of AIDS on the continent in 2003. The disease has brought in its wake famine, mass poverty, and tens of millions of orphans. The question asked by experts around the world is whether the Pope has alleviated the AIDS epidemic or exacerbated the problem.

John Paul was explicit when he addressed more than a thousand scientists, ethicists, and health care workers at a three-day conference on AIDS at the Vatican in 1989. He said then that the answer to the "scourge" was for people to change their high-risk lifestyles and not resort to "morally illicit" means of prevention. He meant, of course, the use of condoms. "It is morally illicit to champion a prevention of the AIDS sickness based on recourse to means and remedies that violate the authentically human sense of sexuality," he said. His position then was clear enough: All other arguments apart, condoms should not be used because they were intrinsically and therefore in every instance wrong. He did not appeal to Scripture, nor even to tradition, to support his case, but to natural law and, by inference, papal authority. Condoms were part of the "culture of death," and there could be no possible circumstance in which they could be used without violating deep principles of sexual ethics.

He repeated the message, and the moral rationale behind it, on his 1994 visit to Kampala, capital of Uganda, where the rate of HIV infection was 12 percent, and as high as 30 percent in some segments of the population. He said: "Actions are like words that reveal our heart. To give one's body to someone is to give oneself entirely to that person." In other words, even if one were liable to transmit a fatal disease, it was better not to use a condom than offend the idealistic principle of giving oneself entirely in sexual intercourse.

John Paul has been able to take a degree of comfort from countries like Kenya and Uganda, where the rates of infection have been reduced, in part at least because of campaigns recommending abstinence. On closer examination, however, these successes have been owed, as many experts point out, to a multidimensional approach: abstinence, faithfulness within marriage, early testing, and visits to AIDS wards to see the consequences of catching the disease—but also, human nature being what it is, an absolute insistence on using condoms where people are not capable of abstaining. The importance of condom use, according to experts working in Africa, applies particularly in the case of married migrant workers, who, being months away from home, are tempted to seek out prostitutes and return to their wives infected.

That John Paul has actually exploited the AIDS tragedy to promote an intransigent ethic against contraception in any circumstances has been evident in Uganda. In July 2000, Archbishop Christophe Pierre, an apostolic nuncio and hence official representative of the Pope, initiated a media campaign in the country, urging youth to ignore government-sponsored calls to use condoms to prevent the spread of the disease. This was in direct opposition to the stance taken by Speciosa Wandir Kazibwe, Uganda's vice president and a medical doctor, who had criticized religious leaders who opposed the use of condoms. Kazibwe also advocates abstinence as an essential part of any successful campaign to reduce AIDS, not because contraception is sinful but because it is a partial practical solution to the problem. The Vatican has shown no embarrassment at its degree of interference in a foreign country's legitimate public health projects.

The notion that avoidance of sin overrides every consideration in attempts to control a pandemic disease above and beyond social, behavioral, and prophylactic measures is a calamitous proposition. The Pope and conservative Catholics are entitled to the view that using condoms is immoral, but to suggest that condoms will not prevent the spread of AIDS *because* their use is sinful is an insidious category confusion. Insofar as the confusion is deliberate, the insistence of the Pope and the Vatican is culpable, involving them in responsibility for the spread of AIDS and the illness, death, and social consequences that have ensued. One notes the Church's treatment of AIDS workers who have attempted, in good conscience, to stem the spread of the disease by prophylactics.

The same month as Archbishop Pierre made his bizarre pronouncements on the sinfulness of condoms in Uganda, a priest in Brazil who had been making condoms available for infected parishioners in his region received a "letter of condemnation" from his archbishop, Laudio Hummes of São Paulo. Hummes said there would be further punitive actions "to correct this regrettable situation" if the missionary, who had spent twenty-two years in Brazil, did not comply with official church teaching. The archbishop said the priest's views and attitudes were "unacceptable" and conflicted with Church doctrine, which has been reaffirmed by Pope John Paul II. The priest, Father Valeriano Paitoni, an Italian, said: "If the condom protects life, there is no reason not to view it as a lesser evil. . . . It deals with a greater good."

Father Paitoni runs three shelters in São Paulo for AIDS sufferers and serves a local parish. At a press conference after the bishop's rebuke, Paitoni, who works among the poor in São Paulo, said that the Catholic Church will see itself forced once again to ask for humanity's forgiveness for the "errors committed with respect to AIDS." He said: "AIDS is a world epidemic, a public health problem that must be confronted with scientific advances and methods that have proven effective. Rejecting condom use is to oppose the fight for life." According to Hummes, reprimands "do not exclude administrative and pastoral measures appropriate for correcting this unfortunate situation." Hummes rejected, moreover, Paitoni's comments that the Brazilian Bishops Conference agreed to take a stand against condoms "because of pressure from the Vatican." Some bishops had previously accepted condom use as "a lesser evil," given the spread of AIDS and ensuing deaths. But they were silenced by the Vatican.

Brazil's Health Ministry came out in Paitoni's defense when sanctions against him appeared imminent, saying the priest is an "important partner" in the fight against the disease. There are currently 530,000 people in the country who are HIV positive, according to Health Ministry data. The homes Father Paitoni runs help an estimated 33,000 of that total, two-thirds of whom are children. Nongovernmental organizations specializing in the AIDS fight defended the priest, calling on the Church to keep Paitoni in Brazil's clerical flock. To date, Archbishop Hummes has taken no action against the priest.

John Paul's determination not to allow condoms even in the most extreme circumstances—when a partner within marriage, for example, has the disease and therefore risks infecting a healthy partner— was again paraded before the world at a special session of the United

Nations, which met in New York on June 25, 2001. The Vatican delegation, which did not have voting rights on the commission's public declaration but which was invited like other religious groups to comment on the language, dissociated itself from the plea for the use of condoms in the battle against HIV/AIDS. The Holy See, according to the Vatican representatives, said it had "in no way changed its moral position with regard to the use of condoms as a means of preventing HIV infection." A personal message from John Paul was presented to the commission. The statement was largely self-promotional: "The Church," said the Pope, "carries out a quarter of the total welfare given to those infected with HIV and AIDS worldwide." Then he went on to insist that the best means of prevention was "training in the authentic values of life, love and sexuality."

A more recent aspect of the papal strategy, however, was to congratulate itself while blaming others. In Rome in the presence of John Paul, the head of the Vatican's office for health care, Cardinal Javier Lozan Barragan, chose World AIDS Day—December 1, 2003—to ram home John Paul's anti-safe-sex policy. First he praised the Pope for what he had done for AIDS victims throughout the world, then he turned his attention to the evil intent of the pharmaceutical companies. Cardinal Barragan said the industry had priced antiretroviral anti-AIDS drugs beyond the pockets of governments and patients: The scandal, the cardinal said, "cries to God for vengeance."

Next he lambasted education programs that favor "policies that foster immoral and hedonistic lifestyles and behavior" rather than "the culture of life and responsible love"—which was code for the conviction that sin caused AIDS and that only nonsinning would cure it. The Catholic Church, he went on, led the world in the fight against the virus. He added that it must be remembered that the Holy Father had insisted that Church efforts should emphasize "fidelity, chastity, and abstinence" in combating AIDS, which was "a pathology of the spirit" aggravated by "a crisis of moral values."

*

Listening to Catholics discuss the AIDS issue in the first years of the new century has been like listening to the grown children of a dysfunctional and abusing father gingerly assuaging him lest they prompt a tantrum.

Clifford Longley, an abrasive and independent-minded leading writer for *The Tablet,* declared himself "ashamed to be a Catholic" in an article he wrote in 2001, because of the Pope's intransigence on condoms and AIDS. And yet we find him tying himself in mental knots so as not to offend papal principles on contraception. Given that a husband has AIDS, he wrote in *The Tablet,* "in using a condom his intent is to perform the subjectively and objectively good act of making love to her while not threatening her life. It is not per se, to prevent conception; he may even regret that the condom also has that effect." These literary contortions by a writer normally known for his boldness evince the huge sense of papal oppression and the difficulty that faithful Catholics, loyal to the Pope, are experiencing.

John Paul, for one, has not been in the least pacified by such ethical gymnastics. In fact, the postmillennial Vatican has seen an example of remarkable ingenuity in defense of the papal position. In the second week of October 2003, Cardinal Alfonso Lopez Trujillo, speaking for the Holy See's Council for the Family and therefore expressing the official view of John Paul on the question, declared that "serious scientific studies" had shown that the HIV virus could pass through latex rubber. He wanted governments around the world to put a health warning on condom packets stating that they were not safe. The HIV virus, he told a BBC program, "is roughly 450 times smaller than the spermatozoon" and "the spermatozoon can easily pass through the 'net' that is formed by the condom." This was the same Cardinal Trujillo who in 1999, again in the Pope's name, told a meeting of the Guild of Catholic Doctors in London that the concepts introduced at the United Nations conferences on population in Cairo in 1994 and on women in Beijing in 1995 had been an attempt to introduce "a new sort of morals," or a new "lifestyle," involving the "trivialization of sex" and the promotion of contraception. The "Battle of Cairo," as he called it, had been "the battle for authentic sexual education."

By questioning the issue of the efficacy of condoms, John Paul's spokesman for "life" issues had once again, and dangerously, laid the ground for confusion in countries where lack of education was a significant part of the AIDS problem, mixing purely pragmatic and scientific considerations with ethical principles. Was using condoms wrong because they did not work? Or was it wrong because they were intrinsically, ethically wrong? If they were proved to be efficacious, would John Paul then change his mind? Not at all: Cardinal Trujillo was combating condoms on both sets of arguments, and indeed a third, since by the summer of 2004 he was arguing that condoms caused AIDS since they promoted promiscuity and sex outside of marriage.

When he was interviewed by the BBC in October 2003, Trujillo stoutly stood his ground on the scientific and medical issue: Condoms don't work. Next, in December, he published a twenty-page document citing his expert sources.

Undaunted, the BBC's investigative unit Panorama checked Trujillo's experts. One after the other, on camera, the cardinal's sources evaporated. Trujillo's principal champion, Dr. Dave Lyttle, who had advised the U.S. government on the efficacy of condoms, denied that his research could be used to reach the Vatican conclusion. He had written that in a test on 470 condoms, only 2.6 percent allowed "one virus at the most" to penetrate, a statistic that Trujillo had seized upon to bolster his argument. But this amounted, Lyttle said, to a "minuscule" risk in relation to the transmission of the HIV/AIDS virus. His data had been "misused" by the Vatican, he went on. Beyond all the obligatory scientific qualifications, he had concluded that the latex of condoms was "essentially impermeable."

The experts lined up to contradict the cardinal, as well they might: The Vatican statement threatened to undo years of investment in teaching safe sex to combat the disease. Penelope Hitchcock, former head of the U.S. condom-efficacy task force, declared that the Church's stance on condoms was "very detrimental to our controlling the epidemic." Dr. Catherine Hankins, chief scientific adviser to the United Nations agency UNAids, confirmed that "latex condoms are impermeable. They do prevent HIV transmission." She also accused the cardinal of disseminating misinformation. Dr. Rachel Baggaley, an HIV specialist for Christian Aid, insisted that consistent and correct condom use cut risk of infection by 90 percent. She added, so as to throw some much-needed realism into the argument, that some 13,000 people become HIV positive each day, mostly in developing countries. "More than half of these are young people under twenty-four—in many countries, a third of boys and girls are sexually active before the age of fifteen."

For good measure, South Africa's foremost group of AIDS activists, Treatment Action Campaign, criticized the Pope's opposition to condoms. "The Church's irrational stance on condoms," said the campaign's chief, Nathan Geffen, "undermines the very good work that it does with regards to caring for people with HIV." Meanwhile, the president of the international council for Médecins Sans Frontières (Doctors Without Borders), Morten Rostrup, has stated that the Catholic Church is now part of the problem. To counsel the rejection of condoms, he said, "was totally unacceptable from a moral, ethical, and medical perspective . . . the ban was helping the spread of a deadly disease." Finally, the World Health Organization confirmed yet again what most experts accepted: that condoms could reduce the risk of infection by 90 percent.

The astonishing feature of John Paul's anticondoms campaign has been the lack of public dissent among the bishops, even though many bishops disagree with him privately. The situation indicates, again, how the strengthening of the center debilitates and weakens the Church's periphery. By 2004, however, there were at last signs of a break in the ranks. In January, Cardinal Archbishop Godfried Daneels of Belgium, well liked by progressives, spoke his mind. Questioned about safe sex and AIDS, he said, "When someone is HIV-infected and his partner says, 'I want to have sexual relations with you,' I would say, do not do it," Daneels said. "But if he does it all the same, he should use a condom. Otherwise, he adds a sin against the fifth commandment, 'Thou shalt not kill,' to a sin against the sixth, 'Thou shalt not commit adultery.'" He went on to say: "It is a matter of prevention to protect oneself against a disease or against death. You cannot judge that morally to be on the same level as using a condom as a method of birth control."

Just one other bishop came out on the question in 2004. Speaking to an audience of academics and clerics at Boston College, Kevin Dowling, bishop of Rustenburg in South Africa, said there were many women in Botswana, where 39 percent of the population was HIV positive, who turned to prostitution as the only alternative to starvation. "We're at risk of losing entire nations to this disease," he said. Known as the AIDS bishop, Dowling had been giving his audience an impression of the extent of the problem, materially and morally. In these circumstances, the Pope's ban on condoms was what he termed a "death-dealing code." In the discussion that followed, Margaret Farley, a Yale University ethicist and campaigner for African women suffering from AIDS, told the audience: "Many African women have very little choice in the exercise of their sexuality. If, for example, a husband wants sex, wives are expected to respond, even if the husband is infected. It seems to make utter sense what Bishop Dowling is saying, to allow and even encourage condoms not as a contraceptive but as an instrument to prevent the spread of disease." Bishop Dowling then said something that constituted a profound rebuttal of the papal stand against safe sex, implicit in John Paul's *Theology of the Body:* "We need to affirm the sacredness of life in the poorest of the poor. What concrete action can we offer as a way out of this misery? To present an impossible ideal is worse than useless, because it creates a sense of hopelessness." He went on: "In its heart, the Church not only pronounces a series of 'no's' to certain types of behavior, but especially proposes a lifestyle that is wholly insignificant for the person." While acknowledging that AIDS was associated with the "phenomena of drug addiction and abuse of sexuality," he insisted that "the necessary prevention against the threat of AIDS is not inspired by fear but instead by the choice of a healthy, free, and responsible lifestyle."

While the Pope congratulated himself for the Church's efforts to care for the victims of AIDS and continued to counsel against condoms in any circumstances, a failure to empathize, to listen, and to take action had been occurring in another dimension of the AIDS crisis.

In 1994, Sister Maura O'Donohue, a qualified physician and member of the Medical Missionaries of Mary, was completing a shocking presentation for the consideration of appropriate Vatican authorities. It concerned a scandal involving the abuse of nuns, mainly in Africa. Sister Maura had spent six years as an AIDS coordinator for the London-based Catholic Fund for Overseas Development. Her report alleged that Catholic clergy in twenty-nine countries were sexually abusing nuns, treating communities as if they were harems for their exclusive use. The background to the scandal was the AIDS pandemic and the belief that virgins were a prophylactic against the disease. Nuns were thus invariably infected by priests in the belief that they would be cured by having sexual relations with them. In one instance, a priest had impregnated a nun, then encouraged her to have an abortion: She died of the procedure and he was a celebrant at her requiem Mass. There were stories of infected nuns leaving their communities and ending up as prostitutes on the streets.

Sister Maura's report was in fact one of several written by women of various religious orders, but it was one of the earliest. Her report landed on the desk of Cardinal Eduardo Martinez, prefect of the Vatican congregation for religious life, on February 18, 1995. Where it sat.

Sister Maura had written:

> Sadly, the sisters also report that priests have sexually exploited them because they too had come to fear contamination with HIV by sexual contact with prostitutes and other "at risk" women . . .
> For example, a superior of a community of sisters in one country was approached by priests requesting that sisters would be made available to them for sexual favors. When the superior refused,

the priests explained that they would otherwise be obliged to go to the village to find women, and might thus get AIDS.

Donohue wrote that her first reaction was "shock and disbelief," but she soon discovered that the problem was one of great magnitude, as she continued to encounter instances through her contacts in a number of countries. She informed the cardinal: "The enormous challenges which AIDS poses for members of religious orders and the clergy is only now becoming evident."

The story that she told Cardinal Martinez was hardly new to him. Another file on his desk related to a case in which a local bishop in Africa had dismissed a complaint by a women's congregation claiming that some thirty sisters had been impregnated by diocesan priests. Sister Maura informed the cardinal: "Groups of sisters from local congregations have made passionate appeals for help to members of international congregations and explain that, when they themselves try to make representations to church authorities about harassment by priests, they simply are not heard."

Four years after Donohue's report, which yielded no action on the part of the Vatican, another report arrived at the Vatican from Sister Marie McDonald of the Missionaries of Our Lady of Africa. The document was titled: "The Problem of the Sexual Abuse of African Religious in Africa and Rome."

Sister McDonald's report stated that "sexual harassment and even rape of sisters by priests and bishops is allegedly common" and that "sometimes when a sister becomes pregnant, the priest insists that she have an abortion." Her report referred to cases mostly in Africa and to African sisters, priests, and bishops, but she claimed that "the problem exists elsewhere too." She added that when a sister became pregnant she was usually punished by dismissal from the congregation, whereas the priest was "often only moved to another parish—or sent for studies."

Among five separate reports brought to the attention of the Vatican in the mid- to late 1990s, one included an account by a Father

Robert J. Vitillo, working for Caritas, and currently the executive director of the U.S. Bishops' Campaign for Human Development. In 1994, Vitillo told a gathering at Boston College that nuns in Africa had routinely been abused by clergy who had frequented prostitutes:

> The last ethical issue which I find especially delicate but necessary to mention involves the need to denounce sexual abuse, which has arisen as a specific result of HIV/AIDS. In many parts of the world, men have decreased their reliance on commercial sex workers because of their fear of contracting HIV . . . As a result of this widespread fear, many men (and some women) have turned to young (and therefore presumably uninfected) girls (and boys) for sexual favors. Religious women have also been targeted by such men, and especially by clergy who may have previously frequented prostitutes. I myself have heard the tragic stories of religious women who were forced to have sex with the local priest or with a spiritual counselor who insisted that this was "good" for both of them.

Father Vitillo then came to the issue that underscores the point of relating this appalling tale in a portrait of John Paul II. "Frequently, attempts to raise these issues with local and international Church authorities have met with deaf ears," he said. "In North America and in some parts of Europe, our Church is already reeling under the pedophilia scandals. How long will it take for this same institutional Church to become sensitive to these new abuse issues which are resulting from the pandemic?"

Yet while the Pope and his leading Vatican officials responsible for sexual ethics continued to expound the evil of contraceptives, nothing was done to redress the abuse of young sisters who had committed themselves to the religious life.

The *National Catholic Reporter* finally declared on March 16, 2001, that the Vatican had been receiving information about the scandal over a period of seven years. A follow-up piece by Marco Politi appeared in *La Repubblica.* Only then did the Vatican, for the first time, acknowledge the problem of sexual abuse of nuns by priests. The Pope's spokesperson, Navarro-Valls, issued a statement on March 20, 2001:

> The problem is known, and is restricted to a geographically limited area. The Holy See is dealing with the question in collaboration with the bishops with the Union of Superiors General and with the International Union of Superiors General. The work has two sides, the formation of persons and the solution of single cases. Certain negative situations cannot cause to be forgotten the frequently heroic fidelity of the great majority of male religious, female religious, and priests.

The reaction is familiar: minimizing the problem while indulging in self-congratulation as if in mitigation of responsibility. As of the time of this writing, three years on, there has been no information forthcoming from the Vatican about measures taken to eliminate abuse of nuns by Catholic clergy, nor the measures it proposes to implement to secure justice for the women who have been abused.

As a result of the information made available through the *National Catholic Reporter,* some sixty Catholic organizations have set up a campaign titled A Call to Accountability. Among its declarations, the campaign stated: "That this sexual violence occurs in the context of the world AIDS pandemic is especially disturbing . . . Therefore, we condemn the hypocrisy of the Church policies that deny life-saving condoms and contraceptives, responsibly chosen by women." The campaign further stated: "We are appalled that Church authorities were formally and fully briefed on these problems in 1995 and up to now have taken no public action to end the abuse, treating the perpetrators with impunity. Vatican secrecy and inaction have surely contributed to sexual abuse. The Vatican must be accountable for these tragedies. Church officials must do all in their power to bring an end to violence against women in the Church."

CHAPTER THIRTY

Founding Fathers

As the Boston crisis broke in 2002, John Paul invoked religious mystification, as if to consign pedophile abuse to the realms of the powers of darkness beyond the veil of appearances. The papacy was behaving like a cargo cult, creating a make-believe haven adrift from reality, rather than seeing the problem for what it was and accepting the need for radical self-criticism.

The problem went right to the heart of the official Church, even into the papal apartment itself. The most remarkable case, within the ambit of John Paul's haven, involved a prominent priest in whom John Paul continued to place trust, and upon whom he bestowed honors, despite credible allegations of abuse by victims who had nothing to gain from their accusations except the consolation of justice delayed.

Standing accused of the serial abuse of seminarians was Father Marcial Maciel, the Mexican founder of the order Legionaries of Christ, born in 1920. Not only was Maciel allowed to evade due process of canon law (statutes of limitations have protected him from civil and criminal actions), but he was honored with tokens of special papal privilege after the accusations had been made. As in the case of the priests running harems of nuns for HIV-free sex in Africa, John Paul allowed the case of Maciel to gather dust for years within the Vatican.

The allegations concerning Father Marcial Maciel went back to the 1950s. Nine former members of the order went public with their accusations in 1997. They sent letters to the Pope and initiated a formal canon law process seeking Father Maciel's censure. Maciel dismissed the accusations as "defamations and falsities with no foundation whatsoever." The accusers, by now in their sixties, included two academics, a lawyer, and a former head of the Legion in the United States, Juan Vaca. They backed their allegations with sworn affidavits. Vaca reported that the abuse began when he was only ten years of age. The nine accusers alleged that Maciel led a double life of religious devotion during the day and taking boys, sometimes two at a time, to bed in the evenings. While Maciel has denied the charges, he has made no attempt to repudiate them by recourse to the law in any country, despite the detailed publication of the allegations in the book *Vows of Silence,* by two distinguished Catholic investigative reporters, Jason Berry and Gerald Renner.

The Legion, an organization specially favored by John Paul, is one of the world's fastest-growing orders, with more than 500 priests and 2,500 seminarians in 15 countries. Maciel has been praised by John Paul as an "efficacious guide to youth." The background to the case, which might go some way to explaining, if not endorsing, John Paul's indulgence, is the Pope's fondness for Catholic sects that emulate Protestant evangelical movements in their apparent self-denying energy, narrow-mindedness, and evangelical enthusiasm. In the run-up to the millennium, John Paul showed special warmth and encouragement toward the Church groups that operate outside the authority of bishops and parishes, professing direct allegiance to the Pope, constantly citing and expounding papal documents and homilies. There is a link, moreover, between the culture of these movements and John Paul's conviction that sexual instincts can be conquered, and purity of heart and body maintained, by a breezy optimistic self-discipline akin to athleticism. Members of the groups are enthusiasts for mass gatherings, chanting, flag waving, and sporting distinctive T-shirts and headgear. On the eve of the third millennium, John Paul greeted an assembly of some sixty affiliated movements on Pentecost Sunday in St. Peter's Square, confirming them in their charisms and declaring that they were "a reply raised up by the Holy Spirit to the dramatic challenge of the new millennium."

In Rome, Legionaries operated under a mission statement that, like that of the lay movements, was based on the conviction that the world is sinking into a morass of hedonism, materialism, and sexual permissiveness. The view was expounded, and found echoes, in the repeated pronouncements of the Holy Father. The Legionaries, who spend fifteen years in highly disciplined formation, are young men who go into battle against the world, giving their all in unquestioning self-sacrifice to God. Whereas most pontifical colleges and universities had taken to wearing lay casual clothes, the Legionaries of Christ were wearing cassocks and Roman collars in the streets, looking for all the world like young Pacelli look-alikes. A directive insisted that they should all, without exception, part their hair on the left side. Whereas the members of many of the national colleges would be out at night drinking in local bars, the Legionaries would stay within their compound to pray and study.

Maciel, the founder, was suspended from his leadership of the order for two years following the 1950s allegations. An investigation was conducted by the Vatican, but no evidence was found against him. He was reinstated in 1958 at just the time when Pius XII died. Students interviewed during the investigation of Maciel recently claimed that they lied during the first investigation out of fear of the founder. The phenomenon of victims covering up for pedophiles was all too common during a period when the laity was overawed by the clergy and accepted that it was wrong to cause scandal.

The allegations of abuse, made against Maciel in the 1950s based on the sworn evidence of nine witnesses, were eventually published in the mid-1990s in the *Hartford Courant,* a respected U.S. daily paper. America's *National Catholic Reporter* also ran the stories, and in 2004, the *New York Review of Books* ran a piece by Garry Wills reviewing *Vows of Silence.* The accusers were not seeking damages and insisted that they were going public only because the Vatican had failed to act on their just complaints. The Legion has to date taken no steps to litigate against the various parties bringing the accusations.

The account of Jason Berry and Gerald Renner depicted a tale of the sacred and the depraved. Until the scandals erupted across America in 2002, such lurid overlaps of contradiction stretched credulity. The stories have become so routine now as to be banal, although this does not necessarily make them true.

Maciel founded the Legionaries in his native Mexico in 1941 after he had been sacked from two seminaries in Mexico as unsuited to a priestly vocation (he found another seminary and was eventually ordained). He was given exactly thirty minutes to leave one of these institutions. Nevertheless, aged only twenty-one, and with little education, he founded a school for junior seminarians in Cuernevaca, undertaking to teach them. An unusual requirement for becoming one of his Legionaries was the adoption of a vow of silence that effectively banned members from criticizing the founder or talking to outsiders about any aspect of the order. By 1950, having started a study center in Rome, Maciel declared that he had been received by Pius XII in private audience and given official encouragement. No record of this endorsement exists, but it was given ample credit by Maciel's benefactors and students.

Maciel's life from those early beginnings has been a picaresque tale of Chaucerian proportions: Now he is depicted engaged in edifying self-denials and marathons of prayer; next he is leaping from Concorde flights onto helicopters. Living in great personal poverty, he is at home in the drawing rooms of the superrich. His congregation and its style of religiosity struck a chord in young men sufficient to attract recruits by the hundreds when most other orders, and the diocesan priesthood, had only defections. But that was not all: The Legionaries, inspired by their leader Father Maciel, were engaged in good works the world over.

By 1990, the order was administering 98 religious communities and admission centers in 15 different countries; it ran more than 80 schools, 10 universities, and 640 lay training centers. At least 65,000 students were enrolled in Legionary institutions. The Pontifical Athenaeum, or university under the direct protection of the Pope in Rome, "Regina Apostolorum," has 356 students from 36 countries. In addition, the lay affiliates in a movement called Regnum Christi (Kingdom of Christ) has 45,000 members around the world. The movement has distributed some $40 million worth of food aid and built some 238 churches and chapels in the past quarter century. By any criterion, this is an impressive accomplishment at a time when churches, schools, and presbyteries have been closing in developed countries, and Europe especially. But what price this whirlwind of energizing evangelization when, sitting on a shelf in a Vatican office at the turn of the millennium 2000, were the reports of nine men, former seminarians and priests, charging Marcial Maciel with sexual abuse? The charges were significant precisely because John Paul believed that the Legionary style of spirituality and discipline was the answer not only to the "culture of death" with which the world was seized but also the phenomenon of pedophile priests. To accept that Maciel may have been as guilty as any of those charged in places like Boston and New Orleans would be to undermine the conviction prevailing from the top down in the Vatican: that old-style disciplines, the cloisters, cassocks, and cummerbunds of both mind as well as body were the answer to priestly abuse.

But now to the allegations as related by Berry and Renner. At the junior seminary in Ontaneda, Spain, founded by Father Maciel (known to his seminarians as Nuestro Padre, Our Father), there was a student, Fernando Perez, age fourteen in 1949. Perez has stated that he was made to sleep on a mattress in Maciel's bedroom for a month. Then one night, Maciel "was lying in bed, naked, covered with a blanket, writhing in pain. He told me to massage his stomach." This led to an act of sexual abuse. According to Perez, Maciel also seduced Perez's younger brother, Jose Antonio Perez Olvera. According to Fernando, Maciel explained that he had been advised by his doctor to release a buildup of semen. A third student in the Spanish seminary, Alejandro Espinosa, was frequently called to the room of Nuestro Padre. "It was very repulsive to me, but I believed my problem was nothing compared to his. I had to be brave . . . I considered myself like a nurse and accepted as a great distinction that he trusted me." A fourth student, Saul Barrales Arellano, resisted Maciel's advances, but he "asked me to manipulate him sexually five or ten times and I refused." Another testimony, published in *Newsweek,* comes from Jose Barba, who was a student, eighteen years of age at the time, at Maciel's college in Rome. He was invited to Maciel's room, where he was informed by Nuestro Padre that Pius XII had given special permission for students to masturbate him. Masturbation and mutual masturbation practices, Barba has charged, were alternated with drug injections of Demerol. Then there was Arturo Jurado, who claims that he both masturbated and injected Nuestro Padre with drugs. "He taught me and forced me to masturbate him. I got an order from a holy man and I obeyed that order without any question. Maciel told them that King David had a lady in the Bible. David called for her to sleep with him; therefore, it was okay to sleep with Maciel."

After one of the key accusers, Juan Amenabar, died in 1995, the others, who had come to his funeral, decided to take their case to Rome under a process of canon law. The statute of limitations had run out, but there was no limit on a provision in canon law known as "complicit absolution," which involves a priest absolving in confession a person with whom he had committed a sin. The circumstance is a sacrilege punishable with excommunication. Accusers had said that they had been obliged to confess to Maciel sexual acts they performed with him.

A Vatican canon lawyer named Martha Wegan agreed to present the case to the appropriate tribunal in Cardinal Ratzinger's Congregation for the Doctrine of the Faith in Rome. In 1998, three of the accusers went to Rome to present the case to one of Ratzinger's secretaries. But they were warned that they should never breathe a word to the media. They agreed not to speak to the press, but the story eventually, and inevitably, leaked. Six years on, at the time of this writing, there has been no Vatican response to their allegations.

At a time when a priest could be suspended as a result of a twenty-five-year-old allegation of inappropriate fondling (as in the case of the distinguished priest Father Michael Hollings in London), Marcial Maciel, because of the favor he finds with the Holy Father, is given the benefit of the doubt. Indeed, John Paul continued to extend him special privileges after the allegations were made.

Of the various responses to this tale of alleged depravity, one is worth noting insofar as it represents a view so closely associated with John Paul as to give a reliable indication of his thinking on the matter. It also answers definitively and in the affirmative the question as to whether John Paul was aware of the charges against Father Maciel. Father Richard John Neuhaus, editor in chief of *First Things* and close friend of John Paul II, awarded himself ample space in his periodical to deliver a lengthy verdict on the Maciel case and John Paul's view of the matter. He began with the familiar comment that the pedophile priest crisis is no more than a symptom of the greed of alleged victims and their lawyers: "Stories about Catholic priests have a certain cachet—and, for trial lawyers, a promise of cash—that is usually lacking in other cases." He then proceeded to opine that even were there any truth in the charges against Maciel, "what can you do to an eighty-two-year-old priest who has been so successful in building a movement of renewal and is strongly supported and repeatedly praised by, among many others, Pope John Paul II?" So praise from the Pope of itself creates amnesty even for crimes of sexual abuse that could result in prison sentences.

But there is something you can do, after all, he continues: "By destroying the reputation of the order's founder you can try to discredit what Catholics call the founding 'charism' of the movement, thus undermining support for the Legionaries of Christ." In other words, the scandal of Father Maciel is not about the charges of sexual abuse but the spiteful aggression of liberal Catholics against the good works of Father Maciel.

Next, Father Neuhaus informs us that he is impressed by the words of Jesus that "by their fruits you shall know them." He has known the Legion for some years and has a high regard for it. More to the personal point, he tells us that he himself has taught in their institutions—clear evidence, we are to take it, of the goodness of their fruit. Strangely, there is no hint that 11,000 victims of priestly abuse of minors in fifty years also indicates a fruit of a very bitter kind.

Now, Father Neuhaus proceeds, he has examined the "endless"

material and, exasperated, has cut to the chase. He has sought the opinion, he tells us, of an unnamed cardinal "in whom I have unbounded confidence and who has been involved in the case who tells me that the charges are 'pure invention, without the slightest foundation.'" In consequence, "I have arrived at a *moral certainty* that the charges are false and malicious." What is moral certainty, one might ask, and how is it acquired? "Moral certainty," he asserts, "is achieved by considering the evidence in the light of the Eighth Commandment, thou shall not bear false witness against your neighbour."

Then he comes to the nub of the whole matter: the reason Father Maciel has not had to answer the allegations of past students against him. "It counts as evidence," he concludes, "that Pope John Paul II, who almost certainly is aware of the charges, has strongly, consistently, and publicly praised Fr. Maciel and the Legion."

Thus, Father Neuhaus unwittingly puts his finger precisely on the responsibility that John Paul shares in the priestly sexual abuse scandal. Father Maciel is innocent because the Holy Father has discerned him to be so, just as the Holy Father judged most of the accused priests to be innocent earlier in the crisis. Hence, there was no need of investigation, no need of self-questioning, no need for apologies, and, above all, no need for change.

Father Neuhaus and his party, however, would adopt a strikingly different attitude of mind when it came to the issue of whether the Church should support the preemptive invasion of Iraq. The unerring discernment of the Pope, it seemed, would have strict limits when the *First Things* coterie decided otherwise.

John Paul and the Iraq War

As the United States and Britain continued to amass troops and military equipment in Kuwait through January 2003 for the threatened invasion of Iraq, John Paul made his thoughts and feelings known on the looming war. On the first day of the year, World Day of Peace, he anticipated the fortieth anniversary of his predecessor John XXIII's encyclical *Pacem in Terris* (*Peace on Earth*). It was as if he was steadying himself to withstand an onslaught of war rhetoric. Once again, he invoked a Pope of the past to sustain his papal vision. "Looking at the present and into the future with eyes of faith and reason," he wrote, "Blessed John XXIII discerned deeper currents at work than international experts of his day."

Although John Paul had made sympathetic declarations for the American victims following the 9/11 attacks, he was not in a mood to budge on his insistence that an invasion of Iraq would be a disaster and wrong. He had come to the same verdict twelve years earlier when Bush Senior and the coalition had invaded Iraq. And he said as much during the attacks on Afghanistan in 2001.

In the second week of January, against a background of frenzied diplomatic activity in the UN and around the Western capitals, John

Paul, addressing his nuncios and the ambassadors to the Holy See, declared: "War is never just another means that one can choose to employ for settling differences between nations." He had sympathetic words for Iraq's hard-pressed people. War, he said, could "strike the people of Iraq, the land of the prophets, a people already sorely tried by more than twelve years of embargo."

Appealing to the United Nations Charter and international law, he said that war could only be decided upon as a "very last option and in accordance with very strict conditions." Which was to say that while he was not a purist pacifist, the conditions for a just war did not obtain in this case. U.S. Defense Secretary Donald Rumsfeld might well have been irritated by this judgment, since the 1991 invasion had the full backing of the UN and had met every criterion for a just war based on the principles of Saints Augustine and Thomas Aquinas—yet John Paul had still denounced it.

As he reached his peroration before the diplomats, John Paul somewhat undermined his argument by making a rambling plea against abortion and the culture of death. Countries should have the courage to say "no to death," and especially for "unborn children; all that weakens the family; all that destroys in children their respect for themselves and others; to everything that makes people protect themselves inside a social or cultural cocoon." Finally, he had harsh words for the lifestyle of the prosperous, making special mention of "the problem of water resources." All of which were important causes, but their inclusion blurred somewhat the focus of his message about the coming war.

The American bishops had been solidly with John Paul against a decision to attack Iraq. The U.S. Conference of Catholic Bishops, speaking as one, pronounced that the war did not and "would not meet the strict conditions of Catholic teaching for the use of military force." Cardinal Pio Laghi, moreover, who had made the journey to Washington, D.C., to plead with President Bush against an invasion, said that there was "great unity on this grave matter on the part of the Holy See, the bishops in the United States, and the church throughout the world." That unity, however, was wishful thinking. John Paul's main promoters in the United States, both lay and clerical, including the *First Things* coterie and Deal Hudson of *Crisis*, were adamant that such a war was not only just but "a moral obligation."

Professor Michael Novak, winner of the Templeton Award for Progress in Religion, who had proved influential with the Pope on the issue of capitalism in the previous decade, flew into Rome to carry the debate to the heart of the Eternal City by giving a public lecture on the American case for war. He was the guest of the U.S. ambassador to the Holy See, and former Republican national chairman, Jim Nicholson. Novak's arguments drove a formation of tanks through John Paul's plea.

The war, Novak told a mixed audience of diplomats, prelates, and theologians, was "a lawful conclusion to the just war fought and swiftly won in February 1991." At the peace table, he pointed out, the UN had insisted that as a condition of his continuation in his presidency, Saddam must disarm and provide proof that he had disarmed, accounting for his weapons of mass destruction. "During the next twelve years, despite constant warnings," said Novak, "Saddam Hussein brazenly flouted all these obligations." He went on to talk of Security Council obligations ignored, and the launching of "asymmetrical warfare" against the United States, aided and abetted by Iraq and other countries in the Middle East that sponsored international terror.

In an explicit swipe at armchair ethicists, which clearly included His Holiness, Novak pointed out that the new *Catechism of the Catholic Church* recognized that primary responsibility for waging war resided not with "distant commentators" but with the appropriate responsible public authorities.

Here was a strange situation. In recent years, Novak, Neuhaus, and Weigel had routinely denounced any critic of the papal viewpoint as "megalomaniac." Now, it seemed, they allowed themselves the privilege of choosing which papal pronouncements and viewpoints were to be unquestioningly accepted and which not.

Invoking subsidiarity, Novak declared that only authorities closest to the facts of the case could take responsibility for going to war,
for only these authorities were "privy to highly restricted intelligence." That argument posed a remarkable hostage to fortune, since
Novak was hardly privy to such intelligence either. The intelligence
claims, as we now know, evaporated within a year. All the same,
Novak lent a Catholic voice to a review of just-war theories in the
light of terror attacks involving mass murder, such as occurred on
9/11, and the insistence that rogue states that were in the business of
acquiring weapons of mass destruction must be checked by preemptive strikes. Cardinal Ratzinger had dismissed the notion of preven-
tive war, which "does not appear in the *Catechism of the Catholic
Church*." But Novak might well have responded that flying civilian
aircraft into skyscrapers to kill thousands of innocent people, and
planning terror attacks with chemical, biological, and nuclear
weapons, did not appear in the catechism either.

John XXIII's *Pacem in Terris* was influenced by the long course of
the Cold War, whereas John Paul was influenced by the nonviolent
revolution in Eastern Europe and the Soviet Union, profoundly
reinforcing his conviction that there were means other than war
of resolving conflict. Michael Novak and his associates could
hardly be blamed for insisting that the world had changed drastically
since September 11, and the nature of war—"asymmetrical warfare"—with it. But that was hardly the point. The point was to bring
pressure on the Vatican, and thereby the Holy Father, to give a
moral boost to the Bush administration's plan to bring down
Saddam Hussein.

John Paul, however, was looking back across the centuries to no
less an authority than St. Augustine, the patron of just-war theorists,
in defense of nonviolence. St. Augustine wrote: "It is a higher glory
still to stay war itself with a word than to slay men with the sword,
and to maintain peace by peace, not by war." It was St. Augustine
who invoked the norms of the just war: just cause, legitimate
authority, and right intention. But the Church had added and refined

other considerations in the Middle Ages: proportionality and the prospect of success and reduction of collateral damage.

John Paul was not only securely within Catholic tradition in seeking restraint in early 2003, but he was in line with popular opinion in Europe and South America, which vociferously questioned the principle of "right intention" and, in view of Bush's jaundiced attitude toward the UN, the issue of "legitimate authority." But the shock of 9/11 within the homeland made all the difference. The American people did not share these views.

In March 2003, the Vatican's assertion that the Church stood together against the war was contradicted by opinion polls showing that Catholics in the United States favored a unilateral attack on Iraq by two to one. That Catholics should pick and choose the lead taken by the Supreme Pontiff and, indeed, all the nation's bishops, should not have been a matter for surprise. After all, Catholics in America, as elsewhere, had become accustomed to ignoring official papal teaching on matters such as contraception. There was also the influence of Novak, Neuhaus, and Weigel, who, through the amplification of the right-wing Catholic media, had substantial reach in America.

Meanwhile, John Paul had decided to engage in some diplomacy of his own, unaware perhaps that he was about to throw some incendiary ingredients into the pot. In mid-February, he dispatched to Baghdad Cardinal Roger Etchegaray, a French Basque and retired head of the Holy See's Council for Justice and Peace. Etchegary had turned eighty-one in 2003. He told journalists: "The Pope is not resigned to war. He has decided to go to the extreme limits of hope, and I am his messenger." Well-meaning, if doddery, the good cardinal revealed a certain lack of realism when he reported that Saddam had listened "long and deeply" to the papal appeal for peace.

But the visit carried a nasty quid pro quo. While Etchegaray was journeying to Iraq, the prime minister of Iraq, the owlish Tariq Aziz, well-known to TV viewers the world over for his cynical double-talk during the Iraqi invasion of Kuwait, was flying to Rome to visit John Paul. John Paul had greeted Aziz on three previous occasions through the mid- to late 1990s, heeding Saddam's plea that sanctions should be dropped against the country. Aziz announced at the airport that he had come to the Holy See to appeal to the Pope in person to help mobilize "all the forces of good against the forces of evil." In a sanctimonious mood (he presents himself as a Catholic), Aziz said: "Everyone who believes in peace and justice, everyone who believes in God, Christian and Muslim, is against this aggression." He was also granted meetings with Secretary of State Angelo Sodano and Jean-Louis Tauran, Secretary for Relations with States. Thus, John Paul dignified Saddam at a time when moral censure of the regime might have brought more pressure upon him. Was John Paul thinking clearly?

At a press conference in Rome's Foreign Press Office afterward, an Israeli correspondent asked Aziz if Iraq would attack Israel in the event of an invasion by America. Aziz instantly became his more familiar poisonous self, responding that he would not have entered the room had he known that a Jew would be present—which provoked spirited boos from the rest of the Vatican and Rome press corps. The Israeli, Menachem Gantz, left the room, whereupon a French reporter repeated the question. "We do not," said Aziz primly, "have the means to attack any country beyond our territory." The exchange with Gantz prompted the mayor of Rome to cancel his meeting with Aziz forthwith.

The Iraqi minister now proceeded in the posture of a pious pilgrim to Assisi to pray at the shrine of St. Francis. On his knees, he listened as a Franciscan priest read the Prayer of St. Francis, which begins: "Lord, make me an instrument of your peace." Then he was handed the "Lamp of Peace," which had been lit by the leaders of world religions the previous January.

Those who knew Aziz better, including Iraqis in exile, protested that the Franciscan friars had been exploited. Afterward, Aziz declared that Saddam Hussein was "a father for his people, who trust in him."

The following week, the British prime minister, Tony Blair, went in to see John Paul and received a sharp pep-talk in contrast to the benign papal reception accorded Aziz. Blair was told of the "special consideration to be given to the Iraqi people, already severely tried by long years of embargo."

On the eve of hostilities, March 16, John Paul spoke animatedly of the "responsibility before God" of war leaders. He said that he did not believe in peace at any price but felt bound to remind the world of the "great, very great responsibility" that world leaders faced.

As the hostilities began in mid-March, John Paul, unmoved by Michael Novak's best efforts to influence the Vatican, condemned the coalition attack. The outbreak of hostilities affected John Paul deeply. Speaking to the personnel of the Catholic television station Telepace (Telepeace), he said, "Peace is the only way to construct a more just and solid society. Violence and arms can never resolve human problems." On the first Sunday of the war, speaking from his office window over St. Peter's Square at the noon Angelus, he prayed to the Virgin Mary for the gift of peace. His speech was blurred, he was barely audible, and he sounded desperately tired.

In the United States, the bishops stood by their original opposition to the war, although they distanced themselves from the opinion of Bishop John Michael Botean of Canton, Ohio, who declared that it was a mortal sin to fight against Iraqis. By the end of March, an American survey by Pew Forum revealed that the United States had never gone to war with so little support from its religious leaders, nor had its religious leaders made so little impression on public opinion. Some 60 percent of the population, the survey claimed, supported the war.

❋

It was not in John Paul's character smugly to inform those who opposed him, "I told you so." But as the year wore on, and after military victory, and as the coalition began to face the onslaughts of insurgents, he might well have pondered the accuracy of his forecasts: that war would be counterproductive, that civilians would suffer greatly, that global terror would be further incited. Angelo Sodano, his Secretary of State, had even gone as far as to draw parallels with Vietnam.

Yet after a long period of virtual silence on Iraq, John Paul and his close aides were inclined to moderate their comments on the occupation despite a horrific attack on Italian troops. In mid-November, a truck bomb exploded outside the Italian army HQ in Nasiriya, killing nineteen soldiers. The attack was all the more tragic because the troops were on policing and training tasks rather than offensive military operations. John Paul joined the Italian bishops in referring to the attack as "wicked work." When a single bishop expressed disgust at the "sanctification" of the Italian military effort in Iraq, he was hauled up before appropriate Vatican cardinals and roundly rebuked.

During the period of national mourning that followed the deaths, there were street demonstrations and widespread insistence that the Italians should be recalled. But Cardinal Camillo Ruini, papal vicar of Rome and president of the Italian Bishops Conference, declared that there should be no withdrawal of Italian troops from their "great and noble mission." When he was asked whether these were soldiers who had died in an unjust war, he said: "They are victims of terrorism, pure and simple."

As the situation grew more grim in Iraq, the Vatican assumed a calm and realistic front. John Paul may well have been thinking how much worse the war might have gone. Speaking to *America* magazine, a high but unattributable Vatican source said: "The Vatican clearly said 'no' to the war. But at a certain point, you have to manage the situation that has been created in the way that does the least damage. If the military pulls out of Iraq now, the country would fall into chaos. The vase had been broken, and we have to try to find a way to mend it. Of course, there is the problem that the more deeply one becomes involved in this project, the greater the tendency to justify that involvement."

CHAPTER THIRTY-TWO

John Paul's Decline

I t was late September 2003, and John Paul had just returned from Slovakia. He had been accompanied on that trip by two doctors, one of whom was a cardiologist. There were oxygen cylinders on board the plane, a defibrillator, and blood in case a transfusion was needed. On returning to Rome, he immediately departed for Naples in a cramped helicopter for an exhausting pastoral visit. On his return, he went straight up to his summer residence at Castel Gandolfo.

The next day, in the midst of a torrid heat wave, the corridors of the Vatican and the Roman restaurants favored by the Curia were buzzing with consternation. The Holy Father had suffered a stomach blockage in the night and Dr. Buzzonetti had been called out. The word was that he had stomach cancer. That day he issued a decree, apparently from his bed, bringing forward the nomination of thirty-one new cardinals by six months: Most of them would be of an age to vote at the next papal election. He was evidently, once again, preparing to embark on his last great papal journey, and leaving nothing to chance in ensuring the security of his vision for the future of the Catholic Church. At supper with me that night, Monsignor Sotto Voce was inclined to dwell rather salaciously on the details of the Pope's condition. The BBC, I was told by the corporation's Rome correspondent, David Willey, had dispatched eighty journalists to Rome in the expectation that he would be dead within a week.

Yet once again, it was a false alarm. Once again, John Paul upset expectations of his imminent demise by rising from his bed and carrying on. A week or so after the scare, having beatified Mother Teresa and greeted the thirty-one new cardinals at a lengthy Mass, he was presiding once more at his public Wednesday audience in the open air in St. Peter's Square. Monsignor Sotto Voce had obtained for me a special pass so I was able to sit just a few feet from the Pope for more than an hour.

I was mesmerized by his frailty. His body was slumped, and he was looking out at the world wonderingly, as if he had just returned from the dead. It had suddenly gotten cold, and he was swaddled in his ample scarlet cloak to fend off a treacherous wind swirling about the vastness of the square. Occasionally, he raised his good right hand to dab his mouth with a handkerchief; occasionally, that hand rose to his skullcap to save it from being whipped off by a sudden freezing blast. The other hand, given to uncontrollable tremors, lay hidden.

I was fascinated that day by the ever-increasing ingenuity of John Paul's mobility engineers. He was deposited by hydraulic mini-elevator from his Popemobile onto the dais, then wheeled a few yards by papal aides to face the faithful. Whereupon the tiny wheels beneath his high-tech chair rose slowly out of sight, lowering the plinth that now formed the base to the papal throne firmly onto the dais. With the weary ripeness of an outpatient stranded on a hospital corridor, he was gazing out upon the city and the world as if to say: "How much longer!" You could feel huge waves of pity from the crowd, who could see him clearly, even far back, on the enormous TV screens placed at intervals through the square. Yet strange things happened, despite the atmosphere of reverence and respect. The cell phone of the woman sitting next to me went off and—just a few feet from the Pope—she started up a loud conversation about a shopping trip. A prelate was glaring at her, but she took no notice. I was also astounded to see a man in a black leather coat lighting up a cigarette.

Following the scare at the end of September, talk of John Paul's resignation was now rife, even at the level of cardinals. The Japanese Cardinal Stephen Fumio Hamao had declared to the media that the Pope should resign.

*

It had been a punishing year. In May, he had traveled to Spain, where he was greeted as "El Torero" (The Bullfighter), the highest compliment a Spaniard can pay anyone, let alone a foreign Pope. At an air-force base outside Madrid, he addressed 500,000 young people, declaring in the sweltering heat that Europe was a "lighthouse" for the world. "Ideas," he thundered, "should not be imposed, but proposed." Not for nothing was he presenting himself as the liberal Pope. Spain was a country that had had its bellyful of dogmatism: Church attendance had dropped from 23 percent in 1998 to 18 percent in 2002. The following month, he was off to Croatia—also a Catholic country where church attendance is plummeting—his third visit to the Mediterranean Balkan country and his one hundredth foreign visit in total. He preached, dressed in heavy robes, in temperatures of 100 degrees F. Once he asked for prayers not only in life but after his soon-to-be-expected death. Then there was Slovakia.

He seemed to bask that autumn day in Rome amid waves of affection and sympathy: This, it seemed, was how he would be remembered, the evangelist, traveling in old age and sickness to the ends of the earth, to the very last. His prayers in public, halting and barely audible, were now focused on the sick, the senile, and the plight of children. He had become a living symbol of the consolations of religion in the face of helplessness and debilitating illness. This man, who once evoked admiration for his handsome looks and energy, betrayed not a scintilla of embarrassment in his broken state. He was demonstrating that courageous acceptance of old age and sickness are in themselves an ennobling sermon to the world.

But to what extent was he still in charge by late 2003? To what extent was he sustaining a visible presence by medicinal cocktails and pontifical smoke and mirrors? Was he still sound enough of mind and body to be at the head of the billion-strong Catholic Church, with its multifarious needs, challenges, tensions, and controversies? His spokespersons and close aides, in statements of staggering denial, were still insisting that he was in "complete control."

But John Paul's dogged hold on power was now beginning to expose some long- and deeply held myths about the papacy. This was a Pope who, immobile and often speechless, was clearly incapable of managing the Church. The question, and it was being asked all over Rome, was this: How much does he understand of the prodigious enterprise over which he presides?

His predicament had become grotesquely false. In just one week in October, he had completed, according to the published papal schedules, enough executive activities to exhaust a man half his age. He met President Vladimir Putin of Russia (still no invitation to Moscow, alas) and President Mary McAleese of Ireland; chaired an international conference on depression; published a statement on cultural difference; appointed a dozen bishops; lectured members of the Polish union Solidarity; and presided over a world congress on pastoral care for migrants and refugees.

Everything had gone out in the Pope's name so that the newspapers and agencies could report "The Pope says this" and "The Pope says that," but one had to wonder precisely who was running the show. When the Pope was a younger man and in good health, insiders used to talk of how he kept in tension the centrifugal problems of the entire universal Church. A pope, in theory, maintains daily contact with all the national bishops in about 110 countries of the world. These bishops, more than three thousand of them, come to Rome for regular "personal meetings" with the pope—their *"ad limina"* visits. Everywhere there is a major crisis. In Latin America is the challenge of poverty, injustice, overpopulation, and the threat of Protestant evangelical missions. In Africa and Asia, cultural forces threaten disintegration of the traditional Catholic mold of belief and worship. In southern Africa, there are calls for safe sex to combat AIDS. In North America, there is the pedophile-priest crisis and contradictions to papal teaching in every area. Across the length and breadth of Europe, there are empty churches, a drastic decline in priestly vocations, anxieties about ecumenism, rows over liturgy, and the rejection of Christianity as a pillar of the new European constitution.

For six years or so, gradually and without public awareness, John

Paul had been leaving more and more of the running of the Church to others. For his condition was up and down, from morning to night and from day to day. A striking example of his occasional memory lapses occurred at the beginning of October 2003, conveyed to me as an item of "eyewitness" gossip by my Monsignor Sotto Voce, who was told the story "very reliably." The Archbishop of Canterbury, Dr. Rowan Williams, came into Rome to visit the Pope accompanied by various Anglican dignitaries. There were mutual blessings, they kissed each other's rings, statements were read (somebody read the Pope's address for him), and exchanges of gifts. After they had gone, the Pope turned to an aide and said: "Tell me, who *were* those people?"

After Mary McAleese, the president of Ireland, met John Paul, she spoke frankly to a journalist, who reported her comments in the British Catholic weekly *The Universe*. "I found him considerably changed," she said. "He has to fight so hard for every word that you become very conscious that even in meeting you it's a good act of generosity, at his age and with his failing health." McAleese said that the Pope struggled to talk about the Irish College in Rome, the seminary for candidates for the priesthood from Ireland. "He wanted to be reminded where the Irish college was, and when he heard that it was very close to St. John Lateran's Basilica he wanted to be reminded where that was too." Since St. John Lateran is the traditional basilica of popes from time immemorial, the memory lapse was equivalent to the Queen of England asking where Windsor Castle is. That same week, he sat speechless through an audience with the president of Uruguay.

Yet, a few days on, at a special Mass celebrating the twenty-fifth year of his pontificate in St. Peter's Square, he looked and sounded amazingly strong again. During the Mass, John Paul spoke from a prepared text about his devotion to Our Lady as he rededicated his papal ministry to Christ: "By the intercession of Mary, beloved Mother, the gift of myself, of the present and future: May all be done according to your will, Supreme Pastor, so that we can advance safely with you to the house of the Father."

The great ceremonies that autumn, those vast public theatricals in which he was center stage, seemed to energize him. The crowds attending the beatification of Mother Teresa, estimated at 300,000, stretched right back to the banks of the Tiber at the end of the Via della Conciliazione. The Pope, visible close-up on the great screens in the square, appeared deeply moved. This beatification brought the number of saints and blesseds created by him to 1,321. He and Mother Teresa were great friends and she visited him frequently in Rome during the halcyon days. The Sisters of Charity, members of Mother Teresa's congregation, were there in force—some 500 of them—and the front rows were filled with some 3,500 poor and sick.

The consistory of cardinals and the beatification ceremonies that autumn were grueling, both lasting about three hours; John Paul soldiered on, managing to bless several hundred people individually at the end of each of the Masses. It was said that he did not recognize some of his oldest friends at these blessings. One bishop remarked that John Paul drew his hand across his throat in a gesture indicating that he was unable to speak. Ironically, at the consistory Mass, Dr. Buzzonetti himself, on standby to keep an eye on John Paul, fainted from sheer exhaustion. He had to be carried off in a great flurry to his own little accident and emergency unit in the Vatican.

And through all these ceremonies great and small, it was noticeable now that the CTV cameras controlled by the Vatican information services, run by Opus Dei and syndicated to the world's news channels, discreetly panned away from the Pope whenever he appeared to be in difficulty or slumped asleep. David Willey, the BBC correspondent, reminded me that a similar editorial control was exerted over the Pontiff by the Communist media on his first visit to Poland. In that instance, it was to avoid revealing the enthusiasm and size of the crowds at his Masses.

*

With Christmas 2003 approaching and yet another "final" health scare receding, I watched John Paul at yet another Wednesday audience. He was like a battered and listing galleon in calmer waters after a storm. The drooling was under control, he was managing a short homily once more (although it was often difficult to understand what he was saying and he would skip whole phrases), and that all-purpose wheel-throne continued to make his presence felt in body, if not completely and consistently in voice, mind, and spirit.

He appeared to be functioning: The yo-yo effect, given his great heart and the cocktail of medicines available for his condition, could continue for years. He had made it known that he was prepared to go on until he dropped. "Christ," he told a general audience of pilgrims, "did not come down from his cross." He would preach the gospel, he told them, until his "last breath." But if the Catholic Church could be run, "business as usual," by a sick and barely present Pope, what was that telling us about the governance of the Church at its Vatican center, and the long-cherished notion that the Pope is always ultimately in charge?

In earlier years, John Paul would have debated each and every current issue with experts over lunch, and raised questions about the papers he was to sign and seal with the fisherman's ring. I had seen a recent example of that signature, a labored spidery scrawl, scratched in black ink on a papal document endorsed at the end of September 2003: It might have been written on a plane in severe turbulence. But, as members of the Curia were now asking with increasing urgency, was the Pope actually reading any of the documents or was he being guided—and, if so, by whom?

*

By December, everybody was talking about the Polish secretary Stanislaw Dziwisz. I had first met him in December 1987 when he scrutinized me before allowing me to meet John Paul. He is a short fellow, softly spoken, gentle-eyed, and with a feminine handshake; but according to the denizens of the Vatican, he has a feline watchfulness masking a will of iron. The Pope made him an archbishop in his sixty-third year, in the summer of 2003, although he has no diocese and no job to go to when the Pope dies.

It had become increasingly clear that the ultimate gatekeeper of the flow, as well as the custodian of visitors allowed through the door of the papal study, was Dziwisz. By all accounts, Dziwisz was getting the Pope through every aspect of his day, from morning until night, and was now the author of most of his homilies, read at general audiences and at his weekly Sunday appearance above St. Peter's Square. He was now the guiding spirit of the documents, advising the Pope what should be signed and what should not be signed.

Cardinal Ratzinger, the Church's doctrinal watchdog, was still seeing the Pope every Friday, and Cardinal Sodano, the Holy See's head of diplomatic, political, and foreign affairs, was seeing him even more regularly. Neither of these high prelates could enter the papal apartment, however, without permission of Dziwisz, who unlocked the door to let them in, accompanied them to the papal presence, and remained throughout the audience.

Amazingly, there were still those who were loath to acknowledge the true predicament of the Pope's ailing health and his incapacities. They would respond cuttingly to suggestions that he was anything but vigorous and in full control. When I had suggested earlier, in an article in the *Sunday Times,* that John Paul was not at his best, Father Richard Neuhaus had accused me of "journalistic malfeasance."

The current administration of the Vatican and the inner clique of the papal court have always been reluctant to admit that a pontificate is lame or at its end, since it prompts discussion of new policies and new personnel at the top. When a pope dies, his appointments die with him. Every papal household factotum, boon companion, and papal favorite is set to be dismissed. The same would go for a papal resignation.

But what was uppermost in the minds of those who cared for John Paul, and loved their Church, was how this great and stricken man might be manipulated in this period of debility, not only by people close to him who had strong views on how the Church should be run, but by influences great and small beyond the Vatican. After Christmas 2003, an episode illustrated just such a predicament, small in itself but symptomatic all the same.

CHAPTER THIRTY-THREE

Mel Gibson's
The Passion

The New Year 2004 saw John Paul dragged into an unedifying rumpus illustrating the extent to which the papal court was playing fast and loose with the papal name and the truth, and the manipulations of the "velvet power" behind the throne, Archbishop Dziwisz. Above all, the brouhaha demonstrated to Vatican observers with a mind to brood on the unthinkable just how much the pontificate was "adrift."

John Paul saw Mel Gibson's film *The Passion of the Christ* spread over two evening viewings on December 5 and 6 in the privacy of his apartment with his secretary, Dziwisz; no doubt in his frail state the film was considered too much of an ordeal for one sitting. By December 17, Gibson's PR people were claiming that Dziwisz had quoted the Pope as saying of the film: "It is as it was." The apparent "endorsement," which delighted the film's people, was reported independently by the *Wall Street Journal*, citing Dziwisz, and the *National Catholic Reporter*, naming a "senior Vatican source." But then—and this was to be the nub of the row—the claim was flatly denied after Christmas. By January 19, Dziwisz was stating emphatically that the Pope had made no such declaration.

The film, as the world knows, depicts the last hours of Jesus Christ, from the Agony in the Garden of Gethsemane to the Crucifixion. It includes a graphic twenty-five-minute scourging scene. The dialogue, in what constitutes the most extraordinarily affected piece of biblical filming in the history of cinema, is in Aramaic and Latin with subtitles. The Jewish priests, in the view of many critics, conform to stock Semitic hate-figure stereotypes. Others hotly denied the anti-Semitic charge, claiming that Gibson had worked hard to eliminate such elements. Gibson let it be known that it was his hands driving in the first nail, supposedly demonstrating that it was Everyman who crucified Christ.

Before the Pope saw the movie, there had been screenings for select audiences from the late summer of 2003 in various parts of the world, presumably to elicit reactions from Catholic centers of influence. In Los Angeles, it was seen by an audience of four hundred Jesuits, who represented a constituency that gave Gibson cause for anxiety. What if the Jesuits had disapproved of it! But according to one young Jesuit present: "If you have four hundred Jesuits you have four hundred opinions. As it happened, the reaction was positive. We loved it." In Rome, it was shown at the college of the Legionaries of Christ before an enthusiastic audience.

As the screenings progressed, Catholics, Protestant Evangelicals, Jews, and an assortment of atheists and agnostics pitched into a war of words over the film's aesthetics, theology, faithfulness to Scripture, and alleged or denied anti-Semitic content. It was an excellent row from Gibson's point of view, since it fueled the conflagration of publicity. Apart from the inclusion of extraneous material—adaptations from the nineteenth-century anti-Semitic visionary Sister Anne Catherine Emmerich—the account of the Passion did not stray far from the Gospel narrative. The main issue for the naysayers was the excess of violence—some even used the term "sadomasochism."

The Holy Father's reaction would be no mere matter of judgment on the aesthetics or scriptural authenticity of the film, since Mel Gibson's relations with the Catholic Church and the Pope were complicated by some strange baggage. Gibson is one of eleven children from a Catholic family in Peekskill, New York. His father, Hutton, was aligned to traditionalist "Sede Vacantists"—disaffected Catholic hard-liners who believe that Pope John XXIII's election was a fraud and his much-vaunted Second Vatican Council a Jewish-Masonic plot, and that the papal throne stands empty to this day. Harking back to the sixteenth-century Council of Trent, Hutton and his associates deplored the loss of the old Latin Mass and rejected a host of liberal reforms that had in their view polluted the Catholic sanctuary with the smoke of Satan. Worse still, it was rumored that Hutton Gibson was into Holocaust denial, an imputation that could only confirm allegations that the movie was anti-Semitic. Gibson had moved to distance himself from such taints—but he was damned if he was going to disown his own dad, as some interviewers invited him to do. Against this background, a favorable endorsement from John Paul could have been misconstrued by the mischievous.

No sooner had the news of John Paul's comment—that *The Passion of the Christ* represented the suffering of Christ "as it was"—been published in the *National Catholic Reporter* than Cindy Wooden of the Catholic News Service claimed on January 19 that Dziwisz had denied that the Pope had made it. Whereupon Gibson's producers, Icon Productions, published a press release insisting that they had a document signed by no less a person than Joaquin Navarro-Valls, the Vatican press officer, confirming the Pope's comments and authorizing their promotion. Then, on January 22, Peggy Noonan in the *Wall Street Journal* claimed that she had seen an e-mail, allegedly from the Vatican press officer, to Steve McEveety, the film's producer, encouraging him to use "again and again and again" the quote attributed to John Paul. Navarro-Valls's actual words referring to the papal comment, in an e-mail dated December 28 at 6 A.M., were: "Nobody can deny it. So keep mentioning it as the authorized point of reference. I would try to make the words 'It is as it was' the leit motive [*sic*] in any discussion on the film. Repeat the words again and again and again." One could not be more explicit than that. So how come the Pope's secretary was denying that the Pope had said any such thing?

Dziwisz's account of the Pope's comment, "It is as it was!" apparently came up, or did not come up, during a conversation between the film's producer, Steve McEveety, and Stanislaw Dziwisz on December 8 in the apostolic palace, just two days after the Pope had seen part two. Also present at this conversation was the film's assistant producer, Jan Michelini. Later that evening, McEveety and Michelini showed the film to Navarro-Valls, whose reaction was obviously one of untrammeled enthusiasm. Naturally, they imparted to Navarro-Valls the Pope's reaction, or alleged reaction, as supposedly reported by Dziwisz.

The status and presence of Jan Michelini needs some explanation, for it was most likely because of him that the Pope came to see the film in the first place. Michelini was more than just an assistant producer on *The Passion*—he had unusual links with the Holy Father. He was born in 1979 while John Paul was making his first trip to Poland. His father Alberto, a politician and distinguished Italian journalist, accompanied John Paul on that visit and happened to tell the Holy Father that he regretted having to be abroad while his twin son and daughter were being born in Italy. John Paul promised that he would make it up to him: He would baptize the children on his return. So Jan Michelini and his sister became the first children to be baptized by Wojtyla after his election to the papacy. And there was something else: Like Navaro-Valls, Alberto Michelini happens to be a leading figure in Opus Dei in Rome, a movement with which Dziwisz also has ties. All of which perhaps explains how Michelini Junior and McEveety came to be in conversation with Dziwisz in the apostolic palace on December 8 and *a casa* Navarro-Valls later that evening.

When Dziwisz finally came to deny the papal endorsement publicly on January 19, he left no room for doubt. Referring to his meeting with McEveety and Michelini on December 8, he stated: "I said clearly to McEveety and Michelini that the Holy Father made no declaration. I said the Holy Father saw the film privately in his apartment but gave no declaration to anyone. He does not make judgments on art of this kind; he leaves that to others, to experts. Clearly, the Holy Father made no judgment of the film."

So where did this leave Michelini, McEveety, and Navarro-Valls, the various senior sources, and the hapless reporters on Vatican affairs?

Michelini issued a public statement on January 21, 2004:

> I confirm what I have already stated: The pope has seen the Passion by Mel Gibson and has appreciated it because it represents a faithful transcription of the Gospel. He has seen the movie together with his secretary, Stanislaw Dziwisz, in his apartment during a strictly private and informal screening. For this reason there never was, nor could there ever have been an official communique, nor a public statement about the screening. Faced with some specious criticism, the secretary of the Holy Father couldn't but deny. It is upsetting to see how the semantic interpretation of the few words said during a private conversation between the secretary of the pope, the producer Steve McEveety, and myself have been incorrectly used by some journalists. This is what I have finally to say regarding this issue.

Navarro-Valls finally delivered himself of his version of events via the Vatican Press Office on January 22, with no reference to his "again and again and again" e-mail to the producers, and telling us everything while saying nothing:

> After having consulted with the personal secretary of the Holy Father, Archbishop Stanislaw Dziwisz, I confirm that the Holy Father had the opportunity to see the film The Passion of Christ. The film is a cinematographic transposition of the historical event of the Passion of Jesus Christ according to the accounts of the Gospel. It is a common practice of the Holy

Father not to express public opinions on artistic works, opinions that are always open to different evaluations of aesthetic character.

The pomposity of the language—"cinematographic transposition" and "evaluations of aesthetic character"—is not just ludicrous evasion intended to put honest inquirers in their place and off the scent. John Allen, Vatican correspondent for the *National Catholic Reporter* and CNN, went back to his source for the original papal comment. Reading through the spin, the source explained what was being said: "A senior Vatican official suggested to me that the word 'declaration' was important, since in Vatican argot it usually means a formal public statement. If so, it would leave open the possibility that the pope said something privately."

Allen, normally mild in his criticisms of the Vatican and a loyal son of the Church, was outraged. He went on to tell his Catholic readers: "Even if officials were acting for the noblest of motives, they have stretched the meaning of words, on and off the record, to their breaking point. Aside from the obvious moralism that it's wrong to deceive, such confusion can only enhance perceptions that the aging John Paul II is incapable of controlling his own staff, that 'no one is in charge' and the church is adrift. These impressions are not healthy in a time when the church's public image, especially in the United States, has already taken a beating on other grounds."

But, in 2004, there was to be evidence of drift in much weightier matters than Mel Gibson's movie.

CHAPTER THIRTY-FOUR

George W. Bush and John Paul

Despite John Paul's determined opposition to the war in Iraq and his stern reaction to the abuses at Abu Ghraib Prison, revealed by the media in 2004, President George W. Bush got a boost from the Pope in the first week of June 2004. The ostensible reason for the presidential visit to Rome was to meet with Italian prime minister Silvio Berlusconi, America's ally in the Iraq war. He was also in Italy to celebrate the sixtieth anniversary of the liberation of Rome, before moving on to France to attend the anniversary of D-Day: a salutary reminder to Europe, ahead of the UN vote on the Iraq constitution, that the continent owed much to the United States of America.

It was Bush's third meeting with John Paul in three years, and, as with the first in 2001, when he made a show of consulting John Paul in advance of stating his policy on embryonic stem-cell research, there were major political gains in the offing. Bush was patently at odds with the Catholic Church on capital punishment, new generations of nuclear weapons, human rights, his administration's policy of preemptive invasion, and the effects of the global economy on the world's poor. But the value to the U.S. electorate of a photograph of himself and the Pope looking friendly was incalculable. With the gruesome images of tortured and degraded Iraqis, and the grinning perpetrators, still fresh in the minds of billions of people the world over, the effect of a Bush-Pope photo op was well worth any minor humiliation the President might have to endure as a result of being ticked off by John Paul. As it was, John Paul's reference to his "concern" about events in Iraq was anodyne and scarcely audible. Correspondents were obliged to follow their "crib sheets" to understand what he was saying.

Back in the United States, Bush's Catholic Democratic rivals, who in normal circumstances might have considered themselves close to the Holy Father on the controversial conduct of the war in Iraq, were embroiled in fierce quarrels with their bishops, and hence John Paul, over pro-life issues and divorce. There had been pressure on Senator John Kerry, the Democratic presidential contender, to not receive communion in public because of his voting record on abortion. At the same time, the governor of New Jersey, James McGreevey, also a Democrat, had bowed to his archbishop and agreed to stop receiving communion because he had remarried without an annulment. The energetic American bishops' campaign against Democrats who allegedly "condoned" abortion had all the appearance of a hierarchical and papal endorsement of Bush and the Republicans in the 2004 presidential elections. Speaking to *Time* magazine, a high but nameless Vatican official had said: "People in Rome are becoming more and more aware that there's a problem with John Kerry and a potential scandal with his apparent profession of his Catholic faith and some of his stances, particularly on abortion."

The question arose: Was a debilitated John Paul being manipulated by both right-wing Catholic journalists and George W. Bush's reelection campaign? Was his visit to the Pope no more than a campaign stop?

If anything, John Paul's position on the situation in Iraq had hardened in previous weeks. Cardinal Pio Laghi, the former papal nuncio to the United States, and a man not known for liberal tendencies, had vehemently criticized the United States at the beginning of

May, warning that the "law of nations" in Iraq would require a cultural understanding of the Arab world that the United States had not achieved. "To bomb a mosque, to enter holy cities, to put women soldiers in contact with naked men, shows a lack of understanding of the Muslim world that I would label astonishing." Laghi, as we have seen, was John Paul's personal emissary to President Bush in March 2003, begging him not to go ahead with a preemptive invasion. Less official, but much in line with feelings in Italy in early May, a senior official in the Vatican Secretariat of State controversially compared the atrocity of the torture of prisoners with the September 11 terror attacks themselves, eliciting an indignant riposte from the U.S. ambassador in Rome.

As he greeted Bush, John Paul's appearance revealed marked physical deterioration. He was shaking uncontrollably in both legs and both hands (in the past, it had been mainly his left hand that shook). Nevertheless, his mind appeared reasonably clear for the occasion. Headlines in many European papers remarked on John Paul's "rebuke" of Bush, but across the United States, the event was presented as a coup for the President. Taking him by the hand, Bush leaned over the Pope and looked into his eyes: This was the Pope's friend, the President in compassionate mood presenting himself in solidarity with the world's moral leader. The ceremony was broadcast live on most of the world's main news channels. In his address, the Pope said that the President was familiar with the "unequivocal position of the Holy See" in regard to "the Middle East, both in Iraq and the Holy Land." But despite this mild reiteration of the papal antiwar stance, the sight of John Paul at one with the President could only send clear signals to the Middle East that John Paul was the chaplain of the West. Twice John Paul said jubilantly, and to the delight of all present: "God Bless America!"

The two met for a second time in the Clementine Hall before journalists and diplomats. At the climax of the encounter, Bush rose from his chair to present John Paul with the Medal of Freedom, America's highest civilian award. He said: "We appreciate the strong symbol of freedom that you have stood for and we recognize the power of the freedom to change societies and to change the world." He also pledged that his government would "work for human liberty and human dignity in order to spread peace and compassion." The citation concluded with the words, "The United States honors this son of Poland who became the Bishop of Rome and a hero of our time."

Whatever was actually on the Pope's mind, the theatricality of the award created a striking contrast between the apparent fragrance of the Republicans and the suspicious odor of the Democrats. Considering the power of the Catholic vote—64 million Catholics, making up 27 percent of the American electorate—apparent papal endorsement of Bush, or at least a semblance of it, was no trivial matter.

While he was by birth and upbringing an Episcopalian (married to a Methodist), educated at Andover and Yale, George W. Bush since 1985 had presented himself as a born-again Christian—converted by Billy Graham, no less, and with a fundamentalist belief in the Bible. "I always laugh when people say that George W. Bush is saying this or that to appease the religious right," his first cousin, John Ellis, has commented. "He *is* the religious right."

Yet his evangelical Protestantism is by no means antagonistic to Protestantism's traditional enemy—popery. He has successfully courted John Paul II and the Catholic vote, which was traditionally Democratic, collecting half of it in 2000. He made a speech to commemorate the opening of the Pope John Paul II Cultural Center at the Catholic University of America, stating that "the Pope reminds us that while freedom defines our nation, responsibility must define our lives. He challenges us to live up to our aspirations, to be a fair and just society where all are welcomed, all are valued, and all are protected. And he is never more eloquent than when he speaks for the culture of life." The mostly Catholic audience gave him a standing ovation. Bush was similarly feted when he gave a speech at Notre Dame University, where he was awarded an honorary degree. Catholic social scientist John Kenneth White of the Catholic University of America has stated that the 2000 election showed that "the more you attend church, the more likely you are to vote Republican." Bush had set up a Catholic task force to address some three million active Catholics in fourteen states with cold telephone calls and mailings emphasizing his agreement with John Paul's ideals on sex, TV violence, gay culture, same-sex marriage, and abortion. With an impressive shrewdness, Bush had appropriated some of the language of John Paul's social doctrine, in particular the principle of subsidiarity from Pius XI's encyclical *Quadragesimo Anno* (1931), which, as we have seen, was reaffirmed in John Paul's encyclical *Centesimus Annus* (1993): that decisions should be made bottom-up, closer to the communities that are most affected by them.

Like Ronald Reagan before him, Bush had been skillful in appropriating the language of religion, depicting his vision for America's foreign policy in terms of the clash between good and evil. He even went so far as to use the loaded word "crusade." As for domestic politics: The clash was between the God-fearing, on the one hand, and the secular, on the other—which was where John Kerry came in.

Kerry's position vis-à-vis the Pope and the Church was best described as similar to that of John F. Kennedy, who said famously: "I believe in an America where the separation of Church and State is absolute." The Christian right in America, which included traditionalist Catholics, had been at pains, however, to depict Kerry not as a defender of a pluralist society so much as a "secularist" promoting indifferentism and moral relativism. This characterization, by implication, had John Paul's support and the support of some American bishops.

Bush's Partial-Birth Abortion Act, which limits late-term abortions, was in line with the Vatican agenda on pro-life issues, but Kerry voted against it. On the abortion act Kerry had said: "This is a dangerous effort to undermine a woman's right to choose, which is a constitutional amendment I will always fight to protect." Kerry had also found himself opposed to the Pope, the Catholic Church, and the Republicans on the issue of recognized gay unions.

What had changed in the intervening years between the Vatican's support of JFK I and its antagonism toward JFK II? It was precisely a marked difference on that fundamental stand made by Kennedy nearly forty-five years earlier. In 2002, John Paul issued a "doctrinal note" that insisted that "a well-formed Christian conscience does not permit one to vote for a political program or an individual law which contradicts the fundamental contents of faith and morals." On the question of abortion, the document asserted that a politician had a "grave and clear obligation to oppose" laws that "attack human life."

One did not have to agree with Kerry on the abortion or gay-union issues, however, to recognize that President Bush's conduct of the war in Iraq had offended the moral principles of many states and religious constituencies in the world, not least the Pope's. But the image of the Pope embracing Bush while Kerry was refused Holy Communion in the United States gave the impression that John Paul saw Bush on the side of the angels while Kerry was going to the devil. And all this in an election year.

And there were deeper issues that united rather than divided Bush and John Paul. Both the President and the Pope believed profoundly that "secular humanism" was debauching American and European life in the form of "moral relativism." Both President and Pope believed in the ongoing struggle between the Powers of Darkness and the Powers of Light; for Bush and the American Christian Right, the elections of 2004 represented an ultimate stage in that cosmic spiritual struggle. Republican congressman Tom Cole of Oklahoma told his supporters that a vote against George W. Bush was a vote for Osama bin Laden. He later amended the comparison to a vote for Adolf Hitler.

Later in the week of the Vatican meeting between the Pope and Bush, John Paul paid tribute to Ronald Reagan, who had recently died at age ninety-three. John Paul made mention of the former president's role in prompting the collapse of Soviet communism. Navarro-Valls, the Pope's spokesman, said: "The Pope recalled the contributions of President Reagan to the historical events that changed the lives of millions of people, especially in Europe." John

Paul said he prayed for the "eternal rest of his soul." It was an interesting moment to recall Graham Greene's comment that John Paul and President Reagan had much in common, both having started life as actors. But there were other links: Reagan used to wonder out loud about biblical prophecies and the end-time. He told the Portuguese parliament in 1985: "In the prayers of simple people everywhere, simple people like the children of Fatima, there resides more power than in all the great armies and statesmen in the world. . . . I would suggest to you that here lies power, here is the final realization to life's meaning and history's purpose." Reagan also subscribed to a form of "nuclear dispensationalism" according to which the righteous will "greet the Lord in the air" and be saved seconds before Armageddon. One day, perhaps, both Reagan and John Paul will be credited with having postponed, one hopes indefinitely, Armageddon. One wonders, though, whether John Paul, in his prayers for Ronald Reagan's soul, considered the former president's diversion of profits from the arms trade for hostages to the illegal war waged in Nicaragua against the Sandinista government, which included four liberation-theology priests.

For some Catholic journalists who had covered events in Latin America, it was a death that prompted somber reflections: Hugh O'Shaughnessy, correspondent for the *Observer* and the *Financial Times* for more than forty years in South America, and a loyal Catholic, wrote that week: "Having spent years observing and reporting on the atrocities that were perpetrated in Central America by [Reagan's] countrymen under his authority in the 1980s, I feel bound first to remember the passing of his victims and recall their fate to others who are not familiar with that region." Not least of his recollections were the files of dead children, men, and women he had seen in the office of Archbishop Oscar Romero, who had been tortured by the Salvadoran army and police "trained and armed by Ronald Reagan's compatriots."

CHAPTER THIRTY-FIVE

John Paul's Grand Design

John Paul's schematic, historico-legendary way of thinking was never more exercised in the course of his papacy than in contemplating his goal to reconcile the Eastern and the Western Churches. The East and the West, the two great lungs of European Christianity, must come together under his aegis as the Slav Pope and universal pastor: St. Peter and St. Paul, St. Cyril and St. Methodius (the ninth-century evangelists to the Slavs)—all wrapped into one. Speaking in the Cathedral of Gniezno during his first trip to Poland on Pentecost Day 1979, he spoke these remarkable words: "This Pope comes here to speak before the whole Church, before Europe and the world, of those often forgotten nations and peoples . . . He comes here to embrace all these peoples, together with his own nation, and to hold them close to the heart of the Church, to the heart of the Mother of the Church, in whom he has unlimited trust."

Here was the unbearable tension between John Paul's regard for the particular (a perspective vital to Polish Catholicism) and for the general, or universal, characteristic of a great, controlling pope. And his schemes, formed in the crucible of an imagination that was both tragically isolated and at the same time outward-reaching, would become ever more determined as they appeared confirmed by the fall of communism, the fulfillment of the Secrets of Fatima, the formation of a greater Europe, and, of course, his survival, despite illness and accident, into the third millennium. Within these schemes were seeds of a hubris that would result in conflict, disillusionment, decay, and divisions. The story of John Paul's spiritual and historic *ostpolitik*, in contradiction to Paul VI's *ostpolitik*, exemplifies all that was most spectacular and all that was most flawed in his character and pontificate.

*

The situation of the Churches in East Europe and Russia after the fall of the Berlin Wall and the coming of Yeltsin was fraught with complexity. There were Latin-rite Catholics in East Europe (notably, the Balkans, Ukraine, Hungary, Lithuania, and even a handful in Russia) who had been oppressed and persecuted under communism as aliens and infiltrators. There were also the Byzantine-rite Catholics within the Soviet republics, and Ukraine especially, who owed allegiance to the pope in Rome but who followed Eastern liturgies, and whose priests could marry. These faithful Catholics, sometimes referred to pejoratively as "Uniates" by the Orthodox, were regarded from time to time as a Trojan horse by their Orthodox religious rivals. These "Uniates" had been especially oppressed and persecuted by the Communists, and at times by the Orthodox, their churches appropriated or destroyed.

But then the ancient Orthodox Churches—Greek, Ukrainian, and Russian—in loose communion with each other, were united in their traditions and spirituality, as well as their ancient distrust of Rome for doctrinal and historic reasons. They were also resentful and suspicious of the Poles, who had been credited with imperialist and proselytizing designs eastward since the sixteenth century. Ask a Russian why John Paul is distrusted, and he will tell you at the head of a substantial catalogue of reasons: "Because he is a Pole!"

The Orthodox Church, in Russia and the Soviet republics, like the Catholics, suffered waves of persecution under Lenin, Stalin, and Khrushchev, and held on by timely accommodations. This bruised, tarnished Church, infiltrated by Communists and KGB agents, which has lost more than anyone could possibly remember or record in eighty years of persecution and repression, nevertheless retains and cherishes a memory of its better ancient soul. Russians refer to the Moscow Church as the "Third Rome." Old Rome, by this notion, is the Latin "First Rome," which stands for rigid discipline, law and order, and aspirations to universal authority under the Pope: God the Father. Constantinople is the "Second Rome," which is doctrinal, theological, seat of the Logos and therefore of the Second Person of the Trinity: Jesus Christ. Constantinople suffered grievously at its fall, but in compensation came Moscow, the "Third Rome," which expresses the charism of the Holy Spirit. Moscow represents in its own eyes the glory of the liturgy, the Eucharist, popular mysticism of an iconic kind, the transfiguration of the cosmos. It is moved neither by legalism nor by logic.

From the Vatican point of view, however, the Russian Orthodox had made too many concessions to communism. Its members had been guilty of collaborating with Stalin in the repression of Catholics, both Latin and "Uniate," of forced conversions to Orthodoxy, and of the appropriation of churches. The Orthodox Church, by this Vatican estimation, was corrupt, and irredeemable by itself. But with the advent of John Paul, that was now all in the past. For had not John Paul, whatever the Orthodox failings, freed their patriarchs, and what was left of their monks, priests, monasteries, cathedrals, and churches, from the Soviet yoke? Had not John Paul given them back their religious liberties by defeating communism? Could they not see the providential merits of the great Slav Pope, unifier of East and West, and endowed with the primacy of Saint Peter?

The Orthodox Churches, individually and as a whole, tended to see matters differently. They had long memories and nourished ancient grudges dating back to the split from Rome in 1054, a doctrinal schism reinforced by detestation following the sack of Constantinople in 1204, the handiwork of the fourth Crusade conducted under the auspices of the papacy. And what need had they of close unity with a pope who claimed primacy over their bishops? They were in proud possession of authentic succession from the apostles, and valid sacraments. Their bishops and clergy were governed by a form of pluralism and consensus—their synods. Then there was everyday religion. They deplored the contraceptive mentality without judging appropriate contraception a sin; they sanctioned valid divorces and remarriage; they allowed their priests to marry (provided they did not aspire to be bishops, unless widowed). Why should they wish to bend the knee to a pope who chose all the bishops in his Church, pried beneath the sheets of the marriage bed, and deprived lay Catholics of the sacraments after divorce? The Russian Orthodox Church had had more than enough of being bullied. And here, on his first visit to his native Poland in 1979, there was evidence, in writing, of John Paul II's grand designs upon them without reference to their own thoughts on the matter. But the declaration at Gniezno was only the beginning.

The following year, in 1980, came his apostolic letter *Egregiae Virtutis*, wherein he proclaimed the Byzantine saints Cyril and Methodius as co-patrons of Europe along with St. Benedict, Patriarch of the West. He talked of unity in diversity. Europe, he wrote, was "the fruit of the action of two currents of Christian tradition, to which were joined two different but at the same time profoundly complementary forms of culture." The implication was that as the Slav Pope he represented both Cyril and Methodius, as well as Benedict: east and west.

Then, on February 14, 1985, on the feast of St. Cyril and Methodius, John Paul stated his intentions explicitly. He published his encyclical *Slavorum Apostoli* (*Apostle to the Slavs*), a marvelously baroque meditation on the cultural and linguistic scope of Christian evangelization from its true center, Rome, and with clear references to the Slav Pope's destiny at the coming new millennium. His road map of evangelization took in Moravia, Slovakia, Pannonia, Bohemia, Poland, the Balkans, Bulgaria, Romania, the "ancient Rus' of Kiev," and, ultimately, the regions that lie "from Moscow eastwards." As Tolstoy might well have quipped: "How much land does a Pope need?"

Then, ten years on, on the feast of St. Athanasius, May 2, 1995, that much closer to the millennium, and after the collapse of the Soviet system, John Paul published yet another remarkable letter, titled *Orientale Lumen* (*The Eastern Light*), signaling his hopes for unity with the Orthodox Churches.

> Mary, "Mother of the star that never sets," "dawn of the mystical day," "rising of the sun of glory," shows us the Orientale Lumen. Every day in the East the sun of hope rises again, the light that restores life to the human race. It is from the East, according to a lovely image, that our Savior will come again. For us, the men and women of the East are a symbol of the Lord who comes again. We cannot forget them, not only because we love them as brothers and sisters redeemed by the same Lord, but also because a holy nostalgia for the centuries lived in the full communion of faith and charity urges us and reproaches us for our sins and our mutual misunderstandings: We have deprived the world of a joint witness that could perhaps have avoided so many tragedies and even changed the course of history.

"Holy nostalgia"! A pregnant phrase, so full of longing. Then the piling up of grandiloquent comparisons, suggesting that it would be the East that would lead the West to unity—the rising sun, the Second Coming, under the star of Mary that never sets. And the comparisons were all the more outlandish, from the Orthodox point of view, as they were cited both in the concrete context of his efforts to enter traditional Orthodox territories on a papal visit replete with youth rallies, flag waving, posters, television coverage, and the full panoply of the cult of papal personality.

The fears of the Orthodox were perfectly understandable. For John Paul repeatedly spoke the language of pluralism while insisting on his role as universal pastor. There was that powerful image of duality, the Eastern and Western Churches as "two lungs," the complementary organs of the one Christian body, breathing in harmony.

As the millennium approached, he even talked of contrition, for-giveness, and mutual understanding—as if to prepare for that part-nership of Churches. But then there came Ratzinger's letter, *Dominus Jesus*, emphatically ratified by John Paul: "Therefore, there exists a single Church of Christ, which subsists in the Catholic Church, gov-erned by the Successor of Peter and by the Bishops in communion with him." It was granted that the Orthodox Churches had apostolic succession, but they were not in "perfect communion" by reasons of their resistance to the claims of the universal pastor. In conse-quence, these Churches "suffer from defects." So at the heart of it all lay that intransigent problem: the difficulty, the virtual impossibil-ity, of John Paul accepting differences in terms that did not sound like submission to his authority. There were two lungs to be sure, but only one heart—and that was the Pope's. One does not have to deny papal primacy to see that the language of *Dominus Jesus* was inappro-priate, and its timing disastrous.

The year after the publication of *Orientale Lumen*, Samuel P. Huntington published his *The Clash of Civilisations and the Remaking of the World Order*. He focused on the Ukraine as the "cleft country" that sits astride Europe's cultural divide; in fact, the very name Ukraine comes from the Slav word for "borderland." John Paul, too, understood the significance of the Ukraine, but rather differently. The Ukraine was the key to his version of East-West unity, and he was determined to lay claim to it in his own way. But he would approach that goal in a roundabout fashion.

In the last week of April 2001, John Paul embarked on his first journey into the lands of the Orthodox Church. He styled it a pil-grimage "in the steps of St. Paul," but it was straightaway seen by the Orthodox as a trespass. His first stop was Athens, where he had been invited by the nation's agnostic president, Constantin Stephanopoulos, since the Greek Orthodox Primate, Archbishop Christodoulos, was against the visit. His church, Christodoulos said, did not wish to "recede from its truths or betray history" by paying court to a pope. He also demanded that on Greek territory the Pope should apologize for "errors committed by Catholics." He met with John Paul at the airport on his departure, and John Paul accordingly apologized for the sack of Constantinople and anything else that irked his separated brethren. They exchanged the kiss of peace and, on John Paul's suggestion, said the Our Father in Greek together. Was there ever a pope in the modern period who knew so well how to charm and beguile? Navarro-Valls, the papal spokesperson, always on hand with the right *mot*, said: "A new era is opening."

Back in Athens, however, members of the Orthodox faithful gathered at a rally on April 25, chanting "Out with the Pope." Some carried banners with John Paul depicted as a horned devil and a legend proclaiming "666," sign of the Beast, to be the Pope's telephone number. Posters went up all over Athens proclaiming "No to the beast of the Apocalypse." An anarchist bomb was exploded on April 28 by a group claiming that the Pope was responsible for the massacres in the Balkans. But John Paul was already off to Syria, to Damascus, where he was received effusively by Muslim leaders and cautiously by Orthodox prelates, then to Malta, a country where the Roman Catholic majority knew how to greet a pope.

But even as John Paul traveled, Patriarch Alexis II of Moscow and all-Rus' made it known that the Pope's apology for "errors committed by Catholics" would be judged by his actions. "It is necessary," he said at a press conference, "to take a look at how this apology will be expressed in deeds." John Paul, in the view of Alexis, was determined to spread Roman Catholicism into Russia rather than support the "sister" Orthodox Church, as the Vatican had professed. Above all, Alexis and Christodoulos were anxious about the Pope's determination to visit the Ukraine in June 2001.

A week after John Paul's "steps of St. Paul" pilgrimage, there were demonstrations in Moscow, backed by the Russian and Greek Orthodox Churches, protesting the Ukraine trip. Orthodox faithful marched on the Kremlin chanting, "No to the visit of the apostle of globalization!" The very day after greeting John Paul and praying with him in Greece, Archbishop Christodoulos appeared to have regretted his symbolic gesture of reconciliation. He flew to Moscow on May 5 to make a joint statement with Alexis deploring the papal Ukraine trip.

There was more, far more, to that visit than met the eye, Alexis wished the world to know. The Ukraine, or more accurately Kiev, was not merely an ex–Soviet satellite with a large population of Catholics; it was the cradle of Christianity for the whole of Russia. It was in Kiev that St. Vladimir led the conversion of Rus' to Byzantine Christianity in 988. For the Orthodox prelates and their faithful, a papal visit to Kiev at the approach of their own millennium celebration was an outrageous spiritual hijack by the Latin-rite supremacist.

Despite the warnings and the pleas of the "Sister Church," John Paul arrived as planned on June 23 for a four-day visit, starting in Kiev and finishing in Lvov, where he presided over two beatification ceremonies and one of his much-loved youth gatherings. He wowed the faithful with his ability to speak a few words of Ukrainian, a language that Poles tend to despise as fit "only for animals." The euphoria of the visit drowned out the demonstrations of the Russian Orthodox in Kiev and other towns, protesting that John Paul was a "wolf in sheep's clothing." The Ukrainian Orthodox Metropolitan, Vladimir of Kiev, made sure he was out of town when John Paul came triumphantly through. In January, Vladimir had written to John Paul informing him of the unanimous decision of the forty-two members of his synod of bishops begging him to delay his visit. He declared that it was "bewildering" that the papal visit was being arranged without notifying his Church and without an invitation from his bishops.

From John Paul's point of view, the Orthodox Christians in the Ukraine had been guilty of occupying many hundreds of Catholic churches, both Latin and Byzantine rite, in the country. Following the fall of communism, many of these churches had been "rightfully" taken back by local Catholics. Vladimir saw it differently. Byzantine-rite Catholics had, in his view, grabbed illegitimately and by force more than a thousand churches currently claimed by the Orthodox, and in consequence three Ukrainian dioceses had been destroyed. Vladimir was convinced that a papal visit would "only seal the existing state of affairs, very unfavorable to our church." Hence, if the Pope came on the dates he proposed, "There would be no meeting between us, and no cleric of our church will take part in the program of the visit."

The visit also came at a delicate time for relations between the Ukrainian Orthrodx Church and its Russian sister. The Moscow Church wanted closer unity with the Kiev Church. John Paul, not averse to engaging with these local concerns, was enthusiastically advocating the separation of the Ukrainian Orthodox from the Russian Church. Completing the impression (to the Orthodox) of papal interference, he delivered a homily in Kiev to young people, telling them not to emigrate to the United States but to stay put in the Ukraine. "Stay in your own country," he cried. "Don't opt for an easy life abroad." To make such speeches in a foreign country demanded an extraordinary degree of assurance as well as a remarkable lapse in irony.

The BBC's editor of the Russian service in Moscow, Konstantin Eggert, a Russian Orthodox by confession, made a significant comment during the Ukraine trip. He noted the tens of thousands of brash posters of the Pope that had been distributed throughout the country, something the Orthodox faithful would never consider doing for the visit of a Patriarch, which is always a low-key affair. They had been supplied, he discovered, by a Western Catholic public relations company. "Orthodoxy," Eggert wrote, "preserves elements of inner democracy rooted in the earliest days of Christianity. The Orthodox Church is ruled by a synod of bishops, who cannot insulate themselves from their flocks. The Patriarch of Moscow and All Russia is the Primate of the Russian Orthodox Church, but his power is much more limited than that of the Pope, and he does not have the right to proclaim dogma. I do not feel that the distance separating me, as an ordinary believer from his Holiness Alexis II, is as huge as that which lies between a Roman Catholic and the Vicar of Christ on earth."

*

The Russian Patriarch was right to ask his people to examine the deeds of John Paul rather than his words. A year after the Ukraine trip, and while planning further trips to Slovakia, Azerbaijan, and Kazakhstan, as if circling the peripheries of former Soviet republics before attempting to plunge into the Russian heartland, John Paul upgraded four "apostolic districts" in Russia—offices that took care of Roman Catholics in Russia—to the status of full Roman Catholic dioceses linked directly with Rome. In the meantime, Archbishop Tadeusz Kondrusiewicz, head of the Catholic Bishops Conference in Russia, was elevated to the rank of "Metropolitan." Such an appropriation of a title special to Orthodoxy, in the view of Alexis II, makes Russia a branch office, or "province," of the Catholic Church. The Vatican has argued that there are more than a million Catholics in Russia in need of spiritual sustenance. Should the Pope who has vigorously defended religious liberty deny Catholics religious liberty in Russia? Should the Russian Orthodox Church be allowed to suppress other Christian denominations and other faiths within that vast country?

Whether there is merit in the Russian Patriarch's complaints against Rome or not, it is surely the perception that matters at a time of dialogue and attempts at mutual understanding. The announcement to create Roman Catholic dioceses in Russia against the pleas of the local "sister" Church was made on February 11. The Vatican newspaper *L'Osservatore Romano* explained that the move was to "respond more concretely to the pastoral needs" of Catholics in Russia. But the Moscow Patriarch called the decision an "unfriendly act" that proved that John Paul was determined to proselytize among the Orthodox faithful. Patriarch Alexis II said the "unnecessary" act was a "challenge leveled at Orthodoxy" despite all the flattering and assuaging words from the Vatican.

The tensions between the Vatican and the Russian Orthodox Church, although by no means entirely created by John Paul, have been largely exacerbated by him: Certainly his deeds contradict, again and again, his words. And what is most strange about his determination is the timing. Maurice Cowling, the Cambridge historian, has remarked on the tendency of Christian denominations in the nineteenth century to engage in proselytizing projects in places far away. Hence a semblance of expansion, renewal, and hope is achieved by ignoring troubles closer to home and hurrying abroad to "alien" and "heathen" regions to spread the Word.

February 2002, the month in which the Russian dioceses were established, was the month in which the pedophile crisis exploded in Boston and elsewhere in the United States. While I am not suggesting a link, in the form of a deliberate attempt to create a diversion, the circumstance illustrates the hubris of a universal pastor setting his eyes upon distant vistas eastward while he has more than enough on his plate in the West.

John Paul has not repined the rebuffs from Moscow. In the past two years, he has continued to pay court to the Russian president, Vladimir Putin, using every wile in his considerable repertoire of persuasion to extract from the Russian leader what Alexis II does not wish to give: sanction for a visit to Moscow. The most intriguing item in the ongoing flirtation is an icon that properly belongs to the Orthodox Church. On November 5, 2003, John Paul met with Putin in the Apostolic Palace and showed him the icon of Our Lady of Kazan, which had been hanging in John Paul's private apartment for some years. John Paul made the sign of the cross over the object and kissed it, then handed it to Putin, who did the same.

Putin almost certainly realized that this was an opening move in a game of chess that would end, John Paul devoutly hoped, with an invitation to Russia. For his offer was to give the icon back, provided that he could bring it in person to Russian soil. Putin made it clear after the meeting that he had not discussed a Russian papal trip.

The icon, however, has had a curious history, with echoes of piety close to John Paul's heart, as well as dubious aspects that make it a poor choice as a "gift" of reconciliation. The object, which is deemed to be miraculous, is said to date from at least as far back as 1579, when, according to Orthodox legend, the Virgin Mary appeared to a nine-year-old girl in Kazan telling her to retrieve the icon from the ashes of her home, which had been burned down. The image of the Virgin came to be known as the "Liberatrix of Russia" and was frequently employed as a protective standard for Russian armies. It was also an important image in the domestic life of Russia; copies were displayed in countless homes. But in 1904, the original was stolen from the Cathedral of Our Lady of Kazan in St. Petersburg. From this point it disappeared for more than half a century before turning up in the Byzantine chapel at Fatima, the shrine that has played such a central role in John Paul's vision of his pontificate and world history.

The icon had been purchased for $3 million by the Blue Army, a wealthy traditionalist group of Fatima devotees numbering some 25 million worldwide and officially recognized by the Pope as an "apostolate." The Blue Army, founded in the United States at the outset of the Cold War, proclaimed its ultimate goal to be the defeat of the Red Army and the conversion of Russia to Roman Catholicism by means of devotion to the rosary: One of its campaigns involved, in emulation of atomic weapons, a "chain reaction" of rosaries. The Blue Army placed the icon in the Byzantine chapel at Fatima on July 21, 1970, feast of Our Lady of Kazan. The celebrant was Bishop Andrew Katkoff, rector of the Russicum, a college within the Vatican that specializes in Byzantine studies. The Blue Army has routinely targeted the Eastern-rite Catholic Churches, which they see as "a bridge, a door, to the conversion of Russia": the Fatima Byzantine chapel and the Vatican's Russicum are focuses of study, prayer, and devotion aimed at the conversion of Russia to Roman Catholicism, which the Blue Army claims was the Virgin of Fatima's ultimate intention.

In 1972, Cardinal Wyszynski paid a visit to Fatima, where he presented Our Lady of Kazan with a companion icon: a copy of the Black Madonna of Czestochowa. As we have seen, John Paul's overarching Marian vision, shot through with prophecy to which he himself is inextricably linked, was demonstrated on March 24, 1984, when, having recovered from the attempt on his life and having read the Third Secret of Fatima, he dedicated the planet to the Immaculate Heart of Mary. "The power of this consecration lasts for all time," he said, "and embraces all individuals, peoples, and nations. It overcomes every evil that the spirit of darkness is able to awaken, and has in fact awakened in our times, in the heart of man and his history." Those acquainted with the Fatima cult understood that the special target of the dedication was the people of Russia. In 1981, the Blue Army had taken the icon from Fatima and presented it to John Paul with the express intention that he would take the object personally on a pastoral visit to Russia after the "conversion of Russia." Members of the army, meanwhile, have been expressing dismay on their web sites at the return of the icon before the fulfillment of this crucial condition.

Small wonder that the Orthodox Church, which, of course, is well apprised of these maneuvers, has doubts about the Pope's true intentions. In the meantime, a problem arose weeks after President Putin's visit. On April 29, 2003, Russia's culture minister, Mikhail Shvydkoi, announced that the icon in John Paul's keeping was a fake—that it was made not in the sixteenth century but in the eighteenth. Following a joint investigation of Russian and Vatican experts, the minister said: "The question is whether this is really the icon that was stolen from Kazan several centuries ago, or if it was painted later. The experts' conclusion is that the icon was made in the eighteenth century." The Vatican has remained silent on the issue, but Curial officials have indicated that even if the icon is merely a copy, the religious value holds good.

*

The very characteristics that have tragically wrecked the chances of greater Christian unity between East and West in the post-Soviet era are related to the reasons why the Roman Catholic community is experiencing a period of great crisis and division. The Pope speaks but does not engage in dialogue; he hears but does not listen; he studies but does not learn. His professions of admiration for the East are entirely in, and on, his terms and not theirs. His respect for the East is couched in poetic historico-legendary metaphor rather than the language of daylight realities. There is no indication that he believes there is anything to be actually learned from the Orthodox Churches, in particular about those matters of religion that impact on everyday life in the contemporary world of the Church: sexuality, marriage, divorce, contraception, homosexuality, married priesthood, and a preparedness to discuss a woman's priesthood; and yet, that is an area where the Roman Catholic community has most to learn and most to gain. By the same token, the reason that John Paul has made so little progress with Orthodox Churches is not unconnected with his failure to make headway with the Anglican Communion.

John Paul's failure to make progress with the "sister" Churches of Christianity tells us much about the deep and growing rifts within his own Church. For just as there are two lungs in Christian Europe, East and the West, so there are two great complementary rhythms within the Roman Community. The importance of these rhythms, and John Paul's failure to address the balance and the harmony that should exist between them, merits the final word: the epilogue.

The Legacy of John Paul II

John Paul will go down in history as the Pope who helped the Polish people oust Communist rule; who helped prompt the process that brought down communism and ended the Cold War, thus making the world a safer place. Of all world figures in the last quarter century, moreover, he stands out as a man of peace. On his deeply emotional final visit to Lourdes in August 2004, he wept at the grotto of the Virgin and prayed for peace. "Join me," he asked the faithful, "in imploring the Virgin Mary to obtain for our world the longed-for gift of peace. May forgiveness and brotherly love take root in human hearts. May every weapon be laid down and all hatred and violence put aside. May everyone see in his neighbor not an enemy to be fought but a brother to be accepted and loved, so that we may join in building a better world."

But what will be his lasting legacy for the Catholic Church? How will his influence be felt among the billion-strong faithful in years to come? And what sort of pope ideally should follow him, immediately or eventually?

Throughout the worldwide Church one finds everywhere vibrant Catholic communities: people working, and dying, for the faith; selfless ministers, sisters, and laity working for the sick and the poor; members of the faithful making the world a better place. The spirit of Vatican II is at work and cannot be quenched. But there are countless millions of Catholics who have fallen away because they have become demoralized and excluded under John Paul II. His major and abiding legacy, I believe, is to be seen and felt in various forms of oppression and exclusion, trust in papal absolutism, and antagonistic divisions. Never have Catholics been so divided; never has there been so much contempt and aggression between Catholics. Never has the local Church suffered so much at the hands of the Vatican and papal center.

John Paul has exhibited from time to time a rhetorical appreciation of the dual role of the two great impulses within the Church in the world, the universal and the local, that should beat in mutual empowerment and understanding, not in competition or rivalry.

In the interests of unity, and faced with what he saw as the centrifugal fragmentation of the Church in the postconciliar era, John Paul emphasized the institution of the universal at the expense of the local. To achieve this end, he wielded the instruments of power available to him—the Petrine office and the outreach of the Curia—binding the local Church more closely to the papacy. And he traveled, treating every nation, diocese, and parish as his own. John Paul had neither doubts nor scruples in this vaulting hubris, because he was convinced that he had divinely ordained mystical endorsement; there were no coincidences—it was all meant from the beginning, foretold, predestined.

But the Catholic Church should exist in its fullness wherever and whenever the Eucharist is celebrated: in every cathedral, in every parish church, and in every chapel. Through the long papacy of John Paul, the Church in its parishes, dioceses, and all its myriad local congregations has been reduced and diminished, sacrificed to the dominance of the papal and Vatican center.

There are aspects of this centralizing policy that are owed to John Paul's character, his temperament, and his personal history. Yet, as Pope, he does not stand outside the tide of history. His agenda, its successes and failures, were part, as we have seen, of the history of the papacy through the modern period since the French Revolution, and of the long tensions and confrontations between the "ultra-montist" centralizers and the progressive devolutionists.

John Paul's ecclesial legacy, then, is a tumescent papal authority that has become a "norm." This legacy, moreover, is presented as "traditional" instead of what it truly is—a modern anomaly that gathered pace in the mid–nineteenth century as the papacy struggled to maintain its power and significance against burgeoning nation-states, many of them antagonistic to Catholicism.

The Second Vatican Council signaled an era in which the local Church would begin to flourish anew, with greater independence and local discretion. At the time of his election, however, the Church appeared to many, even progressives, to be out of control. There was great need of discipline. This explains up to a point why John Paul, while professing himself a Pope of the Council, tightened the reins of papal and Curial authority. While making many necessary correctives, he consistently promised to guide the Church back to the principles of the Council. But his actions consistently belied his words through two decades of his papacy.

At the end of the great Jubilee Year, having closed the Holy Door, he signed his Jubilee apostolic letter. The letter declared that much had been done in reforming the Roman Curia, "but there is much more to be done." Communion, he wrote, must be cultivated and extended at every level of the Church; to this end, "the structures of participation envisaged by canon law, such as the council of priests and the pastoral council, must be ever more highly valued."

Many people took these words, uttered at the dawn of the millennium, as a change of heart: at last! Was he, on the brink of death, about to repudiate the centralizing policies of many years? A year or two into the new century, it became obvious that John Paul was not about to change. His words, yet again, were at variance with his actions.

If a father lives in hope that his children will help him, he gives them a measure of independence, he sets them free. John Paul II has denied the local Church growth toward responsibility. And so, in an era largely hospitable to religious freedom, it is difficult to estimate the full extent of the enfeeblement of the periphery during such a long papacy. But the longer the pontificate, the deeper and more extensive the weakness. There is in consequence no easy solution to the damage that has been done during his reign. John Paul's successor will inherit a dysfunctional Church fraught with problems and yet impatient for change. But in which direction? A progressive pope, a papal Mikhail Gorbachev, could find himself presiding over a sudden and disastrous schism as conservatives refuse to accept the authenticity of progressive reforms; a hardline conservative, however, would likely create a "remnant" catacomb Church after prompting wide-ranging defections and apostasy from a faithful unprepared to take more of the same, or even worse.

Every indication from world history over the past half century suggests that the papacy, which has become ever more absolutist under this Pope, will find itself unable to hold the center unless it reforms itself. The Third World Church, thriving in many regions, will likely come into its own, with potential to spin out of control; and the Church in North America, which has still to count the appalling cost of the pedophile priest crisis in collapsing morale and plummeting vocations, faces a future without priests.

Fortunately, we Catholics who retain a profound belief in Original Sin, the context in which we struggle to attain our ideals, are with grace seldom entirely disillusioned by our failures and hence are never without hope. After all, we believe in the long-term efficacy of the Holy Spirit, even if there are popes who busy themselves making hoops for Him to jump through.

John Paul was Pope during an extraordinary era of disruption and fragmentation in the world and within the Church. He responded to the manifold problems and crises by becoming a superman Pope: He took charge. He saw the Church as a pyramid rather than a group of communities. He saw his papal role as that of a chief executive running the branch offices from the apex. In this he had exemplars in plenty through the twentieth century: Pius X, Pius XI, and Pius XII. There might have been another pope who took worse decisions and perpetrated more calamitous failures. But as John Paul's reign draws to a close and the Church looks forward to a new pontificate in the twenty-first century, we must ask whether the Church is best served by a superman. John Paul never ceased to be a human being—and a remarkable one at that. But his autocratic solutions tempted him to act in ways that eclipsed those human qualities, demoralizing and discouraging large segments of the faithful.

John Henry Newman, the nineteenth-century Anglican convert, theologian, and cardinal, gave warning of the dangers of an autocratic, long-lived papacy. "It is anomaly," he wrote, "and bears no good fruit; he becomes a god, has no one to contradict him, does not know facts, and does cruel things without meaning it." We can only hope that his successor will be first and foremost a bishop among brother bishops, a judge of final appeal presiding in charity over differences and divisions, and a human being who knows, despite his call to leadership, that he remains a pilgrim with all humanity.

Acknowledgments

As a writer fascinated by the Vatican and the papacy for more than two decades now, I've been fortunate to have many friends and acquaintances who have contributed wittingly, and perhaps unwittingly, to the writing of this portrait of John Paul II. Given such a long papacy, many an influence and debt of gratitude has been neglected; but I thank them one and all, and especially: John Allen, Neal Ascherson, Victoria Clark, Eamon Duffy, John Follain, Cathy Galvin, Michael Gilmore, the late Dan Grisewood, Michael Hirst, Nicholas Lash, Archbishop Paul Casimir Marcinkus, John Milbank, Gerry O'Collins, Gerard O'Connell, John Phillips, Catherine Pickstock, Peggy Polk, John Pollard, Tom Reese, Janet Soskice, Jack Valero, Michael Walsh, Marjorie Weeke, Philip Willan, David Willey, John Wilkins, and Tobias Wolff.

This book could never have seen the light of day without the quiet assistance of my "Monsignor Sotto Voce," about whom it should be said: You are not you, and he is not he. I am deeply grateful to John Wilkins, Eamon Duffy, and Michael Walsh for reading the book in manuscript, and to Chris Fortunato. The idiosyncrasies of perspective are entirely my own, as are any errors of fact. My particular thanks also go to Emma Parry and Clare Alexander, my agents in New York and London, and to my editors—Andrew Corbin of Doubleday, New York, and Juliet Annan of Viking, London. As ever, I cannot express sufficient gratitude for the encouragement of Crispin Rope.

A Select List of the Writings
of Pope John Paul II

DRAMA AND POETRY

Collected Poems. Trans. with introductory essay and notes by Jerzy Peter-
  kiewicz. New York: Random House, 1979, 1982.
The Collected Plays and Writings and Theater. Trans. Boleslaw Taborski. Berkeley:
  University of California Press, 1987.

PREPAPAL BOOKS

Acting Person. D. Reidel. Rev. ed. 1977. Trans. Andrzej Potocki. 1979.
Sign of Contradiction. New York: Seabury Press, 1979.
Sources of Renewal: The Implementation of Vatican II. San Francisco: Harper
  and Row. Trans. P. S. Falla. 1980.
Faith According to St. John of the Cross. Jordan Aumann. San Francisco:
  Ignatius Press, 1981.
Love and Responsibility. San Francisco: Ignatius Press. Trans. H. T. Willetts.
  1981.
Lubliner Vorlesungen, 1954–57. Ed. Juliusz Stoynowski. Stuttgart-Degerloch:
  Seewald, 1981.

ENCYCLICALS

Redemptor Hominis, The Redeemer of Man (1979)
Dives in Misericordia, On the Mercy of God (1980)
Laborem Exercens, On Human Work (1981)
Slavorum Apostoli, Apostles to the Slavs (1985)
Dominum et Vivificantem, The Lord and Giver of Life (1986)

Redemptoris Mater, Mother of the Redeemer (1987)

Sollicitudo Rei Socialis, On Social Concern (1987)

Redemptoris Missio, On the Mission of the Redeemer (1990)

Centesimus Annus, On the Hundredth Anniversary of *Rerum Novarum* (1991)

Veritatis Splendor, The Splendor of Truth (1993)

Evangelium Vitae, The Gospel of Life (1995)

Ut Unum Sint, That They May Be One (1995)

Fides et Ratio, On Faith and Reason (1998)

Ecclesia de Eucharistia, The Church from the Eucharist (2003)

APOSTOLIC CONSTITUTIONS, EXHORTATIONS, LETTERS, INSTRUCTIONS

Catechesi Tradendae, Apostolic Exhortation on Catechesis in Our Time (1979)

Sapientia Christiana, Apostolic Constitution on Ecclesiastical Universities and Faculties (1979)

Inestimabile Donum, Instruction Concerning Worship of the Eucharistic Mystery (1980)

Dominica Cenae, On the Mystery and Worship of the Eucharist (1980)

Familiaris Consortio, Apostolic Exhortation on the Family (1981)

Redemptionis Donum, The Gift of Redemption (1984)

Salvifici Doloris, Apostolic Letter on the Christian Meaning of Human Suffering (1984)

Reconciliatio et Paenitentia, Apostolic Exhortation on Reconciliation and Penance (1984)

Duodecimum Saeculum, Apostolic Letter on the Twentieth Century (1987)

Mulieris Digniatem, Apostolic Letter on the Dignity and Vocation of Women (1988)

Christifideles Laici, Apostolic Exhortation on the Vocation and Mission of the Lay Faithful in the Church and in the World (1988)

Ecclesia Dei, Apostolic Letter on the 25th Anniversary of the Constitution on the Sacred Liturgy (1988)

On the Occasion of the Marian Year, Apostolic Letter (1988)

Euntes in Mundum, Apostolic Letter, Go Into All the World (1988)

Redemptoris Custos, Apostolic Exhortation on the Guardian of the Redeemer, St. Joseph (1989)

Ex Corde Ecclesiae, Apostolic Constitution, From the Heart of the Church (1990)

Pastores Dabo Vobis, Apostolic Exhortation, I Will Give You Shepherds (1992)

Letter to Families (1994)

Tertio Millennio Adveniente, Apostolic Letter on the Third Millenium (1994)

Letter to Women (1994)

Orientale Lumen, Apostolic Letter, Light of the East (1995)

Vita Consecrata, Apostolic Exhortation on the Consecrated Life (1996)

Universi Dominici Gregis, Apostolic Constitution on the Vacancy of the Apostolic See and the Election of the Roman Pontiff (1996)

Books and Other Writing from the Papal Period

Fruitful and Responsible Love. New York: Seabury Press, 1979. His 1978 address on the tenth anniversary of *Humanae Vitae,* with contributions by various respondents.

Holy Thursday Letters to My Brother Priests (1979–1994). Princeton/Chicago: Sceptre, 1994.

Blessed Are the Pure of Heart. Boston: St. Paul's, 1980.

Massimiliano Kolbe, patrono del nostro difficile secolo. Vatican City: Liberia Editrice Vaticana, 1982.

"Be Not Afraid!"—André Frossard in Conversation with Pope John Paul II. Trans. from the French (1982) J. R. Foster. London: The Bodley Head, 1984.

Reflections on Humanae Vitae. Boston: St. Paul's, 1984.

Crossing the Threshold of Hope. Ed. Vittorio Messori. New York: Alfred A. Knopf, 1994.

Gift and Mystery: On the Fiftieth Anniversary of My Priestly Ordination. New York: Doubleday, 1996.

Select Bibliography

Accattoli, Luigi. *When a Pope Asks Forgiveness*. New York: St. Pauls, Alba House, 1998.

Allen, John L.. Jr. *Conclave*. New York: Doubleday, 2002.

Bernstein, Carl; Politi, Marco. *His Holiness*. New York: Doubleday,, 1996.

Berry, Jason; Renner, Gerald. *Vows of Silence*. New York: Free Press, 2004.

Carey, George. *Know the Truth*. London: HarperCollins Publishers, 2004.

Collins, Paul, ed. *From Inquisition to Freedom*. London: Continuum, 2001.

Collins, Paul. *Papal Power*. London: Fount, 1997.

Cooke, Bernard, ed. *The Papacy and the Church in the United States*. Mahwah, NJ: Paulist Press, 1989.

Cornwell, John. *A Thief in the Night*. New York: Viking, 1989.

Cornwell, John. *Breaking Faith*. New York: Viking Compass, 2001.

Cornwell, John. *Hitler's Pope*. New York: Viking, 1999.

Cozzens, Donald B. *The Changing Face of the Priesthood*. Minnesota: Liturgical Press, 2000.

Curran, Charles E. *The Catholic Moral Tradition Today: A Synthesis*. Washington, DC: Georgetown University Press, 1999.

Daw, Richard W. *Pope John Paul II*. Washington, DC, National Catholic News Service, 1987.

315

Deedy, John, ed. *The Catholic Church in the Twentieth Century*. Minnesota: Liturgical Press, 2000.

Duffy, Eamon. *Saints & Sinners: A History of the Popes*. London: Yale University Press, 1997.

Dulles, Avery. *The Splendor of Faith*. New York: Crossroad, 1999.

Dupuis, Jacques, S.J. *Toward a Christian Theology of Religious Pluralism*. New York: Orbis Books, 1997.

Flannery, Austin, O.P., ed. *Vatican Council II (Volume 1)*. Dublin: Dominican Publications, 1987.

Flannery, Austin, O.P., ed. *Vatican Council II (Volume 2)*. New York: Costello Publishing, 1982.

Formicola, Jo Renee. *Pope John Paul II: Prophetic Politician*. Washington, DC: Georgetown University Press, 2002.

Fox, Thomas C. *Sexuality and Catholicism*. New York: George Braziller, 1995.

Garton Ash, Timothy. *The Polish Revolution: Solidarity*. Great Britain: Penguin, 1999.

Garton Ash, Timothy. *The Uses of Adversity*. Great Britain: Penguin, 1999.

Garton Ash, Timothy. *We the People*. Great Britain: Penguin, 1999.

Gillis, Chester. *Roman Catholicism in America*. New York: Columbia University Press, 1999.

Gneuhs, Geoffrey, ed. *The Legacy of Pope John Paul II*. New York: Crossroad, 2000.

Granfield, Patrick. *The Limits of the Papacy*. New York: Crossroad, 1987.

Hastings, Adrian, ed. *Bishops and Writers*. Hertfordshire: Anthony Clarke, 1977.

Hastings, Adrian, ed. *Modern Catholicism: Vatican II and After*. London: SPCK, 1991.

Hebblethwaite, Peter. *In The Vatican*. London: Sidgwick & Jackson, 1986.

Hebblethwaite, Peter. *Introducing John Paul II*. London: Fount, 1982.

Hebblethwaite, Peter. *John XXIII: Pope of the Council.* London: Fount, 1994.

Hebblethwaite, Peter. *The Next Pope.* HarperSanFrancisco, 2000.

Hebblethwaite, Peter. *The New Inquisition? Schillebeeckx and Küng.* London: Fount, 1980.

Hebblethwaite, Peter. *Paul VI: The First Modern Pope.* London: HarperCollins, 1993.

Hebblethwaite, Peter. *The Runaway Church.* London: Collins, 1975.

Hogan, Richard M.; and John M. LeVoir. *Covenant of Love.* New York: Ignatius Press, 1992.

John Paul II. *The Gospel of Life: A Message of Hope.* London: Fount, 1995.

John Paul II. *The Theology of the Body: Human Love in the Divine Plan.* Boston: Pauline Books & Media, 1997.

John Paul II. *Words of Certitude.* Mahwah, NJ: Paulist Press, 1979.

Johnson, Paul. *The Papacy.* London: Weidenfeld & Nicolson, 1997.

Kelly, George A. *Keeping the Church Catholic with John Paul II.* New York: Doubleday, 1990.

Kerr, Fergus. *Immortal Longings.* Great Britain: SPCK, 1997.

Küng, Hans. *The Catholic Church: A Short History.* Great Britain: Weidenfeld & Nicolson, 2001.

Küng, Hans. *My Struggle for Freedom.* London: Continuum, 2003.

Kwitny, Jonathan. *Man of the Century: The Life and Times of Pope John Paul II.* London: Little, Brown and Company, 1997.

Lash, Nicholas. *Easter in Ordinary.* London: SCM Press Ltd., 1988.

Lawler, Justus George. *Popes and Politics.* London: Continuum, 2002.

Liebreich, Karen. *Fallen Order: A History.* London: Atlantic Books, 2004.

MacEoin, Gary, ed. *The Papacy and the People of God.* New York: Orbis Books, 1998.

McBrien, Richard P. *Catholicism.* HarperSanFrancisco, 1994.

McClory, Robert. *Power and the Papacy.* Missouri: Triumph, 1997.

McDermott, John M., ed. *The Thought of Pope John Paul II.* Rome: Gregorian University, 1993.

Messori, Vittorio. *Opus Dei: Leadership and Vision in Today's Catholic Church*. Washington, DC: Regnery, 1997.

Milbank, John. *The Word Made Strange*. Oxford: Blackwell, 1997.

Misner, Paul. *Social Catholicism in Europe*. London: Darton, Longman and Todd, 1991.

Oddie, William, ed. *John Paul the Great*. London: The Catholic Herald & The Catholic Truth Society, 2003.

Paczkowski, Andrzej. *The Spring Will Be Ours*. University Park, PA: Penn State University Press, 2003.

Pollard, John F. *The Unknown Pope*. Geoffrey Chapman, 1999.

Quinn, John R. *The Reform of the Papacy*. New York: Crossroad, 1999.

Rahner, Karl. *Visions and Prophecies*. London: Burns & Oates, 1966.

Ratzinger, Cardinal Joseph; Messori, Vittorio. *The Ratzinger Report*. London: Fowler Wright, 1985.

Ratzinger, Cardinal Joseph. *Salt of the Earth*. San Francisco: Ignatius Press, 1997.

Reese, Thomas J. *Inside the Vatican*. London: Harvard University Press, 1996.

Riccards, Michael P. *Vicars of Christ*. New York: Crossroad, 1998.

Rico, Herminio. *John Paul II and the Legacy of Dignitatis Humanae*. Washington, DC: Georgetown University Press, 2002.

Ruane, Kevin. *To Kill a Priest*. London: Gibson Square, 2004.

Schatz, Klaus. *Papal Primary: From Its Origins to the Present*. Minnesota: Liturgical Press, 1996.

Shaw, Russell. *Papal Primacy in the Third Millennium*. Indiana: Our Sunday Visitor, 2000.

Sullivan, Francis A., S.J. *Creative Fidelity*. Dublin: Gill & Macmillan, 1996.

Sullivan, Francis A., S.J. *Magisterium*. Mahwah, NJ: Paulist Press, 1983.

Szulc, Tad. *Pope John Paul II: The Biography*. New York: Scribner, 1995.

Thompson, Damian. *The End of Time*. London: Sinclair-Stevenson, 1996.

Urquhart, Gordon. *The Pope's Armada*. London: Bantam Press, 1995.

Vaillancourt, Jean-Guy. *Papal Power: A Study of Vatican Control Over Lay Catholic Elites*. Berkeley: University of California Press, 1980.

Vidler, Alec R. *Prophecy & Papacy*. London: SCM Press Ltd., 1954.

Walsh, Michael. *John Paul II*. Fount, 1994.

Walsh, Michael. *The Conclave*. Norwich: Canterbury Press, 2003.

Weigel, George. *Witness to Hope*. New York: Cliff Street Books, 1999.

Weigel, George. *The Courage to Be Catholic*. New York: Basic Books, 2002.

Whale, John, ed. *The Pope From Poland: An Assessment*. London: Collins, 1980.

Whitehead, Kenneth D., ed. *John Paul II—Witness to Truth*. Indiana: St. Augustine's Press, 2001.

Wilkins, John, ed. *Understanding Veritatis Splendor*. Great Britain: SPCK, 1994.

Williams, George Huntston. *The Mind of John Paul II*. New York: Seabury Press, 1981.

Williams, Oliver F., Houck, John W. *Catholic Social Thought and the New World Order*. London: University of Notre Dame Press, 1993.

Willey, David. *God's Politician*. London: Faber and Faber Ltd., 1992.

Wills, Garry. *Papal Sin: Structures of Deceit*. New York: Doubleday, 2000.

Woodward, Kenneth L. *Making Saints*. New York: Simon & Schuster, 1990.

Index